# Contents

# Dedication

## Keith Randell (1943–2002)

The *Access to History* series was conceived and developed by Keith, who created a series to 'cater for students as they are, not as we might wish them to be'. He leaves a living legacy of a series that for over 20 years has provided a trusted, stimulating and well-loved accompaniment to post-16 study. Our aim with these new editions is to continue to offer students the best possible support for their studies.

# 1

# The German Revolution 1918–19

**POINTS TO CONSIDER**

The purpose of this chapter is to consider the events that occurred in Germany during the final days of the First World War and the challenges faced by the new democratic Germany during its first months. These were dramatic, but difficult times for German politicians and the German people. The main themes are:

- The collapse of Imperial Germany and the abdication of Kaiser Wilhelm II
- The German Revolution: the establishment of the democratic republic and the failure of the Spartacist revolt
- The establishment of the National Constituent Assembly

**Key dates**

| | | |
|---|---|---|
| 1918 | September | Ludendorff conceded that Germany was defeated |
| | October 3 | Prince Max of Baden appointed chancellor |
| | November 2 | Grand Fleet mutiny at Kiel |
| | November 8 | Bavaria proclaimed a socialist republic |
| | November 9 | Kaiser fled to Holland |
| | | Ebert appointed chancellor |
| | | Germany proclaimed a republic |
| | November 11 | Armistice signed at Compiègne |
| 1919 | January 1 | German Communist Party founded |
| | January 5 | Start of Spartacist uprising in Berlin |
| | February 6 | National Constituent Assembly met at Weimar |

## 1 | The Collapse of Imperial Germany

Key question
Why did Germany lose the First World War?

When war broke out in 1914 it was assumed in Germany, as well as in all the Great Powers, that the conflict would not last very long. However, by late September 1918, after four years of bloody war, Germany faced military defeat. The reasons for its eventual collapse go right back to the early days of August 1914, but the pressures had developed over the years that followed. The main factors can be identified as follows:

- Germany's failure to achieve rapid victory in the summer of 1914. The German High Command's strategy was built upon the notion of a quick victory in order to avoid a long drawn-out conflict with the Allies. By the autumn of 1914 the **Schlieffen plan** had failed to gain a rapid victory.
- Stalemate. Germany was forced to fight the war on two fronts – the east and the west. The balance of military power resulted in a war of stalemate that put immense pressures on **Imperial Germany**. The situation was made particularly difficult for Germany by the Allies' naval blockade, which seriously limited the import of all supplies. And, although the German policy of '**unrestricted submarine warfare**' at first seriously threatened Britain, it did not decisively weaken her.
- Strengths of the Allies. Britain and France were major colonial powers and could call upon their overseas empires for manpower, resources and supplies. Furthermore, from April 1917, the Allies were strengthened by America's entry into the war, which resulted in the mobilisation of two million men.
- Limitations of German war economy. Imperial Germany was totally unprepared for the economic costs of a prolonged war. It made great efforts to mobilise the war effort and arms production was dramatically increased. However, the economy was seriously dislocated, which wrecked the government's finances and increased social tension.

A chance for Germany to escape from the military defeat came when Russia surrendered in March 1918. This immediately enabled Germany to launch a last major offensive on the Western Front. Unfortunately, it was unable to maintain the momentum and, by August, German troops were being forced to retreat. At the same time its own allies, Austria, Turkey and Bulgaria, were collapsing.

## The socio-economic effects of the First World War

In 1914, the vast majority of Germans supported the war and there were no signs of the country's morale and unity breaking down until the winter months of early 1917. Then, the accumulation of shortages, high prices and the black market, as well as the bleak military situation, began to affect the public mood. Social discontent thereafter grew markedly because of:

- Food and fuel shortages. The exceptionally cold winter of 1916–17 contributed to severe food and fuel shortages in the cities. It was nicknamed the 'turnip winter' because the failure of the potato crop forced the German people to rely heavily on turnips, which were normally for animal fodder.
- Civilian deaths. The number of civilian deaths from starvation and hypothermia increased from 121,000 in 1916 to 293,000 in 1918.
- Infant mortality. The number of child deaths increased by over 50 per cent in the course of the war years.

**Key terms**

**Schlieffen plan**
Its purpose was to avoid a two-front war by winning victory on the Western Front before dealing with the threat from Russia. It aimed to defeat France within six weeks by a massive German offensive in northern France and Belgium.

**Imperial Germany**
The title given to Germany from its unification in 1871 until 1918. Also referred to as the Second Reich (Empire).

'**Unrestricted submarine warfare**'
Germany's policy of attacking all military and civilian shipping in order to sink supplies going to Britain.

**Key question**
How did the war affect the living and working conditions of the German people?

**Kaiser**
Emperor. The last
Kaiser of Germany
was Wilhelm II,
1888–1918.

A cartoon drawn in 1918 by the German artist Raemaeker. It underlines the serious situation faced by **Kaiser** Wilhelm II who is held by two ominous figures – war and starvation.

- The influenza epidemic. In 1918 Europe was hit by the 'Spanish flu', which killed between 20 and 40 million people – a figure higher than the casualties of the First World War. It has been cited as the most devastating epidemic recorded, probably because people's resistance to disease was lowered by the decline in living conditions.
- Inflation. Workers were forced to work even longer hours, but wages fell below the inflation rate. Average prices doubled in Germany between 1914 and 1918, whereas wages rose by only 50–75 per cent.
- Casualties. About two million Germans were killed, with a further six million wounded, many suffering disability. The emotional trauma for all these soldiers and their families was not so easy to put into statistics.

Social discontent, therefore, grew markedly in the final two years of the war. Considerable anger was expressed against the so-called 'sharks' of industry, who had made vast profits from the war. Resentment grew in the minds of many within the middle class because they felt that their social status had been lowered as their income declined. Above all, opposition began to grow against the political leaders, who had urged total war. Faced with the worsening situation on the domestic front and the likelihood of defeat on the Western Front, the military leaders – Generals Ludendorff and Hindenburg (below and page 81), recognised the seriousness of Germany's position – and decided to seek peace with the Allies.

## Profile: Erich Ludendorff 1865–1937

| 1865 | – Born in Kruszewnia in the Polish Prussian province of Posen |
| 1882 | – Joined the Prussian army |
| 1894 | – Joined the General Staff and worked closely with Schlieffen |
| 1914 | – Appointed Chief-of-Staff to Hindenburg on the Eastern Front |
| 1916 | – Transferred to Western Front. Promoted to the post of Quartermaster General – virtual military dictator, 1916–18 |
| 1917 | – Responsible for the dismissal of Chancellor Bethmann-Hollweg (1909–17) |
| 1918 | – Masterminded German final offensive |
|      | – Proposed the theory of the 'stab in the back' (see page 5) Fled to Sweden |
| 1919 | – Returned to Germany |
| 1920 | – Took part in Kapp *putsch* (see pages 45–7) |
| 1923 | – Collaborated with Hitler and was involved in Munich *putsch* (see pages 47–50) |
| 1937 | – Died in Tutzing, Bavaria |

Ludendorff was a soldier of considerable ability, energy and enthusiasm. In the campaign in Belgium he showed considerable initiative and was sent, as Chief-of-Staff, to serve with Hindenburg on the Eastern Front. Here he played an important part in the major victories over the Russians. In 1916, the two men were posted to the Western Front and during the years that followed they were able to assume supreme command of the German war effort. By the end of the war, Ludendorff was effectively the wartime dictator of Germany and, when it was clear that Germany had lost the war, he tried to direct the control of the constitutional reform in October 1918. After the war, he dabbled in extreme right-wing politics and became associated with the activities of Hitler's Nazi Party whose racial views he shared. Later, he became disenchanted with Hitler and in his latter years became a pacifist.

**Key term**

*Putsch*
The German word for an uprising (though often the French phrase, *coup d'état*, is used). Normally, a *putsch* means the attempt by a small group to overthrow the government, which usually fails.

## The October reform

Once Ludendorff came to appreciate that an Allied invasion of Germany would lead to destructive internal disturbances, he pushed for political change. Ever since Imperial Germany had been created in 1871, it had been an **autocracy**. Now Ludendorff wanted to change Germany into a **constitutional monarchy** by the Kaiser's handing over political power to a civilian government. In other words, he aimed to establish a more democratic government, while maintaining the German monarchy.

**Key question**
Why did Ludendorff support constitutional reform?

Key terms

**Autocracy**
A system where one person (usually a hereditary sovereign) has absolute rule.

**Constitutional monarchy**
Where the monarch has limited power within the lines of a constitution.

**'Stab in the back' myth**
The distorted *view* that the army had not really lost the First World War and that unpatriotic groups, such as socialists and Jews, had undermined it. The myth severely weakened the Weimar democracy from the start.

*Reichstag*
The German parliament. Although created in 1871, it had very limited powers. Real power lay with the Emperor.

Ludendorff's political turnaround had two aims. First, he wanted to secure for Germany the best possible peace terms from the Allies – it was believed that the Allied leaders would be more sympathetic to a democratic regime in Berlin. Second, he hoped the change would prevent the outbreak of political revolutionary disturbances.

However, Ludendorff had a third and a more cynical ulterior motive. He saw the need to shift the responsibility for Germany's defeat away from the military leadership and the conservative forces, which had dominated Imperial Germany, e.g. landowners and the army. Instead, he intended to put the responsibility and blame for the defeat on the new leadership. Here lay the origins of the **'stab in the back' myth**, which was later to play such a vital part in the history of the Weimar Republic. It was a theme soon taken up by sympathisers of the political right wing (see page 43).

It was against this background that on 3 October 1918 Prince Max of Baden, a moderate conservative, was appointed chancellor. He had democratic views and also a well-established international reputation because of his work with the Red Cross. In the following month a series of constitutional reforms came into effect, which turned Germany into a parliamentary democracy:

- Wilhelm II gave up his powers over the army and the navy to the *Reichstag*.
- The chancellor and his government were made accountable to the *Reichstag*, instead of to the Kaiser.
- At the same time, armistice negotiations with the Allies were opened.

## The key debate

The changes of the October reform have traditionally been portrayed as 'a revolution from above'. This suggests that they were brought about by those in power and not forced as a result of 'a revolution from below'. So a question that historians have debated is:

> To what extent did the constitutional changes represent a revolution from above?

Some historians from the 1970s, like Hans-Ulrich Wehler, regard the events of October 1918 as proving their theory that Germany had long been controlled and manipulated by the conservative traditional forces. He writes: 'The conservative bastions of the monarchy and the army were to be preserved as far as possible behind the façade of new arrangements intended to prevent the radical overthrow of the system and prove acceptable to the Allies'.

However, other historians, such as Eberhard Kolb from the 1980s, have suggested that the steps taken by the military leaders coincided with increasing pressure from the *Reichstag* to bring about political change. The most telling evidence supporting this interpretation is the resolution passed (on the same day as

Ludendorff proposed an armistice) demanding 'the creation of a strong government supported by the confidence of a majority of the *Reichstag*'. Furthermore, Prince Max was appointed only after consultation with the majority parties in the *Reichstag*.

The idea that it was the *Reichstag* that brought about these changes certainly cannot be ignored but, on balance, it would be wrong to read too much into its actions. Over the years the German *Reichstag* had shown no real inclination to seize the initiative. This still applied in 1918. The *Reichstag* suspended proceedings on 5 October and went into recess until 22 October, when it adjourned again until 9 November. These were hardly the actions of an institution that wished to control events decisively. It seems that the October reforms were shaped 'from above' and the *Reichstag* was happy to go along with these. However, it would be an exaggeration to see these as a constitutional revolution. The forces that had dominated Imperial Germany were still in position at the end of the month.

What pushed Germany, in such a short space of time, from political reform towards revolution was the widespread realisation that the war was lost. The shock of defeat, after years of hardship and optimistic propaganda, hardened popular opinion. By early November it was apparent that the creation of a constitutional monarchy would not defuse what had become a revolutionary situation.

**Key dates**

Ludendorff conceded that Germany was defeated: September 1918

Prince Max of Baden appointed chancellor: 3 October 1918

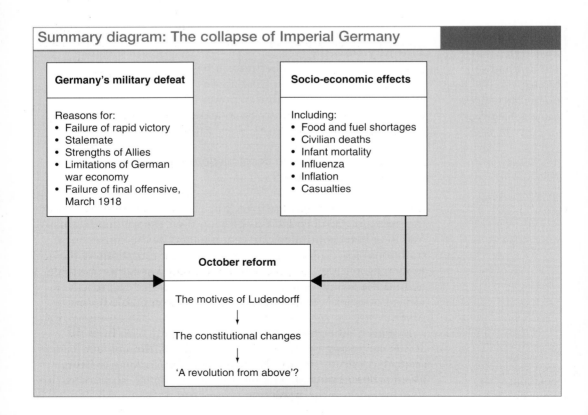

**Summary diagram: The collapse of Imperial Germany**

**Germany's military defeat**

Reasons for:
- Failure of rapid victory
- Stalemate
- Strengths of Allies
- Limitations of German war economy
- Failure of final offensive, March 1918

**Socio-economic effects**

Including:
- Food and fuel shortages
- Civilian deaths
- Infant mortality
- Influenza
- Inflation
- Casualties

**October reform**

The motives of Ludendorff

↓

The constitutional changes

↓

'A revolution from above'?

## 2 | The German Revolution

**Key question**
How and why did the
October reform fail?

On 29 October, a mutiny began to spread among some sailors who refused to obey orders at Wilhelmshaven, near Kiel. Prince Max's government quickly lost control of the political situation and by 2 November sailors gained control of other major ports, such as Kiel and Hamburg. These takeovers had been prompted by a real fear amongst the sailors that their officers were planning a suicide attack on the British fleet, in order to restore the honour of the German navy. The news of the Kiel mutiny fanned the flames of discontent to other ports, Bremen and Lübeck, and soon throughout Germany. By 6 November, numerous workers' and soldiers' councils, similar to the **soviets** that had been set up by the **Bolsheviks** in Russia, were established in the major cities of Berlin, Cologne, and Stuttgart. In Bavaria, the last member of the House of Wittelsbach, King Louis III, was deposed and the socialist Kurt Eisner proclaimed Bavaria an independent democratic socialist republic.

By the end of the first week of November it was clear that the October reforms had failed to impress the German people. The popular discontent was turning into a more fundamental revolutionary movement whose demands were for an immediate peace and the abdication of Kaiser Wilhelm II. The disturbances were prompted by:

- The realisation by troops and sailors that the war was lost and nothing was to be gained by carrying on.
- The sense of national shock when the news came of Germany's military defeat – propaganda and censorship had really delayed the reality for too long.
- The increasing anger and bitterness over socio-economic conditions.

Prince Max would certainly have liked to preserve the monarchy, and possibly even Wilhelm II himself, but the Emperor's delusions that he could carry on without making any more political changes placed the chancellor in a difficult position. In the end, Prince Max became so worried by the revolutionary situation in Berlin that on 9 November he announced that the Kaiser would renounce the throne and that a **coalition** left-wing **government** would be formed by Friedrich Ebert. It was in this chaotic situation that Philipp Scheidemann, one of the provisional government's leaders appeared on the balcony of the *Reichstag* building and proclaimed Germany a republic. (Actually, an hour later Germany was also declared a 'soviet republic' – a statement crucial for the shaping of the next few months of the German Revolution.) It was only at this point in the evening of 9 November that the Kaiser, who was in Belgium, accepted the advice of leading generals. In that way, the Kaiser did not formally abdicate, he simply walked away and went into exile voluntarily in Holland.

**Key terms**

**Bolsheviks**
Followers of
Bolshevism –
Russian
communism.

**Soviet**
A Russian word
meaning an elected
council. Soviets
developed during
the Russian
Revolution in 1917.
In Germany many
councils were set up
in 1918, which had
the support of the
more radical and
revolutionary left-
wing working class.

**Coalition
government**
Usually formed
when a party does
not have an overall
majority in
parliament; it then
combines with more
parties and shares
government
positions.

**Key date**

Kaiser fled to Holland
Ebert appointed
chancellor
Germany proclaimed
a republic:
9 November 1918

## The left-wing movement

A genuinely revolutionary situation existed in Germany in early November 1918. However, the revolutionary wave that swept Germany was not a united force. In fact, the left-wing movement behind it consisted of three main strands (Table 1.1).

**Key question**
In what ways was the left-wing movement divided?

**Table 1.1:** The German left-wing movement

|  | *Moderate socialists* | *Radical socialists* | *Revolutionary socialists* |
|---|---|---|---|
| **Party names** | SPD (German Social Democratic Party) | USPD (German Independent Social Democratic Party) | Spartacists (Spartacus League) |
| **Aim** | To establish a **socialist republic** by the creation of parliamentary democracy | To create a socialist republic governed by workers' and soldiers' councils in conjunction with a parliament | To create a **soviet republic** based on the rule of the workers' and soldiers' councils |
| **Leaders** | Friedrich Ebert Philipp Scheidemann | Karl Kautsky Hugo Haase | Rosa Luxemburg Karl Liebknecht |

### The SPD (German Social Democratic Party)

The SPD represented moderate socialist aims and was led by Friedrich Ebert and Philipp Scheidemann. It dated from 1875. In the election of 1912 it had become the largest party in the *Reichstag* with a membership of over one million. Its fundamental aim was to create a socialist republic, but being wholly committed to parliamentary democracy, it totally rejected anything that might have been likened to Soviet-style communism.

### The Spartacists

On the extreme left stood the Spartacus League (otherwise known as the Spartacists), led by Karl Liebknecht and the Polish-born Rosa Luxemburg, one of the few women to be prominent in German political history (see profile, page 10).

The Spartacists had been formed in 1905 as a minor faction of the SPD. By 1918 it had a national membership of about 5000. From 1914, they had opposed the war and they were deeply influenced by Lenin and Bolshevism. They had come to believe that Germany should follow the same path as Communist Russia. The fundamental aim of the Spartacists was to create a soviet republic based on the rule of the **proletariat** through workers' and soldiers' councils.

**Key terms**

**Socialist republic**
A system of government without a monarchy that aims to introduce social changes for collective benefit.

**Soviet republic**
A system of government without a monarchy that aims to introduce a communist state organised by the workers' councils and opposed to private ownership.

**Proletariat**
The industrial working class who, in Marxist theory, would ultimately take power in the state.

## Key profile: Friedrich Ebert 1871–1925

| | |
|---|---|
| 1871 | – Born in Heidelberg of humble background |
| 1885–8 | – Trained as a saddler |
| 1889 | – Became a trade union organiser and SPD member |
| 1912 | – Elected as a member of the *Reichstag* |
| 1916 | – Chosen as leader of the Party |
| 1918 | – 9 November – became chancellor of the provisional government when Imperial Germany collapsed |
| | – 10 November – Ebert-Groener agreement (see page 11) |
| 1919 | – 11 February – Chosen as the country's first president, a position he held until his death |
| 1925 | – Died at the age of 54 of a heart attack |

Ebert rose from a humble background as a saddler to become the first president of Germany. His character and achievements significantly shaped the development of Weimar democracy.

### The political activist

During his apprenticeship he became quickly involved in trade union work and the socialist movement. His written and spoken skills were soon recognised by the SPD leadership and he advanced through the party covering a range of full-time political jobs such as journalist and secretary. He entered the *Reichstag* in 1912 and just a year later he became chairman of the SPD as he was seen capable of conciliating the developing differences in the Party.

### Leader of the SPD

The First World War divided the SPD fundamentally. Ebert worked really hard to keep it together and in 1916 he was chosen as leader. However, it proved impossible to overcome the differences and a year later the Party split and the USPD was created.

### The German Revolution

When Germany collapsed in autumn 1918, Ebert wanted a democratic parliamentary government with a constitutional monarchy – along English lines – but when events got out of hand in November 1918, the monarchy collapsed and he accepted the chancellorship. It was a major success to manage to hold the first truly democratic German elections, which led to the National Constituent Assembly and the creation of the Weimar Constitution. However, Ebert has been criticised for endorsing the use of the army, the *Freikorps* (see page 44) and other conservative forces to brutally suppress the more radical elements of the left.

### President

He was chosen to be the country's first president by the National Constituent Assembly in February 1919, a position he held until his death. He oversaw the years of crisis and applied the emergency decrees of Article 48 (see page 24) with success. However, he became the focus of scurrilous criticism from the extreme right – which almost certainly contributed to his early death. He was a man of great integrity and decency and, despite the critics, he was a patriot and served his office with distinction and correctness.

**Key term**

*Freikorps* Means 'free corps' who acted as paramilitaries. They were right-wing, nationalist soldiers who were only too willing to use force to suppress communist activity.

## Key profile: Rosa Luxemburg ('Red Rosa') 1871–1919

1870 – Born in Poland of Jewish origins. Badly disabled and walked with a limp, endured continual pain

1905 – Took part in the revolutionary troubles in Russia
– Joined with Karl Liebknecht in Germany to establish the revolutionary group that founded the Spartacist League

1914–18 – Imprisoned for the duration of the war
– Campaigned secretly for a revolutionary end to the war

1917 – Welcomed the Bolshevik revolution in Russia (but soon came to criticise Lenin's repressive methods)

1918 – Freed from prison

1919 – Supported the creation of KPD (German Communist Party) from the Spartacist League
– Opposed the Spartacus uprising in January 1919
– Murdered in police custody in Berlin

After her death, Luxemburg was described as 'arguably one of the finest political theorists of the twentieth century' who famously said, 'Freedom is always for the person who thinks differently'. In 1905, she was one of the founders of the Spartacist League and continued to champion the cause of armed revolution that would sweep the capitalist system away. Ironically, she spoke against the uprising in January 1919 (see page 13) because she felt that Germany was not ready for communism. Although she died a committed revolutionary, she had a humane and optimistic view of communism at odds with the brutality of the Bolsheviks in Russia.

### The USPD (Independent German Social Democratic Party)

The USPD had been formed in 1917 as a breakaway group from the SPD. It was led by Hugo Haase and Karl Kautsky. Although the USPD was a minority of the assembly in the *Reichstag* it had a substantial following of 300,000 members.

The USPD demanded radical social and economic change as well as political reforms. However, as a political movement, it was far from united and internal divisions and squabbles seriously curtailed its influence. The main disagreement was between those who sympathised with the creation of a parliamentary democracy and those who advocated a much more revolutionary democracy based on the workers' councils.

### Ebert's coalition government

Because of the different aims and methods of the socialist movement, there was a lack of unity in Ebert's coalition government. Moreover, it should also be remembered that German society was in a chaotic state of near collapse, so the leading political figures at the time had little room to manoeuvre when they had to make hasty and difficult decisions.

On 9 November 1918 Ebert created a provisional coalition government:

**Key question**
What were the main problems faced by Ebert?

- 'Provisional' in the sense that it was short term until a national election was held to vote for a National Constituent Assembly (parliament).
- 'Coalition' in the sense that it was a combination of parties, the SPD and the USPD.

Ebert himself was a moderate and was frightened that the political situation in Germany could easily run out of control. In Table 1.2, the nature of Ebert's major problems can be seen.

**Table 1.2:** Ebert's main problems

| Socio-economic | Left-wing opposition | Right-wing opposition | Military |
|---|---|---|---|
| **1. Inflation** Wages were falling behind prices, which was increasing social discontent | **1. Strikes** From the autumn of 1918 the number of strikes and lock-outs increased markedly | **1. *Freikorps*** A growing number of right-wing, nationalist soldiers were forming paramilitary units | **1. Demobilisation** About 1.5 million soldiers had to be returned home to Germany |
| **2. Shortages** From the winter of 1916–17 fuel and food shortages were causing real hardship in the cities | **2. German communists** Inspired by the events of 1917–18 in Russia, communists aimed to bring about a revolution in Germany | **2. The army** The army was generally conservative, but also deeply embittered by the military defeat | **2. Allied blockade** The Allies maintained the naval blockade even after the Armistice. Social distress was not relieved until June 1919 |
| **3. Flu epidemic** The 'Spanish flu' killed thousands. It was the most serious flu epidemic of the twentieth century | **3. Workers' and soldiers' councils** Hundred of councils were created and many wanted changes to the army and industries | **3. Nationalists** Nationalist-conservatives were deeply against the abdication of the Kaiser and did not support the creation of a democratic republic | **3. Peace terms** The Armistice was when they agreed to stop fighting, but there was great public concern about the actual effects of the peace treaty |

Ebert's main worry was that the extreme left would gain the upper hand. He recognised the growing number of workers' councils and feared that they might threaten his policy of gradual change. He was determined to maintain law and order to prevent the country collapsing into civil war. He also feared that the return of millions of troops after the Armistice agreement, which was eventually signed on 11 November, would create enormous social and political problems (see Table 1.2). These were the main concerns in the minds of Ebert and the SPD leadership in the months that followed and were the main reasons why they made agreements with the army and industrialists.

**Key date**

Armistice signed between Germany and the Allies at Compiègne in northern France: 11 November 1918

### Ebert-Groener agreement
On 10 November, the day after the declaration of the Republic, General Wilhelm Groener, Ludendorff's successor, telephoned Chancellor Ebert. Their conversation was very significant. The Supreme Army Command agreed to support the new government and to use troops to maintain the stability and security of the new

republic. In return, Ebert promised to oppose the spread of revolutionary socialism and to preserve the authority of the army officers. The deal has become known simply as the Ebert-Groener agreement.

## Stinnes-Legien agreement

A few days later, on 15 November, Karl Legien, leader of the trade unions, and Hugo Stinnes, leader of the industrial employers, held another significant discussion. The Stinnes-Legien agreement was, in effect, a deal where the trade unions made a commitment not to interfere with private ownership and the free market, in return for workers' committees, an eight-hour working day and full legal recognition. Ebert's provisional government endorsed this because the German trade unions were a powerful movement and traditionally closely tied with the SPD.

So, on one level, the agreement to bring about some key, long-desired reforms was a real success. However, these two agreements have been severely criticised over the years, particularly by the left wing. Critics have accused Ebert of having supported compromises with the forces of conservatism. The army was not reformed at all and it was not really committed to democracy. Employers resented the concessions and were unsympathetic to the Weimar system. Nevertheless, there is a counter-argument that Ebert and the SPD leadership were motivated by the simple desire to guarantee stability and a peaceful transition.

## Left-wing splits

By the last days of 1918 it was clear that the SPD had become distanced from its political 'allies' on the left and their conflicting aims resulted in fundamental differences over strategy and policies.

**Key question**
Why did the left-wing movement split?

### USPD

In late December 1918, the USPD members of Ebert's government resigned over the shooting of some Spartacists by soldiers. However, the split had really emerged over the USPD's desire to introduce fundamental social and economic changes that the SPD did not want to adopt.

*Aim*
To create a socialist republic governed by workers' and soldiers' councils in conjunction with a parliament.

*Strategy*
To introduce radical social and economic changes.

*Policies*
To reform the army fundamentally.
To nationalise key industries.
To introduce welfare benefits.

### SPD

The SPD government became increasingly isolated. It moved further to the political right and grew dependent on the civil service and the army to maintain effective government.

*Aim*
To establish a socialist republic by the creation of parliamentary democracy.

*Strategy*
To make arrangements for a democratic *Reichstag* election leading to a National Constituent Assembly.
To introduce moderate changes, but to prevent the spread of communist revolution.

*Policies*
To maintain law and order by running the country with the existing legal and police systems.
To retain the army.
To introduce welfare benefits.

**Key date**

German Communist Party founded: 1 January 1919

## Spartacists

On 1 January 1919, the Spartacists formally founded the *Kommunistische Partei Deutschlands*, the KPD – German Communist Party. It refused to participate in the parliamentary elections, preferring instead to place its faith in the workers' councils, as expressed in the Spartacist manifesto:

> The question today is not democracy or dictatorship. The question that history has put on the agenda reads: bourgeois democracy or socialist democracy? For the dictatorship of the proletariat is democracy in the socialist sense of the word. Dictatorship of the proletariat does not mean bombs, *putsches*, riots and anarchy, as the agents of capitalist profits deliberately and falsely claim. Rather, it means using all instruments of political power to achieve socialism, to expropriate [dispossess of property] the capitalist class, through and in accordance with the will of the revolutionary majority of the proletariat.

*Aim*
To create a soviet republic based on the rule of the workers' and soldiers' councils.

*Strategy*
To oppose the creation of a National Constituent Assembly and to take power by strikes, demonstrations and revolts leading to fundamental social and economic changes.

*Policies*
To replace the army by local militias of workers.
To carry out extensive nationalisation of industries and land.
To introduce welfare benefits.

**Key question**
Why did the Spartacist revolt fail?

### The Spartacist revolt

In January 1919 the Spartacists decided that the time was ripe to launch an armed rising in Berlin with the aim of overthrowing the provisional government and creating a soviet republic.

On 5 January, they occupied public buildings, called for a general strike and formed a revolutionary committee. They denounced Ebert's provisional government and the coming elections. However, they had little chance of success. There were three days of savage street fighting and over 100 were killed. The Spartacist *coup* was easily defeated and afterwards, most notoriously, Liebknecht and Luxemburg were brutally murdered whilst in police custody.

The events of January 1919 showed that the Spartacists were strong on policies, but detached from political realities. They had no real strategy and their 'revolutionaries' were mainly just workers with rifles. By contrast, the government not only had the backing of the army's troops, but also 5000 'irregular' military-style groups, *Freikorps*.

This event created a very troubled atmosphere for the next few months. The elections for the National Constituent Assembly duly took place in February 1919 (see page 18), although the

**Key date**

Start of Spartacist uprising in Berlin: 5 January 1919

continuation of strikes and street disorders in Berlin meant that, for reasons of security, the Assembly's first meeting was switched to the town of **Weimar**. More serious disturbances in Bavaria in April resulted in a short-lived soviet-type republic being established there. The *Freikorps* brought the disturbances under control though, in each case, at the cost of several hundred lives. The infant republic had survived the traumas of its birth.

**Weimar Republic**
Took its name from the first meeting of the National Constituent Assembly in Weimar. The Assembly had moved there because there were still many disturbances in Berlin. Weimar was chosen because it was a town with a great historical and cultural tradition.

Key term

Prost Noske! — — das Proletariat ist entwaffnet!

'Cheers Noske! The Young Revolution is Dead.' A cartoon drawn in 1919 by the German Georg Grosz. Grosz was a communist artist and his images can be stark and disturbing. In this cartoon he satirises the savagery of the *Freikorps*.

## The key debate

After the Second World War, when Germany was divided into east and west, two different interpretations emerged. These raised the question:

> Did Ebert and the SPD leadership betray the German revolution?

In the 1950s and 1960s most historians in West Germany, such as K.D. Erdmann, assumed that there had only ever been two possible options available to Germany at the end of the war: the people had to choose between a communist dictatorship and a parliamentary republic in the style of Weimar. In this light Ebert's decisions were portrayed as those of a heroic figure whose actions had saved Germany from Bolshevism.

In contrast, historians in communist East Germany, 1949–89, saw the actions of the SPD as betrayal of the left-wing movement. Worse, they felt that Ebert had decided to co-operate with the traditional forces of the army and industry. In their view, the real heroes were the Spartacists who had stuck to their true revolutionary ideas and died on the barricades in Berlin.

Following extensive research in the late 1960s and 1970s, these two traditional interpretations have been questioned and a third one has emerged from historians, such as Kolb and Rürup in West Germany. Close analysis of the workers' councils movement throughout Germany has shown that very few fell under the control of the extreme revolutionary left. The vast majority were led by the SPD with USPD support and it was only after January 1919 that the USPD came to dominate. Thus, it is now generally recognised that the threat from the revolutionary communists was grossly exaggerated. They may well have been vocal in putting forward their revolutionary plans, but their actual base of support was minimal. This evidence has, in turn, led to a reassessment of the German Revolution.

Most historians now argue that although the integrity and sincerity of Ebert and the SPD's leadership remain undoubted, their reading of the political situation was poor. Blinded by their fear of the extreme left, they over-estimated the threat from that quarter. This caused them to compromise with the conservative forces of Imperial Germany, rather than asserting their own authority. In that sense, they missed the opportunity to create a solidly based republic built on socialist and democratic principles.

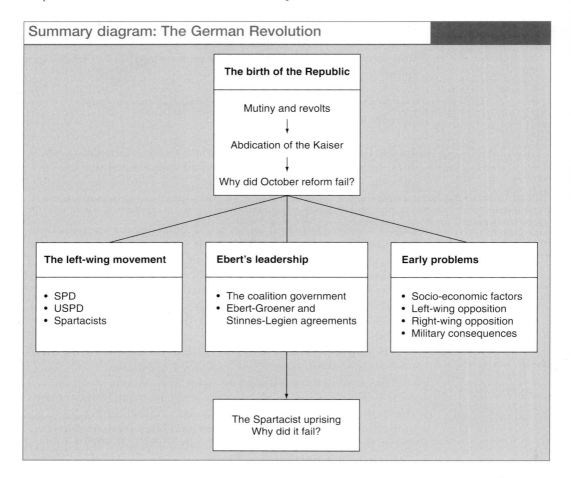

**Summary diagram: The German Revolution**

The birth of the Republic

Mutiny and revolts
↓
Abdication of the Kaiser
↓
Why did October reform fail?

**The left-wing movement**

- SPD
- USPD
- Spartacists

**Ebert's leadership**

- The coalition government
- Ebert-Groener and Stinnes-Legien agreements

**Early problems**

- Socio-economic factors
- Left-wing opposition
- Right-wing opposition
- Military consequences

The Spartacist uprising
Why did it fail?

# 3 | The National Constituent Assembly

Despite the disturbances across Germany, in the months after the collapse of Imperial Germany, the new republic was still able to hold its first elections for a National Constituent Assembly on 19 January 1919. Most political parties took the opportunity to retitle themselves, but new names did not disguise the fact that there was considerable continuity in the structure of the party system (see Table 1.1).

The election results (see Figure 1.1, page 18) quickly led to the creation of the National Constituent Assembly on 6 February. In many respects the results represented a major success for the forces of parliamentary democracy:

- The high turnout of 83 per cent in the election suggested faith in the idea of democracy.
- 76.1 per cent of the electorate voted for pro-democratic parties.
- The solid vote for the three main democratic parties, the SPD, the DDP and the ZP, made it straightforward to form a coalition government, which became known as the 'Weimar Coalition'.

**Key question**
Was the election a success for democracy?

**Key date**
National Constituent Assembly met at Weimar: 6 February 1919

**Table 1.1:** The major political parties in the Weimar Republic

| Party | Leader | Description |
|---|---|---|
| **BVP Bayerische Volkspartei** (Bavarian People's Party) | Leader: Heinrich Held | The BVP was a regional party formed from elements of the ZP in 1919 in order to uphold Bavaria's local interests. It was conservative, but generally supported the Republic. |
| **DDP Deutsche Demokratische Partei** (German Democratic Party) | Leaders: Walther Rathenau and Hugo Preuss | Formed from the National Liberals party in the old *Reichstag*, it attracted support from the professional middle classes, especially the intellectuals and some of the businessmen. The party supported the democratic republic and was committed to constitutional reform. |
| **DNVP Deutschnationale Volkspartei** (German National People's Party) | Leaders: Karl Helfferich and Alfred Hugenberg (see page 80) | The DNVP was a right-wing party formed from the old conservative parties and some of the racist, anti-Semitic groups, such as the Pan-German League. It was monarchist and anti-republican. Generally, it was closely tied to the interests of heavy industry and agriculture, including landowners and small farmers. |
| **DVP Deutsche Volkspartei** (German People's Party) | Leader: Gustav Stresemann (see pages 89–90) | A new party founded by Gustav Stresemann, who was a conservative and monarchist and at first suspicious of the Weimar Republic and voted against the new constitution (see page 24). From 1921, under Stresemann's influence, the DVP became a strong supporter of parliamentary democracy. It attracted support from the protestant middle and upper classes. |
| **KPD Kommunistische Partei Deutschlands** (German Communist Party) | Leader: Ernst Thälmann | The KPD was formed in January 1919 by the extreme left wing, e.g. Spartacists. It was anti-republican in the sense that it opposed Weimar-style democracy and supported a revolutionary overthrow of society. Most of its supporters were from the working class and strengthened by the defection of many USPD members in 1920. |
| **NSDAP Nationalsozialistische Partei Deutschlands** (National Socialist German Workers' Party – Nazi Party) | Leader: Adolf Hitler (see pages 153–4) | Extreme right-wing party formed in 1919. It was anti-republican, anti-Semitic and strongly nationalist. Until 1930 it remained a fringe party with support from the lower middle classes. |
| **SPD Sozialdemokratische Partei Deutschlands** (German Social Democratic Party) | Leaders: Friedrich Ebert (see page 9) and Philipp Scheidemann | The moderate wing of the socialist movement, it was very much the party of the working class and the trade unions. It strongly supported parliamentary democracy and was opposed to the revolutionary demands of the more left-wing socialists. |
| **USPD Unabhängige Sozialdemokratische Partei Deutschlands** (Independent German Social Democratic Party) | Leaders: Karl Kautsky and Hugo Haase | The USPD broke away from the SPD in April 1917. It included many of the more radical elements of German socialism and, therefore, sought social and political change. About half its members joined the KPD during 1919–20 whilst by 1922 most of the others had returned to the ranks of the SPD. |
| **ZP Zentrumspartei** (Centre Party) | Leaders: Matthias Erzberger and Heinrich Brüning (see page 135) | The ZP had been created in the nineteenth century to defend the interests of the Roman Catholic Church. It continued to be the major political voice of Catholicism and enjoyed a broad range of supporters from aristocratic landowners to Christian trade unionists. Most of the ZP was committed to the Republic. From the late 1920s it became more sympathetic to the right wing. |

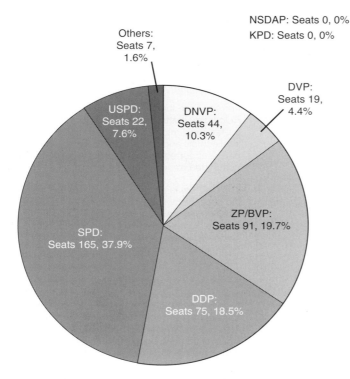

**Figure 1.2:** *Reichstag* election result January 1919
Turnout 83 per cent
Total number of seats 423

However, it should be borne in mind that:

- Although the DNVP gained only 10.3 per cent, it had backing from important conservative supporters, e.g. the landowners, the army officers, industrialists.
- The DVP and its leader, Stresemann, did not support the Weimar Republic in 1919 because they wanted Germany to have a constitutional monarchy.

## What kind of revolution?

By May 1919 a degree of stability had returned to Germany. The revolution had run its course and the Weimar Republic had been established. However, serious doubts remain about the nature and real extent of these revolutionary changes.

Undoubtedly, there existed the possibility of revolution in Germany as the war came to an end. The effects of war and the shock of defeat shook the faith of large numbers of the people in the old order. Imperial Germany could not survive, so Wilhelm II and the other princes were deposed and parliamentary democracy was introduced. These were important changes.

However, in the end, the German Revolution did not go much further than the October reforms and was strictly limited in scope. Society was left almost untouched by these events, for there was no attempt to reform the key institutions.

**Key question**
How fundamental were the changes brought about by the German Revolution?

- The civil service, judiciary and army all remained essentially intact.
- Similarly, the power and influence of Germany's industrial and commercial leaders remained unchanged.
- There were no changes in the structure of big business and land ownership.

Certainly, plans for the improvement of working conditions and the beginnings of a welfare state were outlined by the government, but the SPD leadership hoped that all the changes would follow in the wake of constitutional reform. With hindsight, it seems that more thoroughgoing social and economic changes might well have been a better basis on which to establish democracy. As it was, the divisions on the left played into the hands of the conservative forces. As one historian, M. Hughes, has claim, 'it is more accurate to talk of a potential revolution which ran away into the sand rather than the genuine article'. Indeed, during the first half of 1919 the increasing reliance of the moderate left on the conservative forces of Imperial Germany became a major factor in German politics. These conservative forces were soon to put into doubt the very survival of Weimar democracy.

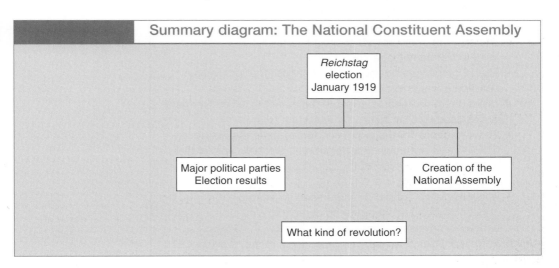

Summary diagram: The National Constituent Assembly

Reichstag election January 1919

Major political parties Election results

Creation of the National Assembly

What kind of revolution?

## Study Guide: AS Questions

### In the style of AQA
Read the following source and answer the questions that follow.

*Adapted from Hinton and Hite,* Weimar and Nazi Germany, *2000.*

Ebert chose the moderate course. He was determined to defend the new democratic system from what he saw as the horrors of Bolshevism. Ebert believed the new government needed the support of the traditional élites and was prepared to co-operate with them.

**(a)** Explain what is meant by 'Bolshevism' in the context of political unrest in Germany in 1918. (3 marks)

**(b)** Explain why the SPD leader, Ebert, opposed the communists in 1918. (7 marks)

**(c)** 'By May 1919 stability had been restored in Germany.' Explain why you agree or disagree with this statement. (15 marks)

*Source: AQA, June 2003*

---

*Exam tips*

*The cross-references are intended to take you straight to the material that will help you to answer the questions.*

**(a)** In question **(a)** you should provide a developed explanation of the concept of 'Bolshevism' linked to the context, for example:
  - German communists wanted to seize power and create a soviet republic (pages 12–13).
  - The unrest arising from economic distress, military failure and the abdication of the Kaiser (pages 2–8).

**(b)** In question **(b)** you have to demonstrate explicit understanding of a range of factors to explain Ebert's hostility to communism and draw conclusions about their relative significance, for example:
  - The influence of the Bolshevik revolution in Russia (page 8).
  - The creation of the soviets (workers' councils) in November 1918 in Germany (page 7).
  - Ebert's precarious position as the chancellor of provisional coalition government (pages 10–11).

**(c)** In question **(c)** you should evaluate the extent to which Germany had stabilised by May 1919. It is important to:
  - Show evidence for the argument, for example the Spartacist uprising was put down; the democratic elections resulted in the successful creation of the Constituent National Assembly (pages 13, 16–18).
  - Show evidence against the argument, for example the opposition of traditional élites to democracy; major social and economic problems (pages 11 and 15–18).

A thoughtful conclusion is vital. You must use a range of evidence to make your judgment, for example it would be useful to point out that Ebert helped to stabilise the situation in Germany in the short term, but made a fatal error in the long term by compromising with the élites.

## In the style of Edexcel

(a) What were the problems faced by Chancellor Ebert and his government immediately after the collapse of Imperial Germany?                                   (15 marks)

(b) Why did the Spartacists fail to create a soviet republic?
                                                              (15 marks)

---

### Exam tips

*The cross-references are intended to take you straight to the material that will help you to answer the questions.*

(a) In question **(a)** you should concentrate on the two months from November 1918. However, this covers a lot of detail, so focus on the most important points and do not just describe the story. Take a thematic approach and identify problems, such as:
- Socio-economic problems (pages 2–3), e.g. inflation, shortages.
- Opposition from the extreme left (pages 12–14), e.g. revolutionary groups.
- Opposition from the extreme right (page 11), e.g. the *Freikorps*.
- Military consequences of defeat (pages 2–3), e.g. Allied blockade.

In a good conclusion you could prioritise the problems.

(b) In question **(b)** you must concentrate on the months November 1918–January 1919, but be aware of the background of the chaotic situation in Germany after the collapse of Imperial Germany. Also describe fully the aim of the Spartacists to create a soviet republic.

You should identify a number of key factors to explain the failure of the Spartacists:
- The divisions of the left-wing movement (pages 8–13).
- The strength of the conservative forces (pages 15–18).
- The weaknesses of the Spartacist leadership (page 13).

A good conclusion will show the interaction of factors and how they combined to bring about the failure of the Spartacists. It is also important to show the relative significance of these factors. It may be helpful to compare the success of the Bolshevik Russian Revolution with the total failure of the Spartacists in Germany.

## In the style of OCR

How far do you agree with the view that, by 1919, 'the German Revolution did not really change Germany'?

---

### Exam tips

*The cross-references are intended to take you straight to the material that will help you to answer the question.*

This question requires you to evaluate the impact the German Revolution had immediately after it had happened. High marks depend on your addressing and answering the question actually set. In order to do this you should show some of the ways in which Germany was changed in the six months after the declaration of the Republic and some of the ways in which it was limited. A good answer will be organised so that different themes – such as institutions, society, government – are evaluated in turn by comparing the extent and limitations of change in each one. Some examples of change are:

- The abdication of the Kaiser and the princes (page 7).
- The creation of the National Constituent Assembly and the commitment to the creation of a parliamentary democracy (pages 16–19).
- The promise to create a welfare state and improved working conditions (pages 12–13).

Some of the ways in which the German Revolution was limited are:

- Ebert's government's over-reliance on the army and the *Freikorps* to crush revolutionary groups (pages 13–14).
- The failure to change the ownership of land and industry (pages 15–18).

Finally, round off your answer by offering an opinion on how far you agree or disagree with the view.

# 2 Two Key Documents

> **POINTS TO CONSIDER**
> In the summer of 1919 two crucial documents were drawn up that influenced the history of the Weimar Republic:
>
> - The Weimar Constitution, which was agreed by the German *Reichstag*
> - The Treaty of Versailles, which was imposed by the Allies
>
> This chapter will examine the terms and significance of each.

### Key dates
| 1919 | February 6 | National Assembly first meeting at Weimar |
|------|------------|-------------------------------------------|
|      | June 28    | Treaty of Versailles signed               |
|      | July 31    | Weimar Constitution adopted by the National Constituent Assembly |
|      | August 11  | Weimar Constitution signed by President Ebert |

## 1 | The Weimar Constitution

### The key terms of the Constitution

Back in November 1918, Ebert invited the liberal lawyer Hugo Preuss to draw up a new **constitution** for Germany and a draft was outlined by the time the National Assembly was established in February 1919. Preuss worked closely with a constitutional committee of 28 members over the next six months, though their discussions were deeply overshadowed by the dispute about the Treaty of Versailles (see pages 29–36).

The proposals for the new constitution were influenced by the long-established democratic ideas of Britain and the USA. Nevertheless, Germany's particular circumstances and traditions were not ignored as, for example, in the introduction of

**proportional representation** and the creation of a **federal structure**. Eventually, on 31 July 1919, the *Reichstag* voted strongly in favour of the constitution (for: 262; against: 75) and on 11 August the president ratified it. The main features of the constitution are outlined below and in Figure 2.1 on page 25.

## Definition

Germany was declared a 'democratic state', although it retained the title of 'Reich' (empire). It was a republic (all monarchies were ended). It had a federal structure with 17 *Länder* (regional states), e.g. Prussia, Bavaria, Saxony.

## President

The people elected the president every seven years. He enjoyed considerable powers, such as:

- The right to dissolve the *Reichstag*.
- The appointment of the chancellor. (Although the president was not obliged, he tended to choose the chancellor as the leader of the largest party in the *Reichstag*. In order to form a workable coalition government, it was necessary to negotiate with the leaders of other political parties.)
- The Supreme Commander of the Armed Forces.
- The capacity to rule by decree at a time of national emergency (**Article 48**) and to oversee the *Reichstag*.

But this created a very complex relationship between the powers of the president and the *Reichstag*/chancellor.

## Parliament

There were two houses in the German parliament:

- The *Reichstag* was the main representative assembly and law-making body of the parliament. It consisted of deputies elected every four years on the basis of a system of proportional representation. The PR system allocated members to parliament from the official list of political party candidates. They were distributed on the basis of one member for every 60,000 votes in an electoral district.
- The *Reichsrat* was the less important house in the parliament. It was made up of representatives from all of the 17 state regional governments (*Länder*), which all held local responsibilities such as education, police, etc. But the *Reichsrat* could only initiate or delay proposals, and the *Reichstag* could always overrule it.

**Key dates**

National Assembly first meeting at Weimar: 6 February 1919

The Weimar Constitution was adopted by the National Assembly: 31 July 1919

**Key terms**

**Constitution**
The principles and rules that govern a state. The Weimar Constitution is a good example. (Britain is often described as having an unwritten constitution. It is not drawn up in *one* document, but built on statutes, conventions and case law.)

**Proportional representation**
A system that allocates parliamentary seats in proportion to the total number of votes.

**Federal structure**
Where power and responsibilities are shared between central and regional governments.

**Article 48**
Gave the Weimar president the power in an emergency to rule by decree and to override the constitutional rights of the people.

## Bill of Rights

The constitution also drew up a range of individual rights. It outlined broad freedoms, for example:

- personal liberty
- the right of free speech
- censorship was forbidden
- equality before the law of all Germans
- religious freedom and conscience (and no State Church was allowed).

In addition to this, the Bill of Rights provided a range of social rights, for example:

- welfare provision, e.g. for housing, the disabled, orphans
- protection of labour.

## Supreme Court

In order to settle different interpretations of law, a Supreme Court was created.

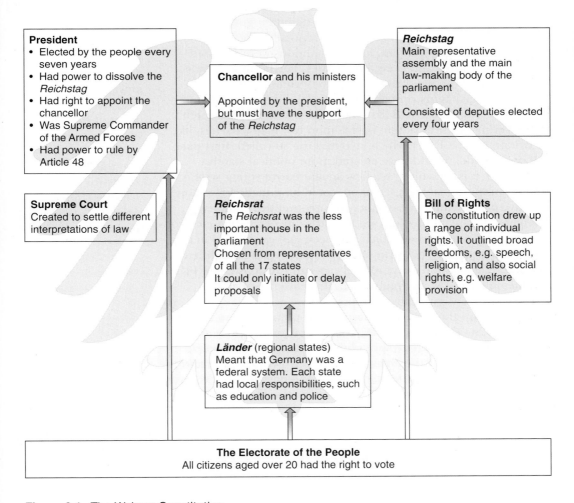

**President**
- Elected by the people every seven years
- Had power to dissolve the *Reichstag*
- Had right to appoint the chancellor
- Was Supreme Commander of the Armed Forces
- Had power to rule by Article 48

**Chancellor** and his ministers

Appointed by the president, but must have the support of the *Reichstag*

**Reichstag**
Main representative assembly and the main law-making body of the parliament

Consisted of deputies elected every four years

**Supreme Court**
Created to settle different interpretations of law

**Reichsrat**
The *Reichsrat* was the less important house in the parliament
Chosen from representatives of all the 17 states
It could only initiate or delay proposals

**Bill of Rights**
The constitution drew up a range of individual rights. It outlined broad freedoms, e.g. speech, religion, and also social rights, e.g. welfare provision

***Länder*** (regional states)
Meant that Germany was a federal system. Each state had local responsibilities, such as education and police

**The Electorate of the People**
All citizens aged over 20 had the right to vote

**Figure 2.1:** The Weimar Constitution

## The issues of controversy

Since the Weimar Republic lasted only 14 crisis-ridden years, it is hardly surprising that its written constitution has been the focus of considerable attention. Some historians have gone so far as to argue that the real causes of the collapse of the Republic and the success of Hitler and National Socialists can be found in its clauses. Such claims are based on three aspects of the constitution. These are:

**Key question**
What were the arguments for and against the terms of Weimar Constitution?

- The introduction of proportional representation.
- The relationship between the president and the *Reichstag* and, in particular, the emergency powers available to the president under Article 48.
- The fact that the traditional institutions of Imperial Germany were allowed to continue.

### Proportional representation

The introduction of proportional representation became the focus of criticism after 1945 because, it was argued, it had encouraged the formation of many new, small splinter parties, e.g. the Nazis. This made it more difficult to form and maintain governments.

In Weimar Germany it was virtually impossible for one party to form a majority government, and so coalitions were required – sometimes of three and even four parties. Furthermore, it was argued that all the negotiations and compromises involved in forming governments contributed to the political instability of Weimar. It is for these reasons that many critics of Weimar felt that a voting political system based upon two major parties, like in Britain (or the USA), which favoured the so-called '**first past the post**' model, would have created more political stability.

However, it is difficult to see how an alternative voting system, without proportional representation, could have made for a more effective parliamentary democracy in early twentieth century Germany. The main problem was the difficulty of creating coalitions amongst the main parties, which had been well established in the nineteenth century. The parties were meant to reflect the different political, religious and geographical views and so a system of PR was the only fair way. By comparison, the existence of all the splinter parties was a relatively minor issue.

There is also the view that, after the economic and political crisis of 1929–33 (see pages 122–5), proportional representation encouraged the emergence of political extremism. However, it now seems clear that the changes in the way people voted and the way they changed their allegiance from one party to another were just too volatile to be kept in check. It may also have been the case that a 'first past the post' system would have actually helped the rise of Nazism and Communism.

**First past the post**
An electoral system that simply requires the winner to gain one vote more than the second placed candidate. It is also referred to as the plurality system and does not require 50 per cent plus one votes. In a national election it tends to give the most successful party disproportionately more seats than its total vote merits.

**Key term**

### The relationship between the president and the *Reichstag*

The relationship created between the *Reichstag* and the president in the Weimar Constitution was meant to have a fair system of checks and balances, but this was very complex.

It was intended to lessen the fears that an unrestricted parliament would become too powerful. Fear of an over-powerful parliament was strong on the right wing, and within liberal circles. It therefore aimed to create a presidency that could provide leadership 'above the parties' and limit the powers of the *Reichstag* (see page 24 and Figure 2.1 on page 25). The president's powers were seen as amounting to those of an *Ersatzkaiser*, a substitute emperor. When the power of the president is compared with the authority of the *Reichstag*, it seems that the attempt to prevent too much power being placed in the hands of one institution resulted in massive power being granted to another. As a result, there was uncertainty in constitutional matters from the start.

The framers of the constitution struggled to keep a balance of power between the president and the *Reichstag*. Was the ultimate source of authority in the democratic republic vested in the representative assembly of the people – the *Reichstag* – or in the popularly elected head of state – the president?

Matters were made more difficult by the powers conferred upon the president by Article 48. This Article provided the head of state with the authority to suspend civil rights in an emergency and restore law and order by the issue of presidential decrees. The intention was to create the means by which government could continue to function in a crisis. However, the effect was to create what the historian Gordon Craig referred to as 'a constitutional anomaly'. Such fears, which were actively expressed by some deputies in the constitutional debate of 1919, later assumed a particular importance during the crisis that brought Hitler to power in 1933. However, it should be remembered that in the crisis of 1923 the presidential powers were used as intended and to very good effect.

## The continuity of traditional institutions

Although the Weimar Constitution introduced a wide range of democratic rights and civil liberties, it made no provision to reform the old traditional institutions of Imperial Germany, such as:

- The civil service was well educated and professional, but tended to conform to the old-fashioned conservative values of Imperial Germany.
- The judiciary continued to enjoy its traditional independence under the Weimar Constitution, but the hearts of many judges did not lie with the Weimar Republic. Bluntly, they were biased and tended to favour the extreme right and condemn the extreme left. Only 28 out of 354 right-wing assassins were found guilty and punished, but 10 of the 22 left-wing assassins were sentenced to death.
- The army enjoyed great status and many of the generals were socially linked with the Prussian landowners. It sought to maintain its influence after 1918 and was generally not sympathetic to democratic Germany. It was the only real authority that had military capacity.
- Universities were very proud of their traditional status and generally more sympathetic to the old political ideas and rules.

In Weimar's difficult early years effective use was made of the established professional skills and educated institutions of the state. However, the result was that powerful conservative forces were able to exert great influence in the daily life of the Weimar Republic. This was at odds with the left wing's wishes to extend civil rights and to create a modern, democratic society. So, whilst the spirit of the Weimar Constitution was democratic and progressive, many of the institutions remained dedicated to the values of Imperial Germany.

## The significance of the Weimar Constitution

With hindsight, it is easy to highlight those parts of the Weimar Constitution that contributed to the ultimate collapse of the Republic. However, it should be remembered that the new constitution was a great improvement upon the previous undemocratic constitution of Imperial Germany and a very large majority voted in favour of it. Indeed, Weimar was initially seen as 'the most advanced democracy in the world'. What the Constitution could not control were the conditions and circumstances in which it had to operate. And the Weimar Republic had other more serious problems than just the Constitution, such as the Treaty of Versailles and its social-economic problems. As Theodor Heuss, the first president of the German Federal Republic in 1949, said: 'Germany never conquered democracy for herself. Democracy came to Germany … in the wake of defeat'.

Therefore, it seems unrealistic to imagine that any piece of paper could have resolved all Germany's problems after 1918. The Weimar Constitution had weaknesses, but it was not fatally flawed – there were many more serious and fundamental problems within the Weimar Republic.

> **Key question**
> Was the Weimar Constitution fatally flawed?

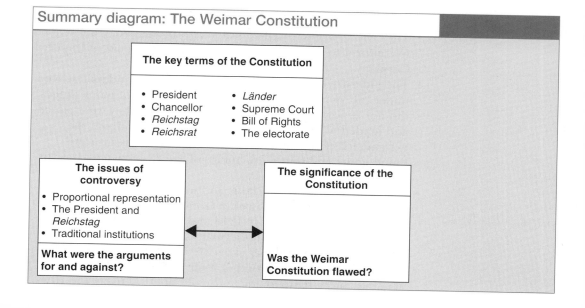

Summary diagram: The Weimar Constitution

**The key terms of the Constitution**

- President
- Chancellor
- *Reichstag*
- *Reichsrat*
- *Länder*
- Supreme Court
- Bill of Rights
- The electorate

**The issues of controversy**

- Proportional representation
- The President and *Reichstag*
- Traditional institutions

**What were the arguments for and against?**

**The significance of the Constitution**

**Was the Weimar Constitution flawed?**

**Key question**
In what ways did the Allies differ over war aims?

**Key date**

The German government signed the Treaty of Versailles: 28 June 1919

# 2 | The Treaty of Versailles

For most Germans the Paris peace settlement of 1919 was a far more controversial issue than the new constitution. It had been generally assumed among German public opinion that the treaty would result in a fair peace. This was partly because defeat had never really been expected, even as late as the summer of 1918, and partly because it was generally assumed that President Wilson's Fourteen Points would lay the basis of the terms.

However, it soon became clear that the peace treaty would not be open for discussion with Germany's representatives. When the draft terms were presented in May 1919 there was national shock and outrage in Germany. In desperation, the first Weimar government led by Scheidemann resigned. The Allies were not prepared to negotiate, which obliged an embittered *Reichstag* finally to accept the Treaty of Versailles by 237 votes to 138 in June. This was because Germany simply did not have the military capacity to resist. And so, on 28 June 1919, the German representatives, led by Hermann Müller, signed the treaty in the Hall of Mirrors at Versailles near Paris.

The Treaty of Versailles was a compromise, but only in the sense that it was a compromise *between* the Allied powers. So the really decisive negotiations were between the so-called 'Big Three':

- Woodrow Wilson, President of the USA
- Georges Clemenceau, Prime Minister of France
- Lloyd George, Prime Minister of Great Britain.

## Woodrow Wilson

He has traditionally been portrayed as an idealist, as he had a strong religious framework. Initially, he had been an academic, but he was drawn into politics when he had campaigned against corruption. At first he had opposed American entry into the war. Once he declared war against Germany in April 1917 he drew up the Fourteen Points in the hope of creating a more just world. His main aims were:

- to bring about international disarmament
- to apply the principle of **self-determination**
- to create a **League of Nations** in order to maintain international peace.

## Georges Clemenceau

He was an uncompromising French nationalist. He had been in his country twice when Germany had invaded and he was deeply influenced by the devastation from the war in northern France. He was motivated by revenge and he was determined to gain

**Key terms**

**Self-determination**
The right of people of the same nation to decide their own form of government. In effect, it is the principle of each nation ruling itself. Wilson believed that the application of self-determination was integral to the Peace Settlement and it would lead to long-term peace.

**League of Nations**
The international body initiated by President Wilson to encourage disarmament and to prevent war.

financial compensation and to satisfy France's security concerns. His main aims were:

- to annex the Rhineland and to create a '**buffer state**'
- to impose the major disarmament of Germany
- to impose heavy reparations in order to weaken Germany
- to get recompense from the damage of the war in order to finance re-building.

## Lloyd George

He may be seen as a pragmatist. He was keen to uphold British national interests and initially he played on the idea of revenge. However, he recognised that there would have to be compromise. In particular, he saw the need to restrain Clemenceau's revenge. His main aims were:

- to guarantee British military security – especially, to secure naval supremacy
- to keep communism at bay
- to limit French demands because he feared that excessively weakening Germany would have serious economic consequences for the European economy.

## The terms of the Treaty of Versailles

The key terms of the Treaty of Versailles can be listed under the following headings: territorial arrangements, war guilt, reparations, disarmament and maintaining peace.

## a) Territorial arrangements

- Eupen-Malmedy. Subject to **plebiscite**, the districts of Eupen and Malmedy to be handed over to Belgium.
- Alsace-Lorraine. Germany to return these provinces to France.
- North Schleswig. Subject to plebiscite, Germany to hand over the North Schleswig.
- West Prussia and Posen. Germany to surrender West Prussia and Posen, thus separating East Prussia from the main part of Germany (creating 'the Polish Corridor').
- Upper Silesia. A plebiscite was to be held in the province of Upper Silesia and as a result it was divided between Poland and Germany.
- Danzig. The German city and port of Danzig (Gdansk in Polish) was made an international 'free city' under the control of the League of Nations.
- Memel. The German port of Memel was also made an international 'free city' under the League.
- Austria. The reunification (*Anschluss*) of Germany with Austria was forbidden.
- Kiel Canal and rivers. All major rivers to be open for all nations and to be run by an international commission.
- Saar area (see 'Reparations' below).
- Rhineland (see 'Disarmament' below).

**Key term**

**Buffer state**
The general idea of separating two rival countries by leaving a space between them. Clemenceau believed that the long-established Franco-German military aggression could be brought to an end by establishing an independent Rhineland state (though this was not implemented because Wilson saw it as against the principle of self-determination).

**Key question**
What were the significant terms of the Treaty of Versailles?

**Key terms**

**Plebiscite**
A vote by the people on one specific issue – like a referendum.

*Anschluss*
Usually translated as 'union'. In the years 1919–38, it referred to the paragraph in the Treaty of Versailles that outlawed any political union between Germany and Austria, although the population was wholly German.

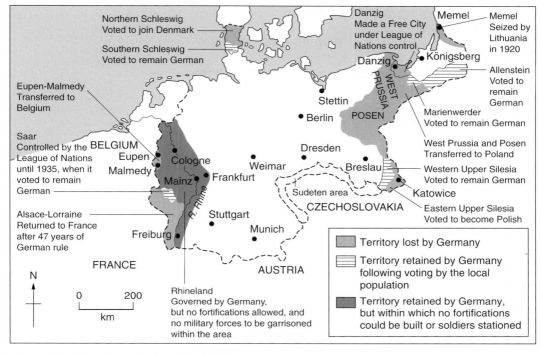

**Figure 2.2:** The Treaty of Versailles 1919

**Mandates**
The name given by the Allies to the system created in the Peace Settlement for the supervision of all the colonies of Germany (and Turkey) by the League of Nations.

- Germany's colonies. All German colonies were distributed as '**mandates**', under control of countries supervised by the League, for example Britain took responsibility for German East Africa.

## b) War guilt
Germany was forced to sign the War Guilt clause (Article 231) accepting blame for causing the war and therefore responsibility for all losses and damage:

Germany accepts the responsibility of Germany and her allies for causing all the loss and damage to which the Allied governments and their peoples have been subjected as a result of the war.

## c) Reparations
- Reparations sum to be fixed later by the IARC (Inter-Allied Reparations Commission). In 1921 the sum was fixed at £6600 million.
- Germany to make substantial payments in kind, e.g. coal.
- The Saar to be under the control of the League until 1935, when there was to be a plebiscite. Until then all coal production was to be given to France.

## d) Disarmament
- Germany to abolish conscription and to reduce its army to 100,000. No tanks or big guns were allowed.
- Rhineland was to be demilitarised from the French frontier to a line 32 miles east of the Rhine. (The Rhineland remained part of Germany.)

- Germany allowed no military aircraft.
- German navy limited to:
  - six battleships, six cruisers, 12 destroyers, 12 torpedo boats
  - no submarines were allowed.
  (The German fleet surrendered to Britain in 1918, but sank its own ships at Scapa Flow on 28 June 1919.)

### e) Maintaining peace
The Treaty also set out the Covenant of the League of Nations, which included the aims and organisation of the League. Germany had to accept the League, but it was initially not allowed to join.

**Table 2.1:** German losses resulting from the Treaty of Versailles

| Type of loss | Percentage of loss |
| --- | --- |
| Territory | 13 per cent |
| Population | 12 per cent (6.5 million) |
| Agricultural production | 15 per cent |
| Iron-ore | 48 per cent |
| Coal | 15 per cent |

### The '*Diktat*'
No other political issue produced such total agreement within Weimar Germany as the rejection and condemnation of the Treaty of Versailles. The Treaty's terms were seen as unfair and were simply described as a '*Diktat*'. Germany's main complaints were as follows:

**Key question**
Why did the Germans view the Treaty as unfair?

*Diktat*
A dictated peace. The Germans felt that the Treaty of Versailles was imposed without negotiation.

Key term

- The Treaty was considered to be very different from President Wilson's Fourteen Points. Most obviously, many Germans found it impossible to understand how and why the guiding principle of self-determination was *not* applied in a number of cases. They viewed the following areas as 'German', but excluded from the new German state and placed under foreign rule:
  Austria
  Danzig
  Posen and West Prussia
  Memel
  Upper Silesia
  Sudetenland
  Saar.
  Similarly, the loss of Germany's colonies was not in line with the fifth of Wilson's Fourteen Points, which had called for 'an impartial adjustment of all colonial claims'. Instead, they were passed on to the care of the Allies as mandates.
- Germany found it impossible to accept the War Guilt clause (Article 231), which was the Allies' justification for demanding the payment of reparations. Most Germans argued that Germany could not be held solely responsible for the outbreak of the war. They were convinced that the war of 1914 had been

fought for defensive reasons because their country had been threatened by 'encirclement' from the Allies in 1914.

- Germans considered the Allied demand for extensive reparations as totally unreasonable. Worryingly, the actual size of the reparations payment was not stated in the Treaty of Versailles – it was left to be decided at a later date by the IARC. From a German viewpoint this amounted to their being forced to sign a 'blank cheque'.

- The imposition of the disarmament clauses was seen as grossly unfair as Britain and France remained highly armed and made no future commitments to disarm. It seemed as if Germany had been **unilaterally disarmed**, whereas Wilson had spoken in favour of universal disarmament.

- Germany's treatment by the Allies was viewed as undignified and unworthy of a great power. For example, Germany was excluded from the League of Nations but, as part of the Treaty, was forced to accept the rules of its Covenant. This simply hardened the views of those Germans who saw the League as a tool of the Allies rather than as a genuine international organisation.

Altogether, the treaty was seen as a *Diktat*. The Allies maintained a military blockade on Germany until the Treaty was signed. This had significant human consequences such as increasing food shortages. Furthermore, the Allies threatened to take further military action if Germany did not co-operate.

## Key term

**Unilateral disarmament**
The disarmament of one party. Wilson pushed for general (universal) disarmament after the war, but France and Britain were more suspicious. As a result only Germany had to disarm.

A cartoon drawn in July 1919 from the German newspaper *Kladderatsch*. It portrays Georges Clemenceau (the French Prime Minister) as a vampire sucking the blood and life from the innocent German maiden.

## Versailles: a more balanced view

In the years 1919–45, most Germans regarded the Treaty of Versailles as a *Diktat*. In Britain, too, there developed a growing sympathy for Germany's position. However, this was not the case in France, where the Treaty was generally condemned as being too lenient. It was only after the Second World War that a more balanced view of the Treaty of Versailles emerged in Europe. As a result, recent historians have tended to look upon the peacemakers of 1919 in a more sympathetic light. Earlier German criticisms of the Treaty are no longer as readily accepted as they once were.

Of course, at the Paris peace conferences Allied statesmen were motivated by their own national self-interests, and the representatives of France and Britain were keen to achieve these at the expense of Germany. However, it is now recognised that it was the situation created by the war that shaped the terms of the Treaty and not just anti-German feeling. The aims and objectives of the various Allies differed and achieving agreement was made more difficult by the complicated circumstances of the time. It should be remembered that the Paris peace settlement was not solely concerned with Germany, so Austria–Hungary, Bulgaria and Turkey were forced to sign separate treaties. In addition, numerous other problems had to be dealt with. For example, Britain had national interests to look after in the Middle East as a result of the collapse of the Turkish Empire. At the same time the Allies were concerned by the threat of Soviet Russia and were motivated by a common desire to contain the Bolshevik menace.

In the end, the Treaty of Versailles was a compromise. It was not based on Wilson's Fourteen Points as most Germans thought it would be, but equally it was not nearly so severe as certain sections of Allied opinion had demanded. It should be borne in mind that:

- Clemenceau, the French representative, was forced to give way over most of his country's more extreme demands, such as the creation of an independent Rhineland and the **annexation** of the Saar.
- The application of self-determination was not nearly so unfair as many Germans believed:
  - Alsace-Lorraine would have voted to return to France anyway, as it had been French before 1871.
  - Plebiscites were held in Schleswig, Silesia and parts of Prussia to decide their future.
  - Danzig's status under the League was the result of Woodrow Wilson's promise to provide 'Poland with access to the sea'.
  - The eastern frontier provinces of Posen and West Prussia were rather more mixed in ethnic make-up than Germans were prepared to admit (in these provinces Germans predominated in the towns, whereas the Poles did so in the countryside – which made it very difficult to draw a clear frontier line).
  - Austria and Sudetenland had never been part of Germany before 1918, anyway.

**Key question**
To what extent was the Treaty of Versailles motivated by anti-German feeling?

**Annexation**
Taking over of another country against its will.

Key term

- Germany was not physically occupied during the war and, as a result, the real damage was suffered on foreign soil, e.g. France and Belgium.
- In comparison the Treaty of Versailles appeared relatively moderate to the severity of the terms imposed by the Germans on the Russians at the Treaty of Brest-Litovsk in 1918, which annexed large areas of Poland and the Baltic states.

## The significance of the Treaty of Versailles

The historical significance of the Treaty of Versailles goes well beyond the debate over its fairness. It raises the important issue of its impact upon the Weimar Republic and whether it acted as a serious handicap to the establishment of long-term political stability in Germany.

The economic consequences of reparations were undoubtedly a genuine concern. The English economist, Keynes, feared in 1919 that the reparations would fundamentally weaken the economy of Germany with consequences for the whole of Europe. However, Germany's economic potential was still considerable. It had potentially by far the strongest economy in Europe and still had extensive industry and resources. As will be seen later (pages 56–7), the Republic's economic problems cannot be blamed on the burden of reparations alone. And it should also be remembered that by 1932 Germany actually received more in loans under the Dawes Plan (see pages 86–7) than it paid in reparations.

It is not really possible to maintain that the Treaty had weakened Germany politically. In some respects, Germany in 1919 was in a stronger position than in 1914. The great empires of Russia, Austria-Hungary and Turkey had gone, creating a power vacuum in central and eastern Europe that could not be filled at least in the short term by a weak and isolated Soviet Russia or by any other state. In such a situation, cautious diplomacy might have led to the establishment of German power and influence at the heart of Europe.

However, on another level, the Treaty might be considered more to blame because, in the minds of many Germans, it was regarded as the real cause of the country's problems and they really believed that it was totally unfair. In the war German public opinion had been strongly shaped by nationalist propaganda and then deeply shocked by the defeat. Both the Armistice and Versailles were closely linked to the 'stab in the back' myth that the German Army had not really lost the First World War in 1918 (see page 5). It may have been a myth, but it was a very powerful one.

As a result, although the war had been pursued by Imperial Germany, it was the new democracy of Weimar that was forced to take the responsibility and the blame for the First World War. Therefore, Weimar democracy was deeply weakened by Versailles, which fuelled the propaganda of the Republic's opponents over the years. Even for sympathetic democrats like Hugo Preuss, Versailles only served to disillusion many into thinking that the gains of the

**Key question**
Did the Treaty of Versailles fundamentally weaken Weimar Germany?

revolution were being undone: '... the German Republic was born out of its terrible defeat ... The criminal madness of the Versailles *Diktat* was a shameless blow in the face to such hopes based on international law and political common sense'. In this way the Treaty of Versailles contributed to the internal political and economic difficulties that evolved in Germany after 1919.

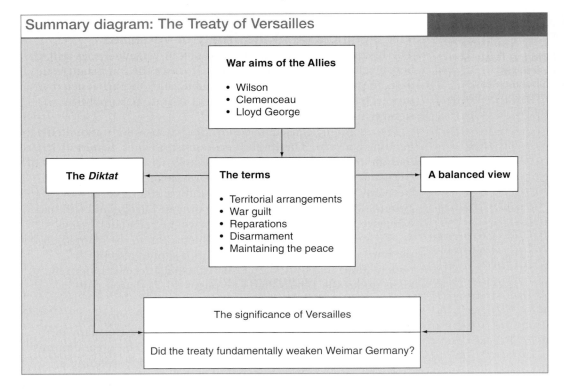

Summary diagram: The Treaty of Versailles

## Study Guide: AS Questions

### In the style of AQA
Study the following source material and then answer the questions that follow.

#### Source A
*Adapted from a book written in 1923 by Hugo Preuss, who drew up the Weimar Constitution.*
... the German Republic was born out of its terrible defeat. This cast from the first a dark shadow on the new political order as far as national sentiment was concerned .... . The criminal madness of the Versailles *Diktat* was a shameless blow in the face to such hopes based on international law and political common sense. The Weimar Constitution was born with this curse upon it.

#### Source B
*From the* Tageszeitung, *a German newspaper, written in May 1919.*
What a peace in accordance with French desires looks like is shown by these conditions, which leave nothing of Germany but

a torn and tattered territory. ... For Germany there is no self-determination. Absolutely German territory is torn off. This peace is unacceptable.

## Source C

*Adapted from P. Alter,* The German Question and Europe, *2000.*

The Germans failed to appreciate the moderating influence exerted by the British on the Allies' deliberations, when they began in Paris in January 1919. Bearing in mind that Germans had willingly started the war and that, during the war, both sides in the conflict had voiced far-reaching plans for annexations, the Versailles Peace Treaty was, in fact, quite moderate. This is often overlooked in the face of the noisy complaints and condemnations made by its critics in later years. All the propaganda against the Treaty was highly exaggerated.

(a) **Use Source A and your own knowledge.**
    Explain briefly the significance of the 'Versailles *Diktat*' in the context of Germany in 1919. (3 marks)
(b) **Use Sources B and C and your own knowledge.**
    Explain how Source C challenges the views put forward in Source B about the Treaty of Versailles. (7 marks)
(c) **Use Sources A, B and C and your own knowledge.**
    Explain the importance of the Treaty of Versailles, in relation to other factors, in weakening Weimar Germany between 1919 and 1923. (15 marks)

*Source: Adapted from AQA, Summer 2003*

---

*Exam tips*
*The cross-references are intended to take you straight to the material that will help you to answer the questions.*

(a) In question **(a)** you should provide a developed explanation of the concept of 'the Versailles *Diktat*' linked to the context of Germany 1919. You should mention:

- That a *Diktat* suggests the treaty was imposed by pressure and without negotiation, e.g. the War Guilt clause; the Allied blockade until the signing of the treaty (pages 30–2).
- And very briefly, that the Versailles Treaty laid down a series of terms that weakened Germany, e.g. disarmament, reparations, territorial losses (pages 30–1).

(b) In question **(b)** you have to concentrate on just these two sources. You must compare them directly, but be careful not to simply describe one source followed by the other. The real skill is to highlight the differences (and any similarities), for example:

- The German newspaper believed Germany was not given self-determination, whereas the historian points out that Germany had started the war and had planned annexations.
- The German newspaper argued that the 'peace is unacceptable' whereas the historian sees it as 'quite moderate'.

However, it is important for high marks to make a judgment about the utility and reliability of the two sources, e.g. the exaggeration by Source B is shaped by the emotional appeal and nationalism written in the week after the publication of the Treaty, whereas Source C is a present-day balanced analysis by a historian.

(c) In question (c) you have to evaluate the extent to which the Weimar democracy was weakened by the Treaty of Versailles in relation to other factors. So, first of all it is very important to use all the three sources:

- Preuss, a supporter of democracy and a moderate, believed that the Versailles Treaty 'cursed' the new democracy.
- The newspaper was convinced that the terms of the Versailles Treaty fundamentally weakened Germany – though its hostility was directed towards France.
- The historian suggests that the complaints about the Versailles Treaty were highly exaggerated.

Then, you can make use of your own knowledge to analyse other factors alongside the Treaty:

- Weimar had many other problems, e.g. economic problems (pages 2, 3 and 56–7).
- The 'stab in the back' myth (page 5)
- Left-wing and right-wing opposition, e.g. Spartacists and Kapp *putsch* (1920) (pages 40–6).

A thoughtful conclusion is vital. You must show an appreciation of the range of evidence to provide a balanced argument and make a judgment.

## In the style of Edexcel

(a) Describe the main features of the Weimar Constitution.

(15 marks)

*Source: Edexcel, June 2001*

(b) Explain why the Weimar Constitution has been regarded as having serious weaknesses. (15 marks)

### Exam tips

*The cross-references are intended to take you straight to the material that will help you to answer the questions.*

(a) Question (a) is relatively straightforward and you should be able to earn good marks as long as you bear in mind that it covers a lot of content and you must not spend more than half of the allocated time on this question (as you can see, question (b) gets the same number of marks, but will require some careful thought and planning). It is important to make reference to all the main five sections – it is not good to write four excellent sections, if you then miss one absolutely vital one.

The five main sections in the Weimar Constitution are:

- Its political status (page 24).
- The parliament (page 24).
- The presidency (page 24).
- The Bill of Rights (page 25).
- The Supreme Court (page 25).

**(b)** In question **(b)** you should concentrate on the features of the Constitution that have been seen as its weaknesses. Explain the reasons for the weakness in turn, but assess whether each one was really that serious or not

- The use of proportional representation (page 26).
- The relationship created between the *Reichstag* and the president (pages 26–7).
- The continuity of traditional institutions of Imperial Germany (page 27).

Then you should be able to provide a good conclusion that shows the interaction of the factors and evaluates the *relative* significance of the weaknesses. It is also worth remembering that you will be able to appreciate the importance of the Constitution, when you complete your studies of the years 1919–29 and see how and why the Weimar Republic collapsed.

## In the style of OCR

'The terms of the Treaty of Versailles were actually reasonable.' How far do you agree?

### Exam tips

*The cross-references are intended to take you straight to the material that will help you to answer the question.*

You should adopt an evaluative approach to this question. High marks depend on you addressing and answering the question actually set. The real skill is to unlock the question and divide the answer into logical sections. In order to do this you should:

- Identify some reasons with evidence to back up the view that the Treaty of Versailles was *not* reasonable (pages 32–4).
- Identify some reasons with evidence to back up the view that the Treaty of Versailles *was* actually reasonable (pages 34–5).
- Draw attention to the ways the German public opinion felt it was a humiliation and how it exerted influence (pages 35–6).

Then you should be able to provide a good conclusion, which evaluates the *relative* significance of the three issues.

# 3 The Threats to Weimar 1919–23

**POINTS TO CONSIDER**
Although the forces of democracy had successfully established the Weimar Republic, Germany remained in turmoil in the years 1919–23. This chapter concentrates on the extent of Weimar's political problems and the range of political threats it faced. It examines:

- The threat from the extreme left
- The threat from the extreme right
- Uprisings of the extreme right
- A republic without republicans: the elections and governments

The country also faced fundamental economic problems, and they will be the focus of the next chapter.

**Key dates**

| 1920 | March | Kapp *putsch* |
|------|-------|---------------|
| 1921 | August | Murder of Erzberger |
| 1922 | June | Murder of Rathenau |
| 1923 | Summer | The 'German October' in Saxony |
| | November | Munich Beer Hall *putsch* |

## 1 | The Threat from the Extreme Left

**Key question**
How serious was the opposition of the extreme left to the Weimar Republic?

After the German revolution of 1918–19 the left-wing movement (see pages 12–13) at first remained in a state of confusion:

- The moderate socialists of the SPD were committed to parliamentary democracy.
- The Communists (the KPD) pressed for a workers' revolution.
- The USPD stood for the creation of a radical socialist society, but within a democratic framework.

This situation became clearer when, in 1920, the USPD disbanded and its members joined either the KPD or the SPD. So, from that time there were two left-wing alternative parties, but with fundamental differences.

The KPD believed that the establishment of parliamentary democracy fell a long way short of its real aims. It wanted the revolution to proceed on **Marxist** lines with the creation of a

**Key terms**

**Marxism**
The political ideology of Karl Marx. His two major books, *Communist Manifesto* and *Capital*, outline his beliefs that the working classes will overthrow the industrial classes by revolution and create a classless society.

**'Red Threat'**
A 'Red' was a loose term used to describe anyone sympathetic to the left and it originated from the Bolshevik use of the red flag in Russia.

**Key date**

The revolutionary uprising in Germany in 1923 is often referred to as the German October, but it is a confusing term. Mass protests started before this, in the summer of 1923, though the uprising did not actually come to a head until October 1923 (which was also emotionally associated with the Bolshevik Revolution in Russia in October 1917)

one-party communist state and the major restructuring of Germany both socially and economically. As a result of the 1917 Russian Revolution, many German communists were encouraged by the political unrest to believe that international revolution would spread throughout Europe.

The KPD's opposition to the Republic was nothing less than a complete rejection of the Weimar system. It was not prepared to be part of the democratic opposition or to work within the parliamentary system to bring about desired changes. The differences between the moderate and extreme left were so basic that there was no chance of political co-operation between them, let alone a coming together into one socialist movement. The extreme left was totally committed to a very different vision of German politics and society, whereas the moderate left was one of the pillars of Weimar democracy.

## KPD opposition

The KPD was indeed a reasonable political force in the years 1919–23. It enjoyed the support of 10–15 per cent of the electorate and there were continuous revolutionary disturbances – protests, strikes and uprisings (see Table 3.1). However, all these actions by the extreme left gave the impression that Germany was really facing a Bolshevik-inspired '**Red Threat**'. Consequently, as a result of right-wing propaganda, many Germans began to have exaggerated fears about the possibility of impending revolution.

**Table 3.1:** Major communist uprisings 1919–23

| Date | Place | Action | Response |
|---|---|---|---|
| January 1919 | Berlin | Spartacist uprising to seize power | Crushed by German army and *Freikorps* |
| March 1919 | Bavaria | Creation of soviet republic | Crushed by the *Freikorps* |
| March 1920 | Ruhr | Formation of the Ruhr Army by 50,000 workers to oppose the Kapp *putsch* (page 45) | Crushed by German Army and *Freikorps* |
| March 1921 | Merseburg and Halle | 'March Operation'. Uprising of strikes organised by KPD | Put down by police |
| Summer 1923 | Saxony | 'German October' A wave of strikes and the creation of an SPD/KPD state government | Overthrown by German army |

Looking back, it is clear that the extreme left posed much less of a threat to Weimar than was believed at the time. So, despite all the disturbances, the revolutionary left was never really likely to be able to seize political power. The main reasons lie in a combination of their own weaknesses and the effective resistance of the Weimar governments:

- Bad co-ordination. Even during the chaos and uncertainty of 1923, the activities of the extreme left proved incapable of mounting a unified attack on Weimar democracy.
- Poor leadership. The repression it suffered at the hands of the *Freikorps* removed some of its ablest and most spirited leaders, e.g. Liebknecht and Luxemburg (see page 13). The later leadership suffered from internal divisions and disagreements on tactics.
- Concessions. The Weimar governments played on the differences within the extreme left by making concessions which split it, e.g. over the Kapp *putsch* in March 1920 (see page 45–8).
- Repression. The authorities systematically repressed the rebels with considerable brutality.

In the end, the extreme left was just not powerful enough to lead a revolution against the Weimar Republic.

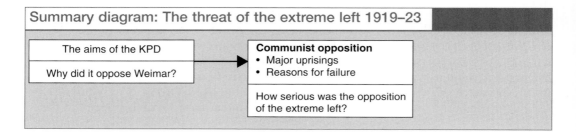

Summary diagram: The threat of the extreme left 1919–23

| The aims of the KPD |
| Why did it oppose Weimar? |

**Communist opposition**
- Major uprisings
- Reasons for failure

How serious was the opposition of the extreme left?

# 2 | The Threat from the Extreme Right

**Key question**
What did the extreme right stand for?

Opposition from the extreme right was very different both in its form and in its extent to that of the extreme left. On the right wing there was a very mixed collection of opponents to the Republic and their resistance found expression in different ways.

## The extreme right in theory

In contrast to Marxist socialism, the extreme right did not really have an alternative organised ideology. It was simply drawn together by a growing belief in the following:

- Anti-democracy: it was united by its rejection of the Weimar system and its principles. It aimed to destroy the democratic constitution because it was seen as weak, which it believed had contributed to Germany's problems.
- **Anti-Marxism**: even more despised than democracy was the fear of communism. It was seen as a real threat to traditional values and the ownership of property and wealth – and when Russian communism was established, it reinforced the idea that communism was anti-German.
- **Authoritarianism**: the extreme right favoured the restoration of some authoritarian, dictatorial regime – though in the early 1920s there was no real consensus on what kind of strong government and leadership would be established.

**Anti-Marxism**
Opposition to the ideology of Karl Marx.

**Authoritarianism**
A broad term meaning government by strong non-democratic leadership.

Key terms

**Nationalism**
Grew from the national spirit to unify Germany in the nineteenth century. Supported a strong policy to embrace all German-speakers in eastern Europe.

**'November criminals'**
Those who signed the November Armistice and a term of abuse to vilify all those who supported the democratic republic.

How did the extreme right manifest itself in different ways?

- **Nationalism**: nationalism was at the core of the extreme right, but Germany's national pride had been deeply hurt by the events of 1918–19. Not surprisingly, from the time of the Treaty of Versailles, this conservative-nationalist response reinforced the ideas of the 'stab in the back' myth and the '**November criminals**'. The war, it was argued, had been lost not because of any military defeat suffered by the army, but as a result of the betrayal by unpatriotic forces within Germany. These were said to include pacifists, socialists, democrats and Jews. Right-wing politicians found a whole range of scapegoats to take the blame for German acceptance of the Armistice.

Worse still, these 'November criminals' had been prepared to overthrow the monarchy and establish a republic. Then, to add insult to injury, they had accepted the 'shameful peace' of Versailles. The extreme right accepted such interpretations, distorted as they were. They not only served to remove any responsibility from Imperial Germany, but also acted as a powerful stick with which to beat the new leaders of Weimar Germany.

## Organisations of the extreme right
The extreme right appeared in various forms. It included a number of political parties and was also the driving force behind the activities of various paramilitary organisations.

### DNVP
The DNVP (German National People's Party) was a coalition of nationalist-minded old imperial conservative parties and included such groups as the Fatherland Party and the Pan-German League. From the very start, it contained extremist and racist elements. Although it was still the party of landowners and industrialists, it had a broad appeal amongst some of the middle classes. It was by far the largest party in the *Reichstag* on the extreme right and was able to poll 15.1 per cent in the 1920 election.

### Racist nationalism
The emergence of racist nationalism, or *völkisch* nationalism, was clearly apparent before 1914, but the effects of the war and its aftermath increased its attraction for many on the right. By the early 1920s there were probably about 70 relatively small splinter nationalist parties, which were also racist and anti-Semitic, e.g. the Nazi Party.

Bavaria became a particular haven for such groups, since the regional state government was sufficiently **reactionary** to tolerate them. One such group was the German Workers' Party, originally founded by Anton Drexler. Adolf Hitler joined the party in 1919 and within two years had become its leader. However, during the years 1919–24, regional and policy differences divided such groups and attempts to unify the nationalist right ended in failure. When, in 1923, Hitler and the Nazis attempted to organise an uprising with the Munich Beer Hall *putsch*, it ended

**Reactionary**
Those opposing change and supporting a return to traditional ways.

in fiasco (see pages 47–50). It was not until the mid-1920s, when Hitler began to bring the different groups together under the leadership of the NSDAP, that a powerful political force was created.

## Freikorps

The *Freikorps* that flourished in the post-war environment attracted the more brutal and ugly elements of German militarism. As a result of the demobilisation of the armed forces there were nearly 200 **paramilitary units** around Germany by 1919.

The *Freikorps* became a law unto themselves and they were employed by the government in a crucial role to suppress the threats from the extreme left. However, as the *Freikorps* was anti-republican and committed to the restoration of authoritarian rule, they had no respect for the Weimar governments. Their bloody actions became known as the '**White Terror**' and showed they were quite prepared to use acts of violence and murder to intimidate others.

**Key terms**

**Paramilitary units**
Informal non-legal military squads.

**'White Terror'**
The 'Whites' were seen as the opponents (in contrast to the Reds). The 'White Terror' refers to the soviet republic in Bavaria.

A cartoon drawn in 1919 by the German artist Grosz. He caricatures the stereotyped right-wing officer. The title, *The White General* relates to the 'White Terror' in opposition to the Reds of the left-wing movement.

**Key dates**

The murder of Matthias Erzberger: 26 August 1921

The murder of Walter Rathenau: 24 June 1922

## Consul Organisation

From 1920 the Weimar governments tried to control the actions of the *Freikorps*, but a new threat emerged from the right wing in the form of political assassination. In the years 1919–22 there were 376 political murders – 22 by the left and 354 by the right. The most notorious terrorist gang was known as the 'Consul Organisation' because it was responsible for the assassination of a number of key republican politicians:

- Matthias Erzberger, Finance Minister 1919–21. Murdered because he was a Catholic and a member of the ZP and had signed the Armistice.
- Walther Rathenau, Foreign Minister, 1921–2 (who drew up the Rapallo treaty with USSR). Murdered because he was Jewish and was committed to democracy.
- Karl Gareis, leader of the USPD. Murdered on 9 June 1921 because he was a committed socialist.

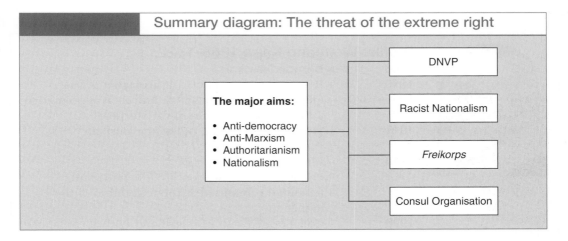

Summary diagram: The threat of the extreme right

DNVP

**The major aims:**
- Anti-democracy
- Anti-Marxism
- Authoritarianism
- Nationalism

Racist Nationalism

*Freikorps*

Consul Organisation

**Key question**
What prompted the Kapp *putsch* and why did it fail?

**Key date**

The Kapp *putsch*: March 1920

## 3 | Extreme Right Uprisings

### The Kapp *putsch*

The *Freikorps* played a central role in the first attempt by the extreme right wing to seize power from the constitutional government. This was because by early 1920 there was considerable unease within the ranks of the *Freikorps* at the demands to reduce the size of the German army according to the terms of the Versailles Treaty.

When it was proposed to disband two brigades of the army, the Ehrhardt Marine Brigade and the Baltikum that were stationed in the Berlin area, Wolfgang Kapp (see profile, page 46) and General Lüttwitz decided to exploit the situation. They encouraged 12,000 troops to march on Berlin and seize the main buildings of the capital virtually unopposed, where they installed a new government.

Significantly, the German army did not provide any resistance to this *putsch*. In spite of requests from Ebert and the Chancellor to put down the rebellious forces, the army was not prepared to become involved with either side. Although it did not join those involved in the *putsch*, it failed to support the legitimate government. General von Seeckt, the senior officer in the Defence Ministry, spoke for many colleagues when he declared:

> Troops do not fire on troops. So, you perhaps intend, Herr Minister, that a battle be fought before the Brandenburger Tor between troops that have fought side by side against a common enemy? When *Reichswehr* fires on *Reichswehr* all comradeship within the officers' corps will have vanished.

The army's decision to put its own interests before its obligation to defend the government forced the latter to flee the capital and move to Stuttgart. However, the *putsch* collapsed. Before leaving Berlin, the SPD members of the government had called for a general strike, which soon paralysed the capital and quickly spread to the rest of the country. After four days, it was clear that Kapp and his government exerted no real authority and they fled the city.

---

### Profile: Wolfgang Kapp 1868–1922

| | |
|---|---|
| 1868 | – Born in New York |
| 1870 | – Returned to Germany with his family |
| 1886–1920 | – Qualified as a doctor of law and then appointed as a Prussian civil servant in various posts |
| 1917 | – Helped to found the right-wing German Fatherland Party |
| 1918 | – Elected to the *Reichstag* |
| | – Opposed the abdication of Wilhelm II and remained committed to the restoration of the monarchy |
| 1920 | – Collaborated with Ehrhardt and Lüttwitz to launch the *putsch*. Briefly appointed chancellor by the leaders of the *putsch*. Fled to Sweden |
| 1922 | – Returned to Germany but died whilst awaiting trial |

Really, only a few points stand out about Kapp. He has been described as 'a neurotic with delusions' or simply a 'crank' who represented the extreme nationalist-conservative views. He did not play any major part in politics of Imperial Germany until the war, when he was one of the founders of the German Fatherland Party. After the war he campaigned for the restoration of Kaiser Wilhelm, but his *putsch* was a fiasco. Interestingly, some of the men involved in his *putsch* had swastika symbols on their helmets.

---

### The aftermath of the Kapp *putsch*

At first sight the collapse of the Kapp *putsch* could be viewed as a major success for the Weimar Republic. In the six days of crisis, it had retained the backing of the people of Berlin and had effectively withstood a major threat from the extreme right. However, what is significant is that the Kapp *putsch* had taken place at all. In this sense, the Kapp *putsch* highlights clearly the

**Key question**
How significant was the Kapp *putsch*?

weakness of the Weimar Republic. The army's behaviour at the time of the *putsch* was typical of its right-wing attitudes and its lack of sympathy for the Republic. During the months after the *coup*, the government failed to confront this problem.

The army leadership had revealed its unreliability. Yet, amazingly, at the end of that very month Seeckt was appointed Chief of the Army Command (1920–6). He was appointed because he enjoyed the confidence of his fellow officers and ignored the fact that his support for the Republic was at best lukewarm. Under Seeckt's influence, the organisation of the army was remodelled and its status redefined:

- He imposed very strict military discipline and recruited new troops, increasingly at the expense of the *Freikorps*.
- However, he was determined to uphold the independence of the army. He believed it held a privileged position that placed it beyond direct government control. For example, he turned a blind eye to the Versailles disarmament clauses in order to increase the size of the army with more modern weapons.

Many within its ranks believed that the army served some higher purpose to the nation as a whole. It had the right to intervene as it saw fit without regard to its obligations to the Republic. All this suggests that the aftermath of the Kapp *putsch*, the Ebert-Groener Pact (see page 11) and the Constitution's failure to reform the structures of army had made it a '**state within a state**'.

The judiciary also continued with the old political values that had not changed since imperial times. It enjoyed the advantage of maintaining its independence from the Weimar Constitution, but it questioned the legal rights of the new republic and reached some dubious and obviously biased decisions. Those involved in the *putsch* of 1920 never felt the full rigour of the law:

- Kapp died awaiting trial.
- Lüttwitz was granted early retirement.
- Only one of the 705 prosecuted was actually found guilty and sentenced to five years' imprisonment.

Over the years 1919–22 it was clear that the judges were biased and their hearts did not lie with the Weimar Republic:

- Out of the 354 right-wing assassins only 28 were found guilty and punished (but no-one was executed).
- Of the 22 left-wing assassins 10 were sentenced to death.

**Key term**

**'A state within a state'**
Where the authority and government of the state are threatened by a rival power base.

## The Munich Beer Hall *putsch*

Although the Munich Beer Hall *putsch* was one of the threats faced by the young republic in the year 1923, the event is also a crucial part of the rise of Hitler and the Nazis. So the details of the events also relate to Chapter 6 on pages 106–9.

In the short term it should be noted that the government of the State of Bavaria was under the control of the ultra-conservative Gustav von Kahr, who blamed most of Germany's problems on the national government in Berlin. Like Hitler, he

**Key question**
Who were the plotters and why did they fail?

**Key date**

The Munich Beer Hall *putsch*:
8–9 November 1923

**Table 3.2:** The plotters in the Munich Beer Hall *putsch*

| Name | Position | Background/attitude | Involvement |
|---|---|---|---|
| Erich von Ludendorff | Retired general | Took part in Kapp *putsch*. Opposed to democracy (see also pages 45–7) | Collaborated with Hitler and supported the *putsch* on 8–9 November |
| Gustav von Kahr | Leader of the Bavarian state government | Deeply anti-democratic and sympathetic to many of the right-wing extremists. Committed to the restoration of the monarchy in an independent Bavaria | Planned with Hitler and Lossow to seize power, but became wary. Forced to co-operate with his rally on 8 November, though did not support the *putsch* on 9 November |
| Otto von Lossow | Commander of the Bavarian section of the German army | Despised Weimar democracy and supported authoritarian rule. Very conservative | Planned with Hitler and Kahr to seize power, but became wary. Forced to co-operate in the rally on 8 November, though did not support the *putsch* on 9 November |
| Adolf Hitler | Leader of the Nazi Party | Extremist: anti-Semitic, anti-democratic and anti-communist. Backed by the Nazi SA | Planned and wholly committed to seize power. Forced the hands of Kahr and Lossow and carried on with the *putsch* on 9 November |
| Hans von Seeckt | General. Chief of the Army Command, 1920–6 | Unsympathetic to democracy and keen to preserve the interests of the army, but suspicious of Hitler and the Nazis (see page 49) | Initially ambiguous attitude in early November. But in the crisis he used his powers to command the armed forces to resist the *putsch* |

wished to destroy the republican regime, although his long-term aim was the creation of an independent Bavaria. By October 1923 General von Lossow, the Army's commander in Bavaria, had fallen under von Kahr's spell and had even begun to disobey orders from the Defence Minister from Berlin. And so it was both of these ultra-conservatives who plotted with Hitler and the Nazis to 'March on Berlin'.

By the first week of November 1923, Kahr and Lossow, fearing failure, decided to abandon the plan. However, Hitler was not so cautious and preferred to press on rather than lose the opportunity. On 8 November Hitler, together with his Nazi supporters, stormed into and took control of a large rally, which von Kahr was addressing in one of Munich's beer halls, and declared a 'national revolution'. Under pressure, Kahr and Lossow co-operated and agreed to proceed with the uprising, but in reality they had lost their nerve when Seeckt used his powers to command the armed forces to resist the *putsch*. So when, on the next day, the Nazis attempted to take Munich they had insufficient support and the Bavarian police easily crushed the *putsch*. Fourteen Nazis were killed and Hitler himself was arrested on a charge of treason.

A cartoon of 1924 derides the judiciary after the trial of Hitler and Ludendorff. The judge simply says 'High treason? Rubbish! The worst we can charge them with is breaking by-laws about entertaining in public'.

## The aftermath of the Munich Beer Hall *putsch*

On one level the inglorious result of the Nazi *putsch* was encouraging for Weimar democracy. It withstood a dangerous threat in what was a difficult year. Most significantly, Seeckt and the army did not throw in their lot with the Nazis – which upset Hitler so much that he described him as a 'lackey of the Weimar Republic'. However, once again it was the dealings of the judiciary that raised so much concern:

**Key question**
How significant was the Munich Beer Hall *putsch*?

- Hitler was sentenced to a mere five years (the minimum stipulation for treason). His imprisonment at Landsberg provided quite reasonable conditions and he was released after less than 10 months.
- Ludendorff was acquitted on the grounds that although he had been present at the time of the *putsch*, he was there 'by accident'!

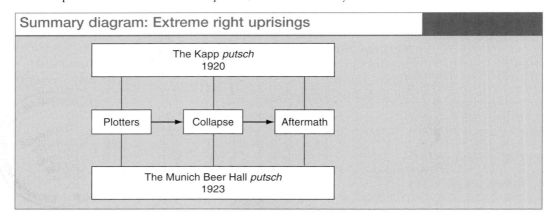

Summary diagram: Extreme right uprisings

## 4 | Weimar Democracy: A Republic Without Republicans

**Key question**
What was the greatest threat to Weimar democracy?

The optimism of the first election of the Republic (see page 18) gave way to concerns in the election of June 1920. The results can be seen in Figure 3.1 on page 51 and they raise several key points:

- The combined support for the three main democratic parties declined dramatically:
  - 1919: 76.1 per cent
  - 1920: 48.0 per cent
  (The figures do not include the DVP under the leadership of Stresemann which voted against the Weimar Constitution at first, but became committed to the Republic from 1921.)
- The performance for each of the pro-democratic parties was as follows:
  - the SPD declined sharply from 37.9 to 21.7 per cent
  - the DDP declined catastrophically from 18.5 to 8.3 per cent
  - the ZP dropped down slightly from 19.75 to 18.0 per cent.
- The support for the extreme left and right increased, especially the DNVP:
  - the DNVP increased from 10.3 to 15.1 per cent
  - the KPD/USPD increased from 7.6 to 20.0 per cent.

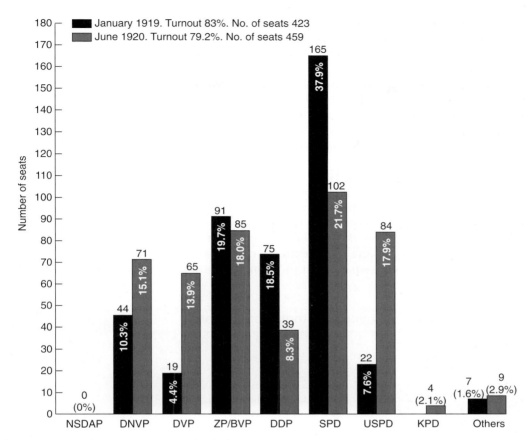

**Figure 3.1:** *Reichstag* election results 1919–20

## Weimar governments

The Weimar Republic not only faced overt opposition from both the extremes but also its democratic supporters struggled with the practical problem of creating and maintaining workable government coalitions. In the four years 1919–23 Weimar had six governments – the longest of which lasted just 18 months (see Table 3.3).

**Table 3.3:** Governments of the Weimar Republic 1919–23

| Period in office | Chancellor | Make-up of the coalition |
| --- | --- | --- |
| 1919 | Philipp Scheidemann | SPD, ZP, DDP |
| 1919–20 | Gustav Bauer | SPD, ZP, DDP |
| 1920 | Hermann Müller | SPD, Centre, DDP |
| 1920–1 | Konstantin Fehrenbach | ZP, DDP, DVP |
| 1921–2 | Joseph Wirth | SPD, DDP, ZP |
| 1922–3 | Wilhelm Cuno | ZP, DDP, DVP |

## Conclusion

The success of the democratic parties in the *Reichstag* elections of January 1919 at first disguised some of Weimar's fundamental problems in its political structure. But opposition to the Republic ranged from indifference to brutal violence and, as early as 1920, democratic support for Weimar began to switch to the extremes. This is shown by the results of the first election after the Treaty of Versailles.

The extent of the opposition from the extreme right to democracy was not always appreciated. Instead, President Ebert and the Weimar governments overestimated the threat from the extreme left and they came to rely on the forces of reaction for justice and law and order. This was partly because the conservative forces successfully exploited the image of the left as a powerful threat. So, in many respects, it was the persistence of the old attitudes in the major traditional national institutions that represented the greatest long-term threat to the Republic. The violent forces of counter-revolution, as shown by the *putsches* of Kapp and Hitler, were too weak and disorganised to seize power in the early years. But the danger of the extreme right was actually insidious; it was the real growing threat to Weimar democracy.

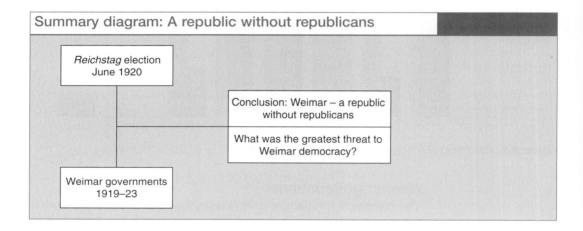

## Study Guide: AS Questions

### In the style of AQA
Study the following source material and then answer the questions that follow.

### Source A
*Adapted from a proclamation by Wolfgang Kapp, 13 March 1920.*
The Reich and nation are in grave danger. With terrible speed we are approaching the complete collapse of law and order. Prices are rising unchecked. Hardship is growing. Starvation threatens. The Government, lacking in authority and in league with corruption, is incapable of overcoming the danger. How are we to escape internal and external collapse? Only by re-erecting a strong State. There is no other way but a government of action which will ruthlessly suppress strikes. Striking is treason to the nation.

## Source B

*From: a poster proclamation issued in the name of the SPD members of the government, 1920.*

Workers, Party comrades! The military *putsch* has started. The achievements of a whole year are to be smashed, your dearly bought freedom to be destroyed. Everything is at stake! The strongest counter-measures are required. No factory must work while the military dictatorship rules! Therefore down tools! Come out on strike! Deprive the military of oxygen! Fight with all means for the Republic!

## Source C

*Adapted from: W. Carr, A History of Germany 1815–1945, 1969.*

The Kapp *putsch* had little hope of ultimate success. What was memorable about it was the attitude taken by the army chiefs. The generals, who had never failed to help Ebert against the threat of Communism, would not move. General von Seeckt spoke for most generals when he bluntly informed Ebert that troops do not fire upon troops. Supporters of the republic were greatly alarmed by these unwelcome signs of right-wing extremism. Despite widespread criticism on the left, little was done to discipline unco-operative officers.

(a) **Use Source C and your own knowledge**
    Explain briefly the significance of 'the threat of Communism' in the context of instability in Germany in the years 1918–20.
    (3 marks)

(b) **Use Sources A and B and your own knowledge**
    Explain in what ways the view of the Kapp *putsch* put forward in Source A is challenged by that presented in Source B.
    (7 marks)

(c) **Use Sources A, B and C and your own knowledge.**
    Explain the ways in which right-wing opposition weakened Weimar democracy in the years 1918–25.      (15 marks)

*Source: AQA, adapted from January 2002*

---

### Exam tips

*The cross-references are intended to take you straight to the material that will help you to answer the questions.*

(a) In question **(a)** you should provide a developed explanation of the concept of 'the threat of Communism' linked to the context of Germany 1918–20. You should mention:
  • That the German communists wanted to seize power and create a soviet republic, e.g. the Spartacist uprising 1919 (pages 13–14).
  • That the instability arose in Germany because of a range of factors, e.g. economic problems, discontent over the Treaty of Versailles (pages 10–11 and 32–3).

(b) In question **(b)** you have to concentrate on just these two sources. You must compare them directly, but be careful not to

simply describe one source followed by the other. The real skill is to highlight the differences (and any similarities), for example:
- The Kapp proclamation opposed any strike, whereas the SPD members of the government encouraged a general strike.
- The SPD members of the government referred to the 'achievements of a whole year', whereas the Kapp proclamation talked of the 'complete collapse of the State'.
- The SPD members of the government upheld the freedom of the new democracy, whereas the Kapp proclamation wanted to 're-erect a strong State'.

However, it is important for top marks to make a judgment about the utility and reliability of the sources, e.g. the exaggeration by Source A and the emotional appeal to freedom by Source B. The two sources clearly reflect very different political standpoints

(c) In question (c) you have to evaluate the extent of the right-wing opposition to Weimar democracy. So, first of all it is very important to use all the three sources, for example:
- The Kapp proclamation believed that the government 'lacked in authority'.
- The SPD members seemed to be frightened of a right wing dictatorship.
- The historian suggested that the German army will not oppose the *putsch*.

Then, you can make use of your own knowledge, for example:
- The Ebert–Groener pact (pages 11–12).
- The government's over-dependence on the Freikorps to suppress the left-wing uprisings (pages 41–2).
- The influence of the traditional élites (pages 27–9).

A thoughtful conclusion is vital. You must show an appreciation of the range of evidence to make judgment, e.g. it could be said that the terms did not really weaken Germany, but many Germans *believed* they were the cause of their problems and Weimar was blamed for the Armistice and Versailles.

## In the style of Edexcel

(a) In what ways did the extreme left and the extreme right pose threats to the Weimar Republic in the years 1919–23?

(15 marks)

(b) Why did the uprisings of the extreme left and the extreme right fail to seize power in the years 1919–23? (15 marks)

### Exam tips

*The cross-references are intended to take you straight to the material that will help you to answer the questions.*

(a) In question (a) you must be careful to make sure you cover the full range of 'threats'. The question does not just expect you to describe the uprisings, but also to refer to:
- The theoretical aims of the extreme left (pages 12–13).

- The theoretical aims of the extreme right (pages 42–4).
- The underlying opposition of the extreme right from the vested interests, e.g. the army (pages 27–9).

**(b)** Question **(b)** covers a lot of content in Chapters 1–4 in a chaotic period, so be certain to choose the material which helps to explain the failure of the extremes very specifically.

Obviously identify:
- The weaknesses of the extreme left-wing movement (pages 41–2).
- The limitations of the extreme right forces (pages 51–2).

But also refer to:
- The strengths of the Weimar governments (despite their many stated weaknesses), e.g. the use of Article 48, Stresemann's leadership in 1923 (page 67).

A good conclusion will show the interaction of factors and how they combined to bring about the failure of the extremists. It is also important to show the relative significance of these factors.

## In the style of OCR

Which was the greater threat to the Weimar Republic in the years 1919–23 – the extreme left or the extreme right?

*Exam tips*

*The cross-references are intended to take you straight to the material that will help you to answer the question.*

You should adopt an evaluative (comparative) approach to this question. High marks depend on your addressing and answering the question actually set and so, the real skill is to bear in mind the key phrase 'the greater threat' all the time. In order to do this, you should show:

- Some of the strengths of the extreme left which threatened Weimar – not only its direct opposition, e.g. the Spartacist uprising, but also its influence, e.g. the Party membership. Bear in mind the extent of its limitations as well (pages 41–2).
- Some of the strengths of the extreme right, which threatened Weimar – not only its direct opposition, e.g. the Kapp uprising, but also its influence, e.g. influence of vested interests. Bear in mind the extent of its limitations as well (pages 51–2).
- A thoughtful conclusion is vital, e.g. it would be useful to point out that the position of the 'threats' was not constant, as they changed over time in the years 1919–23. But justify your choice between the two threats.

# 4 The Great Inflation

**POINTS TO CONSIDER**
1923 became known as the year of the Great Inflation, when Germany's money became totally worthless. For Germans living in the Weimar Republic it was a difficult time for them to understand and it resulted in a further serious loss of confidence in the government. Therefore, to appreciate the significance of the period it is important to consider the main themes:

- The German economic background
- The causes of the inflation – long term, medium term and short term
- The consequences of the inflation
- Stresemann's 100 days and the end of the crisis

**Key dates**

| 1921 | May | IARC (Inter-Allied Reparations Commission) fixed reparations at £6600 million (132 billion gold marks) |
|------|-----|---|
| 1923 | January | Franco-Belgian occupation of the Ruhr Passive resistance proclaimed |
| | Jan–Nov | Period of hyper-inflation |
| | August | Stresemann made chancellor of Germany |
| | Aug–Nov | Stresemann's 100 days |
| | December | Introduction of *Rentenmark* |
| 1924 | April | Dawes Plan proposed and accepted |

## 1 | The Economic Background

**Key question**
How did the First World War weaken the German economy?

In the 20 years before the First World War the German economy grew immensely. By 1914 it had become arguably the most powerful economy on the continent and it was in a position to compete with Britain's supremacy. These strengths were based upon:

- extensive natural resources, e.g. coal, iron-ore
- an advanced and well-developed industrial base, e.g. engineering, chemicals, electronics
- a well-educated population, with special technical skills
- an advanced banking system.

However, the result of four years of **total war** seriously dislocated the German economy. So, although the economy still had many

**Total war**
Involves the whole population in war – economically and militarily.

Key term

natural strengths and great potential, by 1919 it faced fundamental economic problems. The most notable of these were:

- The loss of resources from such territories as the Saar, Alsace-Lorraine and Silesia which, for example, resulted in a 16 per cent decline in coal production, 13 per cent decline in arable agricultural land and 48 per cent loss of iron-ore.
- The cost of paying reparations (set at £6600 million in 1921).
- The growing increase in prices. Between 1914 and 1918 the real value of the mark fell, dropping from 4.2 to 8.9 against the US dollar, while the prices of basic goods increased nearly four-fold.
- The increase in national debt to 144,000 million marks by 1919 compared with 5000 million marks in 1914.

Significantly, Germany had always depended on its ability to export to achieve economic growth. However, between 1914 and 1918 world trade had collapsed and even after 1919 it remained very sluggish.

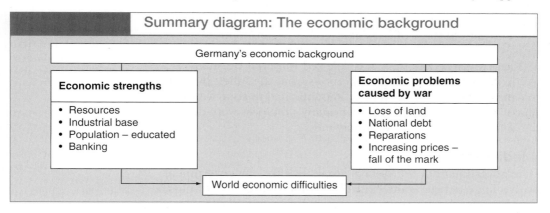

Summary diagram: The economic background

Germany's economic background

**Economic strengths**
- Resources
- Industrial base
- Population – educated
- Banking

**Economic problems caused by war**
- Loss of land
- National debt
- Reparations
- Increasing prices – fall of the mark

World economic difficulties

**Key question**
Why did Germany suffer hyper-inflation?

**Hyper-inflation**
Hyper-inflation is unusual. In Germany in 1923, it meant that prices spiralled out of control because the government increased the amount of money being printed. As a result, it displaced the whole economy.

**'Passive resistance'**
Refusal to work with occupying forces.

Key terms

## 2 | The Causes of the German Inflation

Germany's growing economic problems came to a head in 1923 when prices soared and money values spiralled down. This is often referred to as **hyper-inflation**. However, the crises of that year blinded many to the fact that prices had been rising since the early months of the war. Many Germans glibly assumed it was a result of the Treaty of Versailles and particularly the reparations. Still more unthinking explanations simply blamed it on the financial greed and corruption of the Jews.

However, with hindsight it is clear that the fundamental cause of the inflation was the huge increase in the amount of paper money in circulation, resulting from the government's printing more and more notes to pay off the interest on its massive debts. The causes of the Great Inflation can be divided into three phases:

- long term – the military demands of the First World War (1914–18) led to an enormous increase in financial costs
- medium term – the costs of introducing social reforms and welfare and the pressure to satisfy the demands for reparation payments from 1921
- short term – the French occupation of the Ruhr in 1923 resulted in crisis and the government of Cuno encouraged a policy of **'passive resistance'**.

## Long term

Not surprisingly, Germany had made no financial provision for a long drawn-out war. However, despite the increasing cost of the war, the Kaiser's government had decided, for political reasons, against increases in taxation. Instead, it had borrowed massive sums by selling '**war bonds**' to the public. When this proved insufficient from 1916, it simply allowed the national debt to grow bigger and bigger.

The result of Imperial Germany's financial policies was that by the end of 1918 only 16 per cent of war expenditure had been raised from taxation – 84 per cent had been borrowed.

Another factor was that the war years had seen almost full employment. This was because the economy had concentrated on the supply of military weapons. But, since production was necessarily military based, it did not satisfy the requirements of the civilian consumers. Consequently, the high demand for, and the shortage of consumer goods began to push prices up.

Victory would doubtless have allowed Imperial Germany to settle its debts by claiming reparations from the Allies, but defeat meant the reverse. The Weimar Republic had to cope with the massive costs of war. By 1919, Germany's finances were described by Volker Berghahn as 'an unholy mess'.

## Medium term

The government of the Weimar Republic (like any government with a large deficit) could control inflation only by narrowing the gap between the government's income and expenditure through:

- increasing taxation in order to raises its income
- cutting government spending in order to reduce its expenditure.

However, in view of Germany's domestic situation neither of these options was particularly attractive, as both would alienate the people and cause political and social difficulties, such as increased unemployment and industrial decline.

Consequently, from 1919 the Weimar government guided by Erzberger, the Finance Minister (see page 45), extensively increased taxation on profits, wealth and income. However, it decided not to go so far as aiming to **balance the budget**. It decided to adopt a policy of deficit financing in the belief that it would:

- maintain the demand for goods and, thereby, create work
- overcome the problems of demobilising millions of returning troops
- cover the cost of public spending on an extensive welfare state, e.g. health insurance, housing and benefits for the disabled and orphans
- reduce the real value of the national debt.

Deficit financing means planning to increase the nation's debt by reducing taxation in order to give the people more money to

**Key terms**

**War bonds**
In order to raise more money to pay for the war, Imperial Germany encouraged people to invest into government funds in the belief they were helping to finance the war and their savings would be secure.

**Balanced budget**
A financial programme in which a government does not spend more than it raises in revenue.

**Key term**

**Hard currency**
A currency that the market considers to be strong because its value does not depreciate. In the 1920s the hardest currency was the US dollar.

**Key date**

The IARC (Inter-Allied Reparations Commission) fixed the sum for reparations at £6600 million (132 billion gold marks): May 1921

spend and so increase the demand for goods and thereby create work. The government believed that this would enable Germany to overcome the problems of demobilisation – a booming economy would ensure there were plenty of jobs for the returning soldiers and sailors – and also reduce the real value of the national debt. Unfortunately, an essential part of this policy was to allow inflation to continue.

The reparations issue should be seen as only a contributory factor to the inflation. It was certainly not the primary cause. Nevertheless, the sum drawn up by the Reparations Commission added to the economic burden facing the Weimar government because the reparation payments had to be in **hard currency**, like dollars and gold (not inflated German marks). In order to pay their reparations, the Weimar governments proceeded to print larger quantities of marks and sell them to obtain the stronger currencies of other countries. This was not a solution. It was merely a short-term measure that had serious consequences. The mark went into sharp decline and inflation climbed even higher (see Table 4.1).

**Table 4.1:** The Great Inflation: exchange rate and wholesale prices

| The Great Inflation | Exchange rate of German marks against the dollar | Wholesale price index. The index is created from a scale of prices starting with 1 for 1914 |
|---|---|---|
| 1914 July | 4.2 | 1 |
| 1919 January | 8.9 | 2 |
| 1920 January | 14.0 | 4 |
| 1920 July | 39.5 | N/A |
| 1921 January | 64.9 | 14 |
| 1921 July | 76.7 | N/A |
| 1922 January | 191.8 | 37 |
| 1922 July | 493.2 | 100 |
| 1923 January | 17,792 | 2,785 |
| 1923 July | 353,412 | 74,787 |
| 1923 September | 98,860,000 | 23,949,000 |
| 1923 November | 200,000,000,000 | 750,000,000,000 |

## Short term

Germany had already been allowed to postpone several instalments of her reparations payments in early 1922, but an attempt to resolve the crisis on an international level by calling the Genoa Economic Conference was ill fated. When, in July 1922, the German government made another request for a 'holiday' from making reparations payments, the final stage of the country's inflationary crisis set in.

The French government, at this time led by Raymond Poincaré, suspected German intentions and was determined to secure what was seen as France's rightful claims. Therefore, when in December 1922 the Reparations Commission declared Germany to be in default, Poincaré ordered French and Belgian troops to occupy the Ruhr, the industrial heartland of Germany. In the next few months the inflationary spiral ran out of control – hyper-inflation.

The government, led by Wilhelm Cuno, embarked on a policy of 'passive resistance' and in a way the invasion did help to unite the German people. It urged the workers to go on strike and refuse to co-operate with the French authorities, although it also promised to carry on paying their wages. At the same time, the government was unable to collect taxes from the Ruhr area and the French prevented the delivery of coal to the rest of Germany, thus forcing the necessary stocks of fuel to be imported.

**Key date**

'Passive resistance' in Ruhr against French and Belgian soldiers: 13 January 1923

In this situation, the government's finances collapsed and the mark fell to worthless levels. By autumn 1923, it cost more to print a bank note than the note was worth and the *Reichsbank* was forced to use newspaper presses to produce sufficient money. The German currency ceased to have any real value and the German people had to resort to barter.

**Table 4.2:** Prices in the Great Inflation (in German marks)

| Items for sale in | 1913 | Summer 1923 | November 1923 |
|---|---|---|---|
| 1 kg of bread | 0.29 | 1,200 | 428,000,000,000 |
| 1 egg | 0.08 | 5,000 | 80,000,000,000 |
| 1 kg of butter | 2.70 | 26,000 | 6,000,000,000,000 |
| 1 kg of beef | 1.75 | 18,800 | 5,600,000,000,000 |
| 1 pair of shoes | 12.00 | 1,000,000 | 32,000,000,000,000 |

## Conclusion

The fundamental cause of the German Inflation is to be found in the mismanagement of Germany's finances from 1914 onwards. Certainly, the inflationary spiral did not increase at an even rate and there were short periods, as in the spring of 1920 and the winter of 1920–1, when it did actually slacken. However, at no time was there willingness by the various German governments to bring spending and borrowing back within reasonable limits.

**Key date**

Period of hyper-inflation: January–November 1923

Until the end of 1918 the cost of waging war was the excuse, but in the immediate post-war period the high levels of debt were allowed to continue. It has been argued by some that the inflation remained quite modest in the years 1914–22 and perhaps acceptable in view of all the various difficulties facing the new government. However, the payment of reparations from 1921 simply added to an already desperate situation and the government found it more convenient to print money than to tackle the basic problems facing the economy.

By the end of 1922 hyper-inflation had set in. Cuno's government made no effort to deal with the situation. Indeed, it could be said that Cuno deliberately exacerbated the economic crisis and played on the nationalist fervour brought by the popular decision to encourage 'passive resistance'. It was only in August 1923 when the German economy was on the verge of complete collapse that a new coalition government was formed under Gustav Stresemann. He found the will to introduce an economic policy, which was aimed at controlling the amount of money in circulation.

Summary diagram: The causes of the German inflation

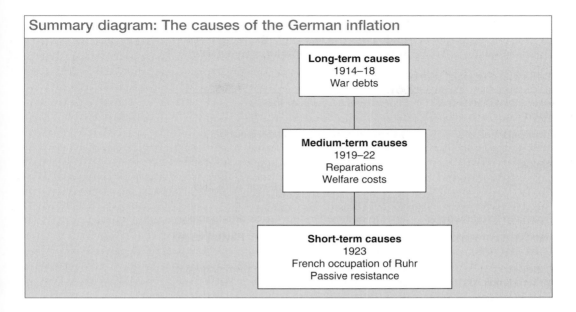

Long-term causes
1914–18
War debts

Medium-term causes
1919–22
Reparations
Welfare costs

Short-term causes
1923
French occupation of Ruhr
Passive resistance

Key question
Why did some
Germans lose and
some win?

## 3 | The Consequences of the Great Inflation

It has been claimed that the worst consequence of the inflation
was the damage done to the German middle class. Stresemann
himself said as much in 1927. Later on in the 1930s it was
generally assumed that the reason a large proportion of the
middle class voted for the Nazis was because of their economic
sufferings in 1923. In the light of recent historical research, such
assumptions have come to be questioned and a much more
complex interpretation has emerged about the impact of the
inflation on the whole of society.

The key to understanding who gained and who lost during the
period of the hyper-inflation lies in considering each individual's
savings and their amount of debt. However, it was not always clearly
linked to class differences. So what did this mean in practice?

The real winners were those sections of the community who
were able to pay off their debts, mortgages and loans with inflated
and worthless money. This obviously worked to the advantage of
such groups as businessmen and homeowners, which included
members of the middle class. Those who recognised the situation
for what it was exploited it by making massive gains from buying
up property from those financially desperate. Some businessmen
profited from the situation by borrowing cheaply and investing in
new industrial enterprises. Amongst these, one of the most
notorious examples was Hugo Stinnes who, by the end of 1923,
controlled 20 per cent of German industry.

At the other extreme, were those who depended on their
savings. Any German who had money invested in bank accounts
with interest rates found their real value had eroded. Most
famously, millions who had bought and invested in war bonds
now could not get their money back. The bonds were worth

nothing. Those living on fixed incomes, such as pensioners, found themselves in a similar plight. Their savings quickly lost value, since any increase was wiped out by inflation (see Table 4.3).

**Table 4.3:** Financial winners and losers

| Financial winners and losers | Explanation of gains or losses |
| --- | --- |
| Mortgage holders | Borrowed money was easily paid off in valueless money |
| Savers | Money invested was eroded |
| Exporters | Sales to foreign countries was attractive because of the rate of exchange |
| Those on fixed incomes | Income declined in real terms dramatically |
| Recipients of welfare | Depended on charity or state. Payments fell behind the inflation rate |
| Long-term renters/landlords | Income was fixed in the long term and so it declined in real terms |
| The German State | Large parts of the government debt were paid off in valueless money (but not reparations) |

## The human consequences

The material impact of the hyper-inflation has recently been the subject of considerable historical research in Germany and, as a result, our understanding of this period has been greatly increased and many previous conclusions have been revised. However, you should remember that the following discussion of the effects of the hyper-inflation on whole classes deals with broad categories, e.g. region and age, rather than individual examples. Two people from the same social class could be affected in very different ways depending on their individual circumstances.

### Peasants

In the countryside the peasants coped reasonably well as food remained in demand. They depended less on money for the provision of the necessities of life because they were more self-sufficient.

### *Mittelstand*

Shopkeepers and craftsmen also seem to have done reasonably good business, especially if they were prepared to exploit the demands of the market.

### Industrial workers

Workers' real wages and standard of living improved until 1922. It was in the chaos of 1923 that, when the trade unions were unable to negotiate wage settlements for their members, wages could not keep pace with the rate of inflation and a very real decline took place. However, as they had fewer savings, they lost proportionally less than those living on saved income. Unemployment did go up to 4.1 per cent in 1923, but it was still at a relatively low level.

**Key question**
Who were the winners and the losers?

**Mittelstand**
Can be translated as 'the middle class', but in German society it tends to represent the lower middle classes, e.g. shopkeepers, craft workers and clerks. Traditionally independent and self-reliant but increasingly felt squeezed out between the power and influence of big business and industrial labour.

**Key term**

Children playing with blocks of worthless banknotes in 1923.

### Civil servants

The fate of public employees is probably the most difficult to analyse. Their income fell sharply in the years 1914–20, but they made real gains in 1921–2. They suffered again in the chaos of 1923 because they depended on fixed salaries, which fell in value before the end of each month. They tended to gain – if they were buying a property on a mortgage – but many had been attracted to buy the war bonds and so lost out.

### Retired

The old generally suffered badly because they depended on fixed pensions and savings.

### Businessmen

Generally, they did well because they bought up property with worthless money and they paid off mortgages. They also benefited if they made sales to foreign countries, as the rate of exchange was very attractive.

## Other social effects

By merely listing the financial statistics of the Great Inflation, there is a danger of overlooking the very real human dimension. As early as February 1923 the health minister delivered a speech to the *Reichstag*:

**Key question**
In what other ways did the Great Inflation affect people's lives?

> … It is understandable that under such unhygienic circumstances, health levels are deteriorating ever more seriously. While the figures for the Reich as a whole are not yet available, we do have a preliminary mortality rate for towns with 100,000 or more inhabitants. After having fallen in 1920–1, it has climbed again for the year 1921–2, rising from 12.6 to 13.4 per thousand inhabitants … thus, oedema [an unpleasant medical condition which occurs when water accumulates in parts of the body] is reappearing, this so-called war dropsy, which is a consequence of a bad and overly watery diet. There are increases in stomach disorders and food poisoning, which are the result of eating spoiled foods. There are complaints of the appearance of scurvy, which is a consequence of an unbalanced and improper diet. From various parts of the Reich, reports are coming in about an increase in suicides … More and more often one finds 'old age' and 'weakness' listed in the official records as the cause of death; these are equivalent to death through hunger.

Even more telling than the health minister's description about Germany's declining health were the possible effects on behaviour, as people began to resort to desperate solutions:

- a decline in law and order
- an increase in crime
- a decline in 'morality', for example, more prostitution
- a growth in suicides
- an increase in prejudice and a tendency to find scapegoats, e.g. Jews.

It has often been suggested that such social problems contributed to people's lack of faith in the republican system. The connection is difficult to prove, as it is not easy to assess the importance of morality and religious codes in past societies. However, it would be foolish to dismiss out of hand their effects upon German society and its traditional set of values. At the very least, the loss of some old values led to increased tensions. Even more significantly, when another crisis developed at the end of the decade, the people's confidence in the ability of Weimar to maintain social stability was eventually lost. In that sense the inflation of 1923 was not the reason for the Weimar Republic's decline, but it caused psychological damage that continued to affect the Republic in future years.

## The key debate

Traditionally, the German inflation of 1923 has been portrayed as an economic catastrophe with damaging consequences that paved the way for the collapse of the Weimar Republic and the rise of

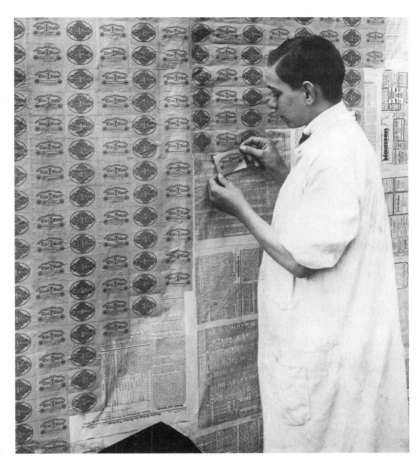

Wallpapering with German marks. Owing to the collapse of the German currency, it was cheaper to paper a wall with banknotes than to buy wallpaper.

Hitler's National Socialists. However, a number of economic historians from the 1980s have begun to perceive the event differently, so the question is:

## Was the Great Inflation a disaster for Germany?

In an interesting analysis the historian Holtfrerich maintains that in the years up to the end of 1922 Weimar's economic policy amounted to a 'rational strategy ... in the national interest'. His interpretation is that by not reducing the budget deficits, the Weimar Republic was able to maintain economic growth and increase production. He argues that the German economy compared very favourably with other European economies that also went into post-war **recession** in 1920–1, for example:

**Key term**

**Recession**
Period of economic slowdown, usually accompanied by rising unemployment.

- Low unemployment. Whereas Britain had an unemployment rate of nearly 17 per cent in 1921, Germany had nearly full employment with only 1.8 per cent unemployed.
- Rising wage levels. After the war the real wages of industrial workers increased between 1918 and 1922, which helped to secure popular support for the new Republic.
- Growing foreign investment. Similarly, after the dislocation it was difficult to encourage domestic investors, but foreigners'

capital, particularly from USA, provided an important stimulus to economic activity.

• Industrial production. Figures of the index for industrial production nearly doubled from 1919 to 1922 (albeit from a very low base because of the war).

Holtfrerich does not accept that the economic policy was a disaster. In fact, he sees it as the only way that could have ensured the survival of the Weimar Republic. He argues that, in the early years of 1921–2, any policy that required cutting back spending would have resulted in the most terrible economic and social consequences – and perhaps even the collapse of the new German democracy. In this sense the inflation up to 1923 was actually beneficial.

This interpretation remains controversial and many have found it difficult to accept. Holtfrerich has been criticised for drawing an artificial line at 1922 – as if the years up to 1922 were those of modest and 'good' inflation, whereas the year 1923 marked the start of hyper-inflation with all the problems arising from that date. This seems a rather doubtful way of looking at the overall development of the Great Inflation, bearing in mind the long-term build-up and the nature of its causes. It also tends to separate the inflation from the drastic measures that were eventually required to solve it. Finally, an assessment of the Great Inflation must pay regard to all the other important considerations, such as the social and psychological. There is always a danger that economic historians tend to rely largely on a study of economic and financial data.

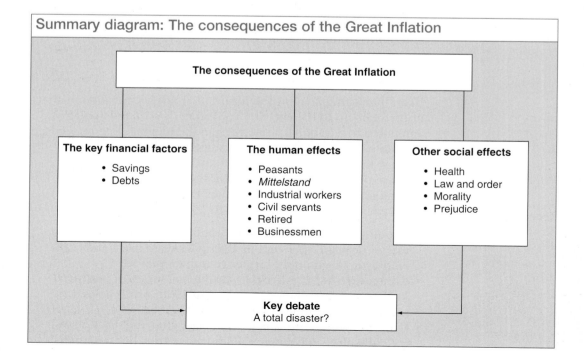

Summary diagram: The consequences of the Great Inflation

**The consequences of the Great Inflation**

| The key financial factors | The human effects | Other social effects |
|---|---|---|
| • Savings<br>• Debts | • Peasants<br>• *Mittelstand*<br>• Industrial workers<br>• Civil servants<br>• Retired<br>• Businessmen | • Health<br>• Law and order<br>• Morality<br>• Prejudice |

**Key debate**
A total disaster?

**Key question**
How did the Weimar Republic survive the crisis of 1923?

# 4 | Stresemann's 100 Days

In the summer of 1923 the problems facing the Weimar Republic came to a head and it seemed close to collapse:

- the German currency had collapsed and hyper-inflation had set in
- French and Belgian troops were occupying the Ruhr
- the German government had no clear policy on the occupation, except for 'passive resistance'
- there were various left-wing political disturbances across the country – in Saxony the creation of an SPD/KPD regional state government resulted in an attempted Communist uprising (page 41)
- the ultra-conservative state government in Bavaria was defying the national government. This finally resulted in the Munich Beer Hall *putsch* (see page 47–50).

Yet, only a few months later a semblance of calm and normality returned. The Weimar Republic's remarkable survival illustrates the telling comment of the historian Peukert that even 1923 shows 'there are no entirely hopeless situations in history'.

**Key dates**

Stresemann appointed chancellor: 12 August 1923

Stresemann's 100 days of leadership: August–November 1923

## Stresemann's achievements

It is important to recognise that, during the summer of 1923, things had just been allowed to slide. Nevertheless, the appointment of Gustav Stresemann as chancellor in August 1923 resulted in the emergence of a politician who was actually prepared to take difficult political decisions. Stresemann led a broad coalition of DVP, DDP, ZP and SPD and aimed to resolve Germany's economic plight and also tackle the problem of her weakness internationally.

Within a few weeks Stresemann made a series of crucial initiatives:

- Firstly, in September, he called off the 'passive resistance' in the Ruhr and promised to resume the payment of reparations. He needed to conciliate the French in order to evoke some sympathy for Germany's economic and international position.
- Under the guidance of Finance Minister, Hans Luther, the government's expenditure was sharply cut in order to reduce the deficit. Over 700,000 public employees were sacked.
- He appointed the leading financial expert Hjalmar Schacht to oversee the introduction of a new German currency. In December 1923 the trillions of old German marks were replaced and a new stable currency, the *Rentenmark* was established.
- He evoked some sympathy from the Allies for Germany by the 'miracle of the *Rentenmark*' and his conciliatory policy. He therefore asked the Allies to hold an international conference to consider Germany's economic plight and, as a result, the Dawes Committee was established. Its report, the Dawes Plan, was published in April 1924. It did not reduce the overall reparations bill, but for the first five years it fixed the payments in accordance with Germany's ability to pay (see pages 86–7).
- The extremists of the left and the right were defeated (pages 41 and 49).

**Key dates**

Introduction of the *Rentenmark*: December 1923

Dawes Plan proposed and accepted: April 1924

## The survival of Weimar

Although Stresemann's resolute action in tackling the problems might help to explain why the years of crisis came to an end, on its own it does not help us to understand why the Weimar Republic was able to come through. The Republic's survival in 1923 was in marked contrast to its collapse 10 years later when challenged by the Nazis.

Why, then, did the Republic not collapse during the crisis-ridden months before Stresemann's emergence on the political scene? This is a difficult question to answer, though the following factors provide clues:

- Popular anger was directed more towards the French and the Allies than towards the Weimar Republic itself.
- Despite the effects of inflation, workers did not suffer to the same extent as they did during the mass unemployment of the 1930s.
- Similarly, employers tended to show less hostility to the Republic in its early years than they did in the early 1930s at the start of the depression.
- Some businessmen did very well out of the inflation, which made them tolerant of the Republic.

If these suggestions about public attitudes towards the Republic are correct, then it seems that, although there was distress and disillusionment in 1923, hostility to the Weimar Republic had not yet reached unbearable levels – as it was to do 10 years later.

Moreover, in 1923 there was no obvious political alternative to Weimar. The extreme left had not really recovered from its divisions and suppression in the years 1918–21 and, in its isolated position, it did not enjoy enough support to overthrow Weimar. The extreme right, too, was not yet strong enough. It was similarly divided and had no clear plans. The failure of the Kapp *putsch* served as a clear warning of the dangers of taking hasty action and was possibly the reason why the army made no move in 1923.

In analysing why the Weimar Republic survived its post-war years of crisis, it is worth remembering that during this period the democratic governments of other countries did not fare well. For example, Italy fell under the control of the Fascist leader Mussolini in 1922; and Hungary and Poland both became military authoritarian regimes in 1920 and 1926, respectively. Up to 1923, the Republic had weathered the storm. Was this a sign of its growing political strength and stability? If so, perhaps it could now begin to build on its achievements as it moved into the calmer waters of the mid-1920s.

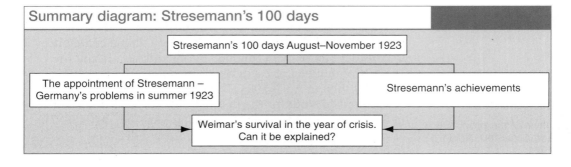

Summary diagram: Stresemann's 100 days

Stresemann's 100 days August–November 1923

The appointment of Stresemann – Germany's problems in summer 1923

Stresemann's achievements

Weimar's survival in the year of crisis. Can it be explained?

## Study Guide: AS Questions

### In the style of AQA

Read the following and then answer the questions which follow.

*Adapted from: Comments on Germany to the Disarmament Commission, given by General John Hartment Morgan, December 1923.*

Inflation has destroyed the balance of society. It has ruined the middle classes and impoverished the workers. Inflation has undermined the political basis of the Republic.

**(a)** What was meant by 'inflation' in the context of the economic situation of Germany in the years 1922 to 1923? (3 marks)

**(b)** Explain why the Weimar Republic was economically stronger in 1925 than it had been in 1919. (7 marks)

**(c)** 'The political instability of the Weimar Republic in the years 1919 to 1923 was the result of its economic difficulties.' Explain why you agree or disagree with this statement.

(15 marks)

*Source: AQA, May 2002*

---

### Exam tips

*The cross-references are intended to take you straight to the material that will help you to answer the questions.*

**(a)** In question **(a)** you should provide a developed explanation of the concept of 'inflation' linked to the context of Germany in 1922–3, for example:
- inflation was caused by a cumulative range of causes – war debts, budget deficits (pages 57–9)
- the printing of money ran out of control, particularly after the French invasion of the Ruhr in 1923, leading to hyper-inflation (pages 59–60).

**(b)** In question **(b)** you have to demonstrate a range of factors to explain why the problems had declined and why Germany's confidence had started to recover, for example:
- inflation had been tackled by the *Rentenmark* and the reduction of government expenditure (pages 67–8).
- economic stability had improved because of Dawes Plan and US investment (pages 86–7).

Do not describe all the details of Germany's economic problems from 1919. But it could be very good to mention that economic weaknesses persisted from 1924, despite the recovery.

**(c)** In question **(c)** you should evaluate the extent to which Germany had suffered *political* instability because of its *economic* problems. It is important to:
- show evidence for the argument, e.g. the loss of resources after Versailles, the effect of reparations, war debts (pages 32–3)
- show evidence against the argument – other factors and examples, e.g. left-wing opposition (the Spartacists); the right-wing opposition (Kapp *putsch*); the discontent of the traditional elites; hostility of some foreign powers (pages 32–3).

A thoughtful conclusion is vital. You must use a range of evidence to make your balanced judgment, e.g. it would be useful to show a clear *link* between the economic and political problems.

## In the style of Edexcel

**(a)** Why was 1923 a year of crisis? (15 marks)
**(b)** In what ways did Germany manage to overcome the year of crisis? (15 marks)

---

### Exam tips

*The cross-references are intended to take you straight to the material that will help you to answer the questions.*

**(a)** You must be very careful in question **(a)** about the date. Although the title of the question makes reference to the year 1923, you should not limit your study to the event of that year. You must look at the causes for the year of crisis, which go back before 1923. So examine and refer to:
- the long-term economic problems that led to the hyper-inflation (pages 57–60)
- the internal weaknesses inherent in Weimar Germany (pages 57–60)
- the reasons for right-wing discontent that led to the activities of the extremists, such as the Nazis (pages 42–50).

A good conclusion will show the interaction of causes and how they combined to bring about the inflation. It is also important to show the relative significance of these factors.

**(b)** You must refer to the importance of Stresemann from August 1923 and you must consider:
- all the steps taken to solve the financial dilemma (page 67)
- the defeat of the extremists and the restoration of law and order (pages 42–50)
- Stresemann's conciliatory approach in foreign affairs (pages 67, 86–7).

It will also be helpful to consider Stresemann's success as saviour of Weimar in 1923 (page 67).

---

## In the style of OCR

How far were the consequences of the German Inflation disastrous for Germany in 1923?

---

### Exam tips

*The cross-references are intended to take you straight to the material that will help you to answer the question.*

In this question you should evaluate the extent to which the Great Inflation was a disaster for Germany by:
- assessing the financial factors supported with some examples as evidence (page 61)
- assessing the effects on the different social classes and how some won and some lost, supported with some examples as evidence (page 62)
- distinguishing between the mild inflation of 1919–22 and the hyper-inflation of 1923 (pages 64–6).

Finally, round off your answer by offering an opinion on how far you agree or disagree with the view that it was disastrous for Germany.

# Weimar: The Years of Stability 1924–9

## 1 | The Economic Recovery

It is often claimed that after the hyper-inflation, the introduction of the new currency – the *Rentenmark* – and the measures brought about by the Dawes Plan ushered in five years of economic growth and affluence. Certainly the period stands out between the economic chaos of 1922–3 and the **Great Depression** of 1929–33. So, for many Germans looking back from the end of the 1920s, it seemed as if Germany had made a remarkable recovery.

### The strengths of the German economy

In spite of the loss of resources as a result of the Treaty of Versailles, heavy industry was able to recover reasonably quickly and, by 1928, production levels reached those of 1913. This was

**Key term**

**Great Depression**
The severe economic crisis of 1929–33 that was marked by mass unemployment, falling prices and a lack of spending.

**Key question**
What were the strengths of the German economy?

the result of the use of more efficient methods of production, particularly in coal-mining and steel manufacture, and also because of increased investment. Foreign bankers were particularly attracted by Germany's high interest rates.

At the same time, German industry had the advantage of being able to lower costs because of the growing number of **cartels**, which had better purchasing power than smaller industries. For example, IG Farben, the chemicals giant, became the largest manufacturing enterprise in Europe, whilst Vereinigte Stahlwerke combined the coal, iron and steel interests of Germany's great industrial companies and grew to control nearly half of all production.

Between 1925 and 1929, German exports rose by 40 per cent. Such economic progress brought social benefits as well. Hourly wage rates rose every year from 1924 to 1930 and by as much as five to 10 per cent in 1927 and 1928.

**Cartel**
An arrangement between businesses to control the market by exercising a joint monopoly.

Key term

## The benefits of social welfare

There were striking improvements in the provision of social welfare. The principles of a welfare state were written into the new Weimar Constitution and in the early 1920s generous pensions and sickness benefits were introduced. In 1927, a compulsory unemployment insurance covering 17 million workers was created, which was the largest scheme of its kind in the world. In addition, state subsidies were provided for the construction of local amenities such as parks, schools, sports facilities and especially council housing. All these developments, alongside the more obvious signs of wealth, such as the increasing number of cars and the growth of the cinema industry, supported the view that the Weimar Republic's economy was enjoying boom conditions. However, it should be borne in mind that the social costs had economic implications (see page 73–4).

## The weaknesses in the German economy

From the statistics for 1924–9 it is easy to get an impression of the 'golden twenties'. However, the actual rate of German recovery was unclear:

**Key question**
Was the Weimar economy fundamentally weak?

- There was economic growth, but it was uneven, and in 1926 production actually declined. In overseas trade, the value of **imports** always exceeded that of **exports**.
- Unemployment never fell below 1.3 million in this period. And even before the effects of America's financial crisis began to be felt (see pages 122–5), the number of unemployed workers averaged 1.9 million in 1929.
- In agriculture, grain production was still only three-quarters of its 1913 figure and farmers, many of whom were in debt, faced falling incomes. By the late 1920s, income per head in agriculture was 44 per cent below the national average.

**Imports**
Goods purchased from foreign countries.

**Exports**
Goods sold to foreign countries.

Key terms

### Fundamental economic problems

The economic indicators listed above suggest that the German economy had fundamental problems in this period and it is therefore important to appreciate the broader view by looking at the following points.

**Tariffs**
Taxes levied by an importing nation on foreign goods coming in, and paid by the importers.

**GNP**
Gross national product is the total value of all goods and services in a nation's economy (including income derived from assets abroad).

- World economic conditions did not favour Germany. Traditionally, Germany had relied on its ability to export to achieve economic growth, but world trade did not return to pre-war levels. German exports were hindered by protective **tariffs** in many parts of the world. By the Treaty of Versailles, they were also handicapped by the loss of valuable resources in territories, such as Alsace-Lorraine and Silesia (see page 30). German agriculture also found itself in difficulties because of world economic conditions. The fall in world prices from the mid-1920s placed a great strain on farmers, who made up one-third of the German population. Support in the form of government financial aid and tariffs could only partially help to reduce the problems. Most significantly, this decline in income reduced the spending power of a large section of the population and this led to a fall in demand within the economy as a whole.

- The changing balance of the population. From the mid-1920s, there were more school leavers because of the high pre-war birth rate. The available workforce increased from 32.4 million in 1925 to 33.4 million in 1931. This meant that, even without a recession, there was always likely to be an increase in unemployment in Germany.

- Savings and investment discouraged. Savers had lost a great deal of money in the Great Inflation and, after 1924, there was less enthusiasm to invest money again. As a result, the German economy came to rely on investors from abroad, for example the USA, who were attracted by the prospect of higher interest rates than those in their own countries. Germany's economic well-being became ever more dependent on foreign investment.

- Government finances raised concern. Although the government succeeded in balancing the budget in 1924, from 1925 it continually ran into debt. It continued to spend increasing sums of money and by 1928 public expenditure had reached 26 per cent of **GNP**, which was double the pre-war figure. The government found it difficult to encourage domestic savings and was forced to rely more and more on international loans. Such a situation did not provide the basis for solid future economic growth.

## The key debate

In the late 1970s a vigorous argument developed on the performance of the German economy in the period 1924–9, which has raised an important question among economic historians:

Was the Weimar economy a fundamentally sick economy?

In the late 1970s, the German economic historian Karl Borchardt was the first to argue that, during the years 1925–9, Germany was living well beyond her means and that her public spending was out of control. He maintained that the government intervention in the **labour market** showed an over-sympathetic attitude towards the trade unions since wage levels were rising without being matched by increases in production.

Borchardt also argued that the higher contributions required from employers towards social insurance both increased production costs and left less money available for investment, as well as making employers less willing to take on workers. This slowed economic growth. By 1927–8, the prospect of falling profits had so badly affected business that there were already signs that the 'points were set to depression'. So, in his assessment, the Weimar Republic's economy was 'an abnormal, in fact a sick economy, which could not possibly have gone on in the same way, even if the world depression had not occurred'.

Carl Holtfrerich, a left-wing German historian in the 1980s, thought differently. He threw doubt on Borchardt's view that excessive wage increases were at the heart of the Weimar Republic's economic problems and he did not blame trade union greed. Instead, he believed that the real cause lay with the business leaders who discouraged industrial and agricultural investment. Consequently, growth remained at low levels and there was no means of creating new jobs. As a result, Holtfrerich concluded, the German economy was not in a chronic condition, but only temporarily 'off the rails'.

All this evidence suggests that before the start of the depression in 1929 the problems of the German economy were hidden by the flood of foreign capital and by the development of an extensive social welfare system. However, it was clear that the German economy was already in a very poor state and it seems safe to offer several key conclusions:

- The German economy's dependence on foreign loans made it liable to suffer from any problems that arose in the world economy.
- Investment was too low to encourage growth.
- The cost of the welfare state could be met only by the government's taking on increasing debts.
- Various sectors of the German economy had actually started to slow down from 1927 and the agricultural sector faced serious problems from the mid-1920s.

Whether this amounts to proof of Borchardt's view of a 'sick' economy is controversial, and to assess what might have happened without a world economic crisis can only be guesswork. However, it is interesting that Stresemann wrote in 1928: 'Germany is dancing on a volcano. If the short-term credits are called in, a large section of our economy would collapse'. So, on balance, the evidence suggests that by 1929 the Republic was already facing serious difficulties and was heading for a major economic crisis. In that sense, the German economy faced a 'crisis before the crisis', when America's financial collapse in October 1929 added to an already grave situation.

**Labour market**
Comprises the supply of labour (those looking for work) and the demand for labour from employers. These two forces within the labour market determine wage rates.

*Key term*

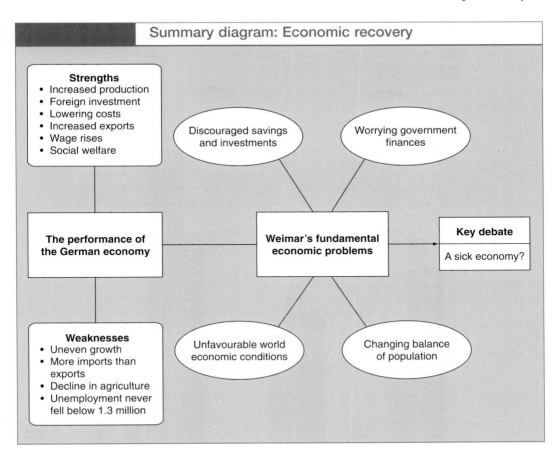

Summary diagram: Economic recovery

**Strengths**
- Increased production
- Foreign investment
- Lowering costs
- Increased exports
- Wage rises
- Social welfare

Discouraged savings and investments

Worrying government finances

**The performance of the German economy**

**Weimar's fundamental economic problems**

**Key debate**

A sick economy?

**Weaknesses**
- Uneven growth
- More imports than exports
- Decline in agriculture
- Unemployment never fell below 1.3 million

Unfavourable world economic conditions

Changing balance of population

**Key question**
Did the general election results of 1924–8 reflect optimism about the Weimar Republic among German voters?

## 2 | Political Stability

The election results during the middle years of the Weimar Republic gave grounds for cautious optimism about its survival (see Figure 5.1, page 76). The extremist parties of both left and right lost ground and altogether they polled less than 30 per cent of the votes cast. The DNVP peaked in December 1924 with 103 seats (20.5 per cent of the vote) and fell back to 73 (14.2 per cent) in May 1928. The Nazis lost ground in both elections and were reduced to only 12 seats (2.6 per cent) by 1928. The KPD, although recovering slightly by 1928 with 54 seats (10.6 per cent), remained below their performance of May 1924 and well below the combined votes gained by the KPD and USPD in June 1920 (see page 51).

In comparison, the parties sympathetic to the Republic maintained their share of the vote and the SPD made substantial gains, winning 153 seats (29.8 per cent) in 1928. As a result, following the 1928 election, a 'Grand Coalition' of the SPD, DDP, DVP and Centre was formed under Hermann Müller, the leader of the SPD. It enjoyed the support of over 60 per cent of the *Reichstag* and it seemed as if democracy was at last beginning to emerge in Weimar politics.

**Key date**

Müller's 'Grand Coalition' formed: May 1928

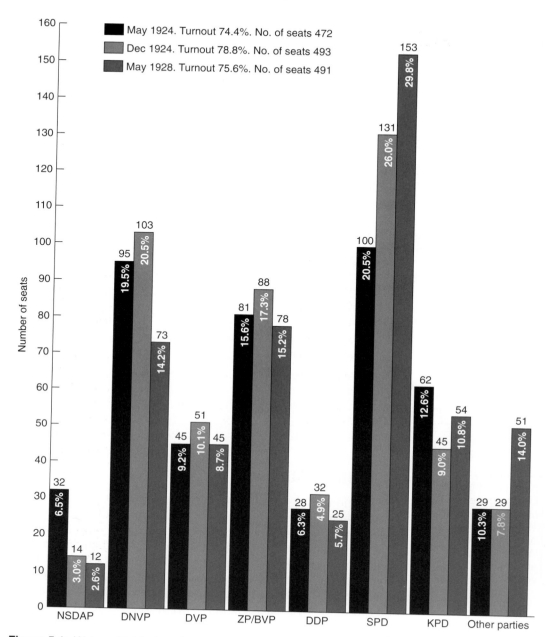

**Figure 5.1:** Weimar *Reichstag* election results 1924 and 1928

## Coalition politics

The election of 1928 must not be regarded as typical in Weimar history – and it should not hide the continuing basic weaknesses of the German parliamentary system. These included not only the problems created by proportional representation (see page 26), but also the ongoing difficulty of creating and maintaining coalitions from the various parties. In such a situation each party tended to put its own self-interests before those of the government.

**Key question**
Why did the political parties find it so difficult to co-operate?

The parties tended to reflect their traditional interests – in particular, religion and class. So attempts to widen their appeal made little progress. As a result, the differences between the main parties meant that opportunities to form workable coalitions were very limited.

- There was never any possibility of a coalition including both the SPD and the DNVP because the former believed in parliamentary democracy whereas the latter fundamentally rejected the Weimar political system.
- The Communists, KPD, remained totally isolated.
- A right–centre coalition of Centre, DVP and DNVP created a situation in which the parties tended to agree on domestic issues, but disagree on foreign affairs.
- On the other hand, a broad coalition of SPD, DDP, DVP and Centre meant that these parties agreed on foreign policy, but differed on domestic issues.
- A minority government of the political centre, including the DDP, DVP and Centre, could only exist by seeking support from either the left or right. It was impossible to create a coalition with a parliamentary majority that could also consistently agree on both domestic and foreign policy.

In this situation, there was very little chance of democratic government being able to establish any lasting political stability. Of the seven governments between 1923 and 1930 (see Table 5.1), only two had majorities and the longest survived just 21 months. In fact, the only reason governments lasted as long as they did was that the opposition parties were also unable or unwilling to unite. More often than not, it was conflicts within the parties that formed the coalition governments that led them to collapse.

**Table 5.1:** Governments of the Weimar Republic, 1923–30

| Period in office | Chancellor | Make-up of the coalition |
| --- | --- | --- |
| 1923–4 | Wilhelm Marx | Centre, DDP, DVP |
| 1924–5 | Wilhelm Marx | Centre, DDP, DVP |
| 1925 | Hans Luther | Centre, DVP, DNVP |
| 1926 | Hans Luther | Centre, DDP, DVP |
| 1926 | Wilhelm Marx | Centre, DDP, DVP |
| 1927–8 | Wilhelm Marx | Centre, DDP, DNVP |
| 1928–30 | Hermann Müller | SPD, DDP, Centre, DVP |

## The responsibility of the parties

The attitude of the Weimar Republic's political parties towards parliamentary government was irresponsible. This may well have been a legacy from the imperial years. In that time the parties had expressed their own narrow interests in the knowledge that it was the Kaiser who ultimately decided policy. However, in the 1920s, parliamentary democracy needed the political parties to show a more responsible attitude towards government. The evidence suggests that no such attitude existed, even in the most stable period of the Republic's history.

## The SPD

Until 1932 the SPD remained the largest party in the *Reichstag*. However, although firm in its support of the Republic, the Party was divided between its desire to uphold the interests of the working class and its commitment to democracy. Some members, and especially those connected with the trade unions, feared that joining coalitions with other parties would lead to a weakening of their principles. Others, the more moderate, wanted to participate in government in order to influence it. At the same time, the Party was hindered by the old argument between those committed to a more extreme left-wing socialist programme and those who favoured moderate, gradual reform.

As a result, during the middle years of the Republic the SPD did not join any of the fragile government coalitions. This obviously weakened the power base of those democratic coalitions from 1924 to 1928. The SPD remained the strongest party during those years: although it was committed to democracy, it was not prepared to take on the responsibility of government until 1928.

## The Centre Party

It therefore fell to the Centre Party to provide real political leadership in Weimar politics. The ZP electoral support was solid and the party participated in all the coalition governments from 1919 to 1932 by taking ministerial posts. However, its support did not increase because its appeal was restricted to traditional Catholic areas. Further, its social and economic policies which aimed at bridging the gaps between the classes led to internal quarrels.

In the early years, such differences had been put to one side under the strong left-wing leadership of Matthias Erzberger and Josef Wirth. However, during the 1920s, the Party moved decisively to the right and the divisions within the Party widened. In 1928, the leadership eventually passed to Ludwig Kaas and Heinrich Brüning, who appealed more to the conservative partners of the coalition than to the liberal or social democratic elements. This was a worrying sign both for the future of the Centre Party and for Germany herself.

## The liberal parties

The position of the German liberals was not a really strong one. The DDP and DVP joined in all the coalition governments of this period and in Gustav Stresemann, the leader of the DVP, they possessed the Republic's only really capable statesman. However, this hid some worrying trends. Their share of the vote, though constant in the mid-1920s, had nearly halved since 1919–20, when it had been between 22 and 23 per cent.

The reasons for the liberals' eventual collapse after 1930 were already established beforehand. This decline was largely a result of the divisions within both parties. The DDP lacked clear leadership and its membership was involved in internal bickering over policy. The DVP was also divided and, despite Stresemann's

**Key question**
In what ways was the SPD divided?

**Key question**
What were the limitations of the Centre Party?

**Key question**
What were the weaknesses of the German liberal parties?

efforts to bring unity to the Party, this remained a source of conflict. It is not really surprising that moves to bring about some kind of united liberal party came to nothing. As a result, German liberalism failed to gain popular support – and after 1929 its position declined dramatically.

## The DNVP

**Key question**
How did the DNVP change over time?

One promising feature of German party politics came unexpectedly from the conservative DNVP. Since 1919, the DNVP had been totally opposed to the Republic and it had refused to take part in government. In electoral terms, it had enjoyed considerable success, and in December 1924, gained 103 seats (20.5 per cent). However, as the Republic began to recover after the 1923 crisis (see pages 67–8), it became increasingly clear that the DNVP's hopes of restoring a more right-wing government were diminishing. The continuous opposition policy meant that the Party had no real power and achieved nothing. Some influential groups within the DNVP realised that if they were to have any influence on government policy, then the party had to be prepared to participate in government. As a result, in 1925 and 1927, the DNVP joined government coalitions. This more sympathetic attitude towards the Weimar Republic was an encouraging development.

**Key date**
Hugenberg leader of DNVP: October 1928

However, that more conciliatory policy was not popular with all groups within the Party. When, in the 1928 election, the DNVP vote fell by a quarter, the more extreme right wing asserted its influence. Significantly, it elected Alfred Hugenberg, an extreme nationalist, as the new leader (see profile, page 80). Hugenberg was Germany's greatest media tycoon – he owned 150 newspapers, a publishing house and had interests in the film industry. He utterly rejected the idea of a republic based on parliamentary democracy. He now used all his resources to promote his political message. The DNVP reverted to a programme of total opposition to the Republic and refused to be involved in government. A year later, his party was working closely with the Nazis against the Young Plan (see pages 89 and 126).

## President Hindenburg

**Key question**
Was the appointment of Hindenburg as president a good or a bad sign for Weimar democracy?

A presidential election was due in 1925. It was assumed that President Friedrich Ebert would be re-elected. So his unexpected death in February 1925 created political problems. There was no clear successor in the first round of the election and so a second round was held. It did result in the choice of Hindenburg as president, but the figures clearly underlined the divisions in German society (see Table 5.2).

**Key date**
Hindenburg elected president: 1925

**Table 5.2:** Presidential election, second round, 26 April 1925

| Candidate (party) | Votes (millions) | Votes % |
|---|---|---|
| Paul von Hindenburg (DNVP) | 14.6 | 48 |
| Wilhelm Marx (ZP) | 13.7 | 45 |
| Ernst Thälmann (KPD) | 1.9 | 6 |

## Profile: Alfred Hugenberg 1865–1951

| | |
|---|---|
| 1865 | – Born in Hanover |
| | – Civil servant, banker, industrialist and 'press baron' |
| 1894 | – Founder of Pan-German League |
| 1920 | – *Reichstag* DNVP deputy |
| 1927 | – Leader of UFA, Germany's largest film company |
| 1928 | – Leader of DNVP until 1933 |
| 1929 | – Campaigned against the Young Plan |
| 1931 | – Joined the *Harzburg Front* against Brüning (see page 134) |
| 1933 | – Member of Hitler's coalition, but replaced in June |
| 1945 | – Survived (his fortune intact) and was not prosecuted by the Allies |
| 1951 | – Death |

Hugenburg was strongly against the Weimar Republic from the outset. He played a crucial role in forming the DNVP in 1919 from various established conservative-nationalist parties and he became a member of the *Reichstag* in 1920. Most significantly, he used his massive fortune to finance the DNVP and several other campaigns against reparations and the Treaties of Versailles and Locarno. Once he became leader of the Party he began to fund Hitler and the Nazis and in 1931–3 his political and financial power were instrumental in Hitler's rise to power. However, although he remained a member of the *Reichstag*, he lost his political power and influence when Hitler established the Nazi dictatorship from mid-1933 and no longer needed him and the DNVP.

The appointment of President Hindenburg has remained controversial. On the one hand, on Hindenburg's coming to power there was no immediate swing to the right. The new president proved totally loyal to the constitution and carried out his presidential duties with correctness. Those nationalists who had hoped that his election might lead to the restoration of the monarchy, or the creation of a military-type regime, were disappointed. Indeed, it has been argued that Hindenburg as president acted as a true substitute kaiser or **Ersatzkaiser** (so although Wilhelm II had abdicated and Germany had lost its monarchy, Hindenburg was seen by monarchists as, in effect, fulfilling the role of sovereign). In that sense, the status of Hindenburg as president at last gave Weimar some respectability in conservative circles.

On the other hand, it is difficult to ignore the pitfalls resulting from the appointment of an old man. In his heart, Hindenburg had no real sympathy for the Republic or its values. Those around him were mainly made up of anti-republican figures, many of them from the military. He preferred to include the DNVP in government and, if possible, to exclude the SPD. From the start, Hindenburg's view was that the government should move towards the right, although it was really only after 1929 that the serious implications of his outlook became fully apparent for Weimar democracy. As the historian A.J. Nicholls put it: 'he refused to betray the republic, but he did not rally the people to its banner'.

## Profile: Paul von Hindenburg 1847–1934

| | |
|---|---|
| 1847 | – Born in Posen, East Prussia |
| 1859 | – Joined the Prussian army |
| 1866 | – Served in Austria |
| 1870 | – Fought in the Franco-Prussian war |
| 1911 | – Retired with the rank of General |
| 1914 | – Recalled at start of First World War |
| | – Won the victory of the Battle of Tannenberg on Eastern Front |
| 1916 | – Promoted to Field Marshal and war supremo |
| 1918 | – Accepted the defeat of Germany and retired again |
| 1925 | – Elected president of Germany |
| 1930–2 | – Appointed Brüning, Papen and Schleicher as chancellors, who ruled by presidential decree |
| 1932 | – Re-elected president |
| 1933 | – Persuaded to appoint Hitler as chancellor |
| 1934 | – Death. Granted a national funeral |

### Background
Hindenburg was born into a Prussian noble family that could trace its military tradition back over many centuries. Described as 'steady rather than exceptional', he was regularly promoted.

### First World War
In 1914, he was recalled from retirement. His management of the campaign against the Russians on the Eastern Front earned him distinction. However, Hindenburg, who was distinguished in appearance and 'looked the part', did not have great military skills and was outshone by his chief-of-staff, Ludendorff.

### War dictator
After 1916, his partnership with Ludendorff was less successful against the British and French on the Western Front. During the years 1917 and 1918, the two men were effectively the military dictators of Germany.

### Appointment as president of Weimar Republic
After the war, Hindenburg briefly retired but in 1925 he was elected president of Germany, a position he held until 1934. He was not a democrat and looked forward to the return of the monarchy and in many respects he only accepted the post reluctantly. Nevertheless, he took up the responsibility of his office and performed his duties correctly.

### Rise of Hitler
From 1930 Hindenburg's political significance increased when Weimar faced growing political and economic crisis. As president, he was responsible for the appointment of all the chancellors from 1930–4, though he became a crucial player in the political intrigue of the competing forces. Given his authority, he must be held ultimately responsible for the events that ended with the appointment of Hitler, but by that time he was 85 years old.

## The limitations of the political system

During this period the parliamentary and party political system in Germany failed to make any real progress. It just coped as best it could. Government carried out its work but with only limited success. There was no *putsch* from left or right and the anti-republican extremists were contained. Law and order were restored and the activities of the various paramilitary groups were limited.

However, these were only minor and very negative successes and, despite the good intentions of certain individuals and groups, there were no signs of any real strengthening of the political structure. Stable government had not been established. This is not surprising when it is noted that one coalition government collapsed in 1926 over a minor issue about the use of the national flag and the old imperial flag. Another government fell over the creation of religious schools.

Even more significant for the future was the growing contempt and cynicism shown by the people towards party politics. This was particularly connected with the negotiating and bargaining involved in the creation of most coalitions. The turn-out of the elections declined in the mid-1920s compared to 1919 and 1920. There was also an increasing growth of small fringe parties. The apparent stability of these years was really a deception, a mirage. It misled some people into believing that a genuine basis for lasting stable government had been achieved. It had not.

**Key question**
Was Weimar's political recovery a 'false stability'?

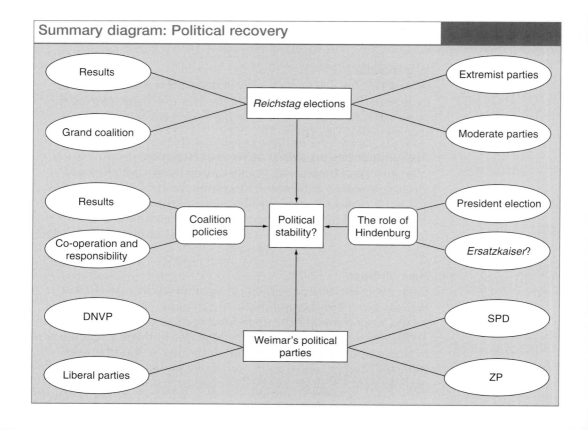

**Summary diagram: Political recovery**

# 3 | The Beginnings of Weimar Foreign Policy 1919–23

The foreign policy of the Weimar Republic was dominated by a determination to revise the Treaty of Versailles. On no other issue was there such agreement as in the desire to erase the memory of the 'shameful peace'. However, while there was agreement on this fundamental aim of German foreign policy, there was a wide division of opinion about how it should be achieved.

## The 'hardliners'

**Key question**
What were the foreign policy objectives of the 'hardliners'?

The term 'hardliners' refers to those who believed that the treaty's terms should be resisted wherever possible. They thought that:

- the reparations should not be paid
- the disarmament clauses of the treaty should be disregarded
- the territorial clauses should be rejected (see map, page 30) and steps taken to achieve:
  - the liberation of the Rhineland and the Saar area
  - the abolition of the Polish Corridor and the regaining of Polish Upper Silesia
  - the *Anschluss* of German Austria
  - the abolition of the Rhineland Demilitarised Zone
- a future military conflict with France and her allies was almost unavoidable and therefore Germany needed to be in a state of military readiness.

Typical of such views were those of Colonel Stülpnagel, who wrote a memo to the Foreign Office in 1926 with the approval of Hans von Seeckt, the head of the German Army or *Reichswehr* (page 46):

> The immediate aim of German policy must be the regaining of full sovereignty over the area retained by Germany, the firm acquisition of those areas at present separated from her, and the re-acquisition of those areas essential to the German economy.

## The 'moderates'

**Key question**
What were the foreign policy objectives of the 'moderates'?

The 'moderates' were those who recognised that the weak domestic position of Germany would prevent their pursuing such an ambitious foreign policy. For this reason, they believed that Germany should follow the twin policies of economic development at home and reconciliation abroad. It was only by working with the Allies that they could hope to reduce the burden of reparations that was holding back the German economy. Further, it was only by restoring her economic strength that Germany could hope to regain her past influential voice in international affairs.

# Weimar foreign policy 1919–23

This policy of moderate **revisionism** came to be known as '**fulfilment**' and is most closely associated with the names of Josef Wirth, German chancellor between May 1921 and November 1922, and Gustav Stresemann, chancellor from August to November 1923 and afterwards foreign minister until his death in October 1929.

Wirth's 'fulfilment' policy was extremely unpopular in right-wing nationalist circles and its supporters became targets in the political violence of the early 1920s (page 45). Also, popular backing for the policy was hard to obtain in the developing inflationary crisis, which many Germans put down to reparations. In these early years, too, there was little sympathy from the Allies, since they received such a small amount of money from Germany's reparations payments. In this sense 'fulfilment', alongside financial and currency problems, failed. As a result, at the end of 1922, Wirth resigned and foreign policy became more hardline.

## The Treaty of Rapallo

One important aspect of Wirth's period of office was the signing of the Soviet–German Treaty of Rapallo in April 1922. This was not an alliance, but a treaty of friendship establishing full diplomatic relations between the two countries. In addition, it was agreed that they would drop all claims for war damage and reparations against each other, whilst secret clauses arranged for future collaboration in military matters.

At the time, the Allies were horrified by what they regarded as an 'unholy alliance'. The treaty was seen as a German-led conspiracy against the Versailles settlement, and it is certainly true that German hardliners in the army and the foreign office supported a pro-Soviet policy. They believed that an improvement in Russo-German relations would reduce the need for 'fulfilment' with the Allies. It might also result in combined military action against Poland which would weaken the entire Versailles settlement.

However, the significance of the hardliners has been exaggerated above the influence of the key figures, such as Wirth and Rathenau, who regarded the Treaty of Rapallo as part of a broader plan. Certainly, the moderates wanted Germany to escape from the isolation of the post-war years and they wanted to counter the French influence in Europe. However, they never intended that the Rapallo Treaty should be pursued in isolation and at the expense of 'fulfilment'. They considered Rapallo in the east as going hand in hand with 'fulfilment' in the west.

**Key question**
Why did 'fulfilment' fail at first?

**Key terms**

**Revisionism**
In general terms, the aim to modify or change an agreement. In the context of Germany in the 1920s it refers specifically to the policy of changing the terms of the Treaty of Versailles (pages 30–1).

**Fulfilment**
The policy of conforming to the terms of a treaty, like Versailles.

**Key date**

The Treaty of Rapallo: 1922

**Key question**
Why was 'fulfilment' restored in autumn 1923?

## Fulfilment restored

Wirth's foreign policy had only limited success. During the year of crisis of 1923, foreign affairs were controlled by the hardliners in the government led by Cuno who started a policy of 'passive resistance' (see page 59). Though such a policy may have satisfied certain nationalistic feelings, the limitations of that approach were highlighted by the events of 1923. With the reparations problem unsolved, Germany descended into a period of hyper-inflation. Those German diplomats and politicians who had hoped to make a stand against the Allies and Versailles succeeded only in underlining Germany's military and diplomatic weakness. In August 1923, at the height of the crisis, Stresemann was appointed chancellor and the policy of 'fulfilment' was restored.

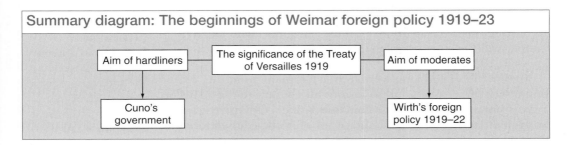

**Summary diagram: The beginnings of Weimar foreign policy 1919–23**

Aim of hardliners — The significance of the Treaty of Versailles 1919 — Aim of moderates

Cuno's government

Wirth's foreign policy 1919–22

**Key question**
How did Stresemann's career change and develop?

## 4 | Gustav Stresemann's Achievements

Before 1921–2, there was little to suggest that Stresemann was to become the mainstay of Weimar democracy. In the years before 1914 his nationalism found expression in his support of the Kaiser's **Weltpolitik** and from the start of the First World War, Stresemann was an ardent supporter of the **Siegfriede**. He campaigned for 'unrestricted submarine warfare' and opposed supporters of peace in 1917 (page 2).

By 1918 his support for the military regime and the Treaty of Brest-Litovsk had earned him the title of 'Ludendorff's young man' (see pages 4–6). And when the war came to an end in defeat, Stresemann was deliberately excluded from the newly created DDP and, so, was left no real option but to form his own party, the DVP. At first, his party was hostile to the revolution of 1918 and the Republic and campaigned for the restoration of the monarchy.

### Turning point

Indeed, it was only after the failed Kapp *putsch* and the murders of Erzberger and Rathenau (page 45) that Stresemann led his party into adopting a more sympathetic approach towards the Weimar Republic. His sudden change of heart has provided plenty of evidence for those critics who have regarded his support of the Weimar Republic as sham. This charge is not entirely fair. Despite the conservatism of his early years, Stresemann's

**Key terms**

*Weltpolitik*
'World policy' – the imperial policy of Kaiser Wilhem II to make Germany a great power by overseas expansion.

*Siegfriede*
'A peace through victory' – referring to Germany fighting the First World War to victory and making major land gains.

subsequent career shows that he was a committed supporter of constitutional government.

Stresemann's ideal was a constitutional monarchy. But that was not to be. By 1922 he had become convinced that the Republic and its constitution provided Germany with its only chance of preventing the dictatorship of either left or right. This was his realistic assessment of the situation and why he was referred to as a *Vernunftrepublikaner*, a rational republican, rather than a convinced one.

## Stresemann's aims

From the time he became responsible for foreign affairs at the height of the 1923 crisis, Stresemann's foreign policy was shaped by his deep understanding of the domestic and international situations. He recognised, unlike many nationalists, that Germany had been militarily defeated and not simply 'stabbed in the back'. He also rejected the solutions of those hardliners who failed to understand the circumstances that had brought Germany to its knees in 1923.

Stresemann's main aims were to free Germany from the limitations of Versailles and to restore his country to the status of a great power, the equal of Britain and France. Offensive action was ruled out by Stresemann and so his only choice therefore was diplomacy. As he himself once remarked, he was backed up only by the power of German cultural traditions and the German economy. So, at first, he worked towards his main aims in the 1920s by pursuing the following objectives:

- To recognise that France did rightly have security concerns and that France also controlled the balance of power on the continent. He regarded Franco-German friendship as essential to solving outstanding problems.
- To play on Germany's vital importance to world trade in order to earn the goodwill and co-operation of Britain and the USA. The sympathy of the USA was also vital so as to attract American investment into the German economy.
- To maintain the Rapallo-based friendship with the USSR. He rejected out of hand those 'hardliners' who desired an alliance with Soviet Russia and described them as the 'maddest of foreign policy makers'. Stresemann's strategy was in the tradition of Wirth's fulfilment.
- To encourage co-operation and peace, particularly with the Western powers. This was in the best interests of Germany to make it the leading power in Europe once again.

## Stresemann and foreign affairs 1923–9

### The Dawes Plan

The starting point of Stresemann's foreign policy was the issue of reparations. As chancellor, he had called off 'passive resistance' and agreed to resume the payment of reparations. The result of this was the US-backed Dawes Plan (see Figure 5.2 on page 87), which has been described as 'a victory for financial realism'. Despite opposition from the right wing it was accepted in April 1924.

**Key question**
What were Stresemann's aims and objectives?

*Vernunftrepublikaner*
'A rational republican' – used in the 1920s to define those people who really wanted Germany to have a constitutional monarchy but who, out of necessity, came to support the democratic Weimar Republic.

Key term

**Key question**
What were the strengths and weaknesses of the Dawes Plan?

**Key date**

The US-backed Dawes Plan was accepted by the German government: April 1924

---

**THE DAWES PLAN 1924**

**The reorganisation of German currency**
- One new *Rentenmark* was to be worth one billion of the old marks.
- The setting up of a German national bank, the *Reichsbank*, under Allied supervision.

**An international loan of 800 million gold marks to aid German economic recovery**
- The loan was to be financed mainly by the USA

**New arrangements for the payment of reparations**
- Payment to be made annually at a fixed scale over a longer period.

**Figure 5.2:** The Dawes Plan

Although the Dawes Plan left the actual sum to be paid unchanged, the monthly instalments over the first five years were calculated according to Germany's capacity to pay. Furthermore, it provided for a large loan to Germany to aid economic recovery. For Stresemann, its advantages were many:

- For the first time since the First World War, Germany's economic problems received international recognition.
- Germany gained credit for the cash-starved German economy by means of the loan and subsequent investments.
- It resulted in a French promise to evacuate the Ruhr during 1925.

In the short term, the Dawes Plan was a success. The German economy was not weakened, since it received twice as much capital from abroad as it paid out in reparations. The mere fact that reparations were being paid regularly contributed to the improved relations between France and Germany during these years. However, the whole system was dangerously dependent on the continuation of American loans, as can be seen in Figure 5.3. In attempting to break out of the crisis of 1923, Stresemann had linked Germany's fortunes to powerful external forces, which had dramatic effects after 1929.

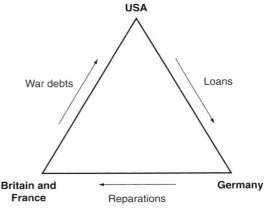

**Figure 5.3:** The reparations triangle

## The Locarno Pact

The ending of the occupation of the Ruhr and the introduction of the Dawes Plan showed that the Great Powers were prepared to take Germany's interests seriously. However, Stresemann continued to fear that Anglo-French friendship could lead to a military **alliance**. In order to counter this concern, Stresemann proposed an international security pact for Germany's western frontiers. Although France was at first hesitant, Britain and the USA both backed the idea. This formed the basis for the Locarno Pact.

In October 1925 a series of treaties were signed which became known as the Locarno Pact. The main points were:

* A **mutual guarantee agreement** accepted the Franco-German and Belgian-German borders. These terms were guaranteed by Britain and Italy. All the five countries renounced the use of force, except in self-defence.
* The **demilitarisation** of the Rhineland was recognised as permanent.
* The **arbitration** treaties between Germany, Poland and Czechoslovakia agreed to settle future disputes peacefully – but the existing frontiers were not accepted as final.

To see the territories affected by the Treaty of Locarno, refer to the map on page 31.

The Locarno treaties represented an important diplomatic development. Germany was freed from its isolation by the Allies and was again treated as an equal partner. Stresemann had achieved a great deal at Locarno at very little cost.

He had confirmed the existing frontiers in the west, since Germany was in no position to change the situation. In so doing he had also limited France's freedom of action since the occupation of the Ruhr or the possible **annexation** of the Rhineland was no longer possible. Moreover, by establishing the beginnings of a solid basis for Franco-German understanding, Stresemann had lessened France's need to find allies in eastern Europe. The Poles viewed the treaties as a major setback, since Stresemann had deliberately refused to confirm the frontiers in the east.

## Further diplomatic progress

Stresemann hoped that further advances would follow Locarno, such as the restoration of full German rule over the Saar and the Rhineland, a reduction in reparations, and a revision of the eastern frontier. However, although there was further diplomatic progress in the years 1926–30 it remained limited:

* Germany had originally been excluded from the League of Nations (see page 32) but, in 1926, she was invited to join the League and was immediately recognised as a permanent member of the Council of the League.
* Two years later in 1928 Germany signed the Kellogg-Briand Pact, a declaration that outlawed 'war as an instrument of

**Key question**
Why were the Locarno treaties so significant?

**Key date**

Locarno Pact: the conference was held in October 1925 and the treaties were signed in December

**Key terms**

**Alliance**
An agreement where members promise to support the other(s), if one or more of them is attacked.

**Mutual guarantee agreement**
An agreement between states on a particular issue, but not an alliance.

**Demilitarisation**
The removal of military personnel, weaponry or forts. The Rhineland demilitarised zone was outlined by the Treaty of Versailles (pages 30–2).

**Arbitration treaty**
An agreement to accept the decision by a third party to settle a conflict.

**Annexation**
Seizing the territory of another country against international law.

**Key date**

Kellogg–Briand Pact:
August 1928

national policy'. Although of no real practical effect it showed
that Germany was working with 68 nations.

- In 1929 the Allies agreed to evacuate the Rhineland earlier
  than intended, in return for a final settlement of the
  reparations issue. The result was the Young Plan, which further
  revised the scheme of payments. Germany now agreed to
  continue to pay reparations until 1988 although the total sum
  was reduced to £1850 million, only one-quarter of the figure
  demanded in 1921 (see page 31).

**Key question**

How was Stresemann
able to reach
agreements with both
the USSR and the
West?

## The Treaty of Berlin

Although Stresemann viewed friendship with the West as his
priority, he was not prepared to drop the Rapallo treaty. He was
still determined to stay on good terms with the USSR. As a result,
the two countries signed the Treaty of Berlin in April 1926 in
order to continue the basis of a good Russo-German relationship.
This was not double-dealing by Stresemann, but was simply a
recognition that Germany's defence needs in the heart of Europe
meant that she had to have understanding with both the East and
the West. The treaty with the Soviet Union therefore reduced
strategic fears on Germany's eastern front and placed even more
pressure on Poland to give way to German demands for frontier
changes. It also opened up the possibility of a large commercial
market and increased military co-operation.

## Profile: Gustav Stresemann 1878–1929

| | |
|---|---|
| 1878 | – Born in Berlin, the son of a publican and brewer |
| 1900 | – Graduated from Berlin University in Political Economy and went into business |
| 1907 | – Elected as a National Liberal – youngest member of *Reichstag* |
| 1914–18 | – Unconditional nationalist and supporter of the war. Worked politically closely with Hindenburg and Ludendorff |
| 1919 | – Formed the DVP and became its leader, 1919–29. Initially opposed the creation of the Weimar Republic |
| 1921 | – Decided to work with the Weimar Republic and became a *Vernunftrepublikaner*, a republican by reason |
| 1923 | – Chancellor of Germany |
| 1923–9 | – Foreign Minister in all governments; major successes: |
| |     1924 – Dawes Plan |
| |     1925 – Locarno Pact |
| |     1926 – Treaty of Berlin |
| |            – Germany entry into League of Nations |
| |     1928 – Kellogg-Briand Pact |
| |     1929 – Young Plan |
| 1926 | – Awarded the Nobel Peace Prize |
| 1929 | – Death at the age of 51 |

Stresemann was born in Berlin, the son of a publican, who successfully entered university to study economics. He went into business and quickly earnt a reputation as a skilled trade negotiator, which laid the basis for his political outlook. His wife was the daughter of a leading Jewish family with strong social and business contacts.

### Political background 1878–1918

Stresemann joined the old National Liberals and was elected in 1907 to the *Reichstag* at the age of just 29. He was a committed monarchist and nationalist and in the years before 1914 he supported the Kaiser's *Weltpolitik*. In the war, Stresemann was an ardent supporter of the *Siegfriede* and more expansionist policies with the result that he was forced to leave his old party.

### His turning-point 1919–22

Stresemann was appalled by the defeat of Germany in the First World War and the Treaty of Versailles. In his heart, he remained a monarchist and hoped to create a constitutional monarchy. So, in the years 1919–21, he formed the DVP and opposed the Weimar Republic. However, by 1921 he came to recognise the political reality and finally committed himself and his party to the Republic.

### Chancellor 1923

In the year of crisis Stresemann was made chancellor, and it is generally recognised by historians that it marked the climax of his career. All the problems were confronted: the occupation of the Ruhr, the hyper-inflation and the opposition from left and right wing extremists. So, although his term in office lasted for just three months it laid the basis for the recovery 1924–9.

### Foreign Minister 1923–9

Stresemann was Foreign Minister in all the Weimar governments and was the 'main architect of republican foreign policy' (Kolb). Most significantly, he showed a strength of character and a realism which allowed him to negotiate with the Allies. Stresemann achieved a great deal in securing Germany's international position. Nevertheless, it should be remembered that that he failed to generate real domestic support for Weimar. So, it is still questionable whether he could have saved the Weimar Republic from Nazism.

## The key debate

In 1926 Stresemann was awarded the Nobel Peace Prize (along with his British and French counterparts Aristide Briand and Austen Chamberlain). Only three years later, at the early age of 51, he died suddenly of a heart attack. However, the emergence of the Weimar Republic's only statesman of quality has always been the focus of controversy. He has been regarded as both a fanatical nationalist and a 'great European' working for international reconciliation. He has been praised for his staunch support of parliamentary government, but condemned for

**Key date**

Death of Gustav Stresemann in the same month as the Wall Street Crash: October 1929

pretending to be a democrat. He has also been portrayed as an idealist on the one hand and an opportunist on the other. So the key question remains:

### Did Stresemann fail or succeed?

Stresemann achieved a great deal in a short time to change both Germany's domestic and international positions. Moreover, the improvement had been achieved by peaceful methods. When one also considers the dire situation he inherited in 1923 with forces, both internal and external, stacked against him, it is perhaps not surprising that his policy has been described by the leading German historian E. Kolb in 1988, as 'astonishingly successful', a perception upheld by the leading English historian Jonathan Wright in 2004, who entitles his biography *Stresemann: Weimar's Greatest Statesman*.

However, it should be borne in mind that the circumstances in the years 1924–9 were working strongly in Stresemann's favour. Another German historian, Walsdorff in 1971, is more critical of Stresemann for failing to achieve his fundamental aims to revise Versailles. He argues, firstly, that Stresemann over-estimated his ability to establish friendly relations with other powers. Walsdorff's second suggestion is that the limits and slow pace of the changes had come to a dead end – and there was no hint of any revision of the Polish frontier.

'He looks to the right, he looks to the left – he will save me'. A German cartoon drawn in 1923 portrays Stresemann as the guardian angel of the young Republic. However, it is worth noting that the little boy is the German Michael – a stereotype for the naïve German.

Despite such debates on Stresemann, historians agree in one sense that where Stresemann's policies failed they did so because he did not generate real domestic support for Weimar. The right wing was always totally against 'fulfilment' and, although a minority, they became increasingly loud and influential in their criticism. They were also connected with powerful groups in society and, by the time of Stresemann's death, the nationalist opposition was already mobilising itself against the Young Plan. Even more significantly, it seems that the silent majority had not really been won over by Stresemann's policy of conciliation. Consequently, by 1929, his policy had not had time to establish itself and so generate sufficient support to survive the different circumstances of the 1930s.

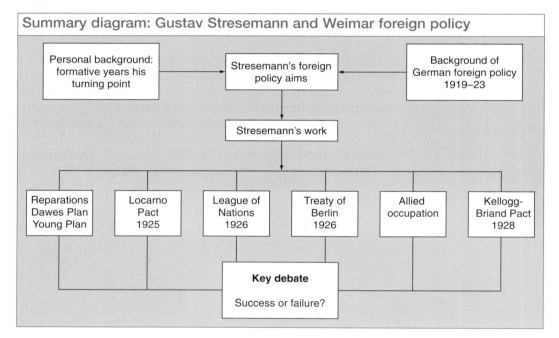

Summary diagram: Gustav Stresemann and Weimar foreign policy

# 5 | Weimar Culture

Key question
Why was the 1920s a culturally rich period?

The Weimar years witnessed an explosion of culture that affected many aspects of German life. This is not a surprise since it was a reaction to the turmoil that followed the war, the defeat and the peace settlement, and the ongoing political and economic crises from 1918 to 1923. The period was also one of dramatic changes in communication and the media – for this decade saw the emergence of film, radio and the car.

There was one other different aspect to post-war Germany. The Kaiser's Germany was a conservative society. It was politically authoritarian and also socially set in established rules and codes. In contrast the Weimar Republic was a liberal society that upheld **toleration** and reduced the levels of censorship. This encouraged many cultural artists to express themselves openly in Weimar Germany – and, so, influence and shape the new society. All these factors contributed to the image of the 'golden years', as

**Toleration**
To accept alternative political, religious and cultural views.

Key term

expressed by William Shirer, the European correspondent of the American newspaper, the *Chicago Tribune*:

> A wonderful ferment was working in Germany. Life seemed more free, more modern, more exciting than in any place I had ever seen. Nowhere else did the arts or the intellectual life seem so lively … In contemporary writing, painting, architecture, in music and drama, there were new currents and fine talents. And everywhere there was an accent on youth … They were a healthy, carefree, sun worshipping lot – politicians, writers, editors, artists, professors, students, businessmen, labour leaders – struck you as being democratic, liberal, even pacifist.

**Key question**
What was *Neue Sachlichkeit* and how did it express itself?

**Key term**

**New functionalism** A form of art that developed in post-war Germany, it tried to express reality with a more objective view of the world.

## The new cultural ferment

It is dangerous to try to define and identify Weimar culture because it had so many different aspects. However, the term generally used to reflect all the developments was *Neue Sachlichkeit*. It can be translated as 'new practicality' or '**new functionalism**' – which means essentially it desired to show reality and objectivity. These words are best explained by looking at some of the major examples of different art forms.

### Art

Artists in favour of the 'new objectivity' broke away from the traditional nostalgia of the nineteenth century. They wanted to understand ordinary people in everyday life – and by their art they aimed to comment on the state of society. This approach was epitomised by Georg Grosz and Otto Dix in the post-war era in the 1920s. Their paintings and caricatures had strong political and social messages and in their artistic approach they showed a seedy, ugly and aggressive style.

A painting from 1927 by the German artist Otto Dix. Dix's war service deeply influenced his experiences and this piece underlines the contrast between the good-life of the affluent and the seedier side of the poor and disabled.

*Pillars of Society*: a painting from 1926 by the German artist Georg
Grosz. Grosz was wounded in the war and in 1918 he joined the KPD.
The title is an ironic comment on the dominant social forces in Germany,
as he mocks the image of the soldier, the priest, the banker.

## Architecture and design

One of the most striking artistic developments in Weimar Germany was the Bauhaus school led by the architect Walter Gropius, which was established in 1919 in the town of Weimar itself. The Bauhaus movement was a new style that influenced all aspects of design – furniture, urban planning, pottery, textiles and graphics. Its approach was functional and it emphasised the close relationship between art and technology, which is underlined by its motto 'Art and Technology – a new unity'. It used materials such as steel, cement and plastic, and geometric shapes. They were profoundly resisted among more conservative circles.

The *Weißenhofsiedlung* was built on the Killesberg in Stuttgart in 1927. It is one of the best examples of the 'new architecture' in Germany and formed part of the exhibition *Die Wohnung* ('The flat') organised by the German *Werkbund*.

## Literature

There was such a rich range of literary styles, forms and subjects in Weimar culture that it is unwise to generalise. Not all writers were **expressionists** influenced by the *Neue Sachlichkeit*. For example, the celebrated Thomas Mann, best known for his book *The Magic Mountain* (1924), which won the Nobel Prize for literature, cannot be classified as expressionist. It should be remembered that the best sellers were the authors who wrote traditional nostalgic literature – such as, most famously, the writer Hans Grimm. In the more *avant garde* style were the works of Arnold Zweig and Peter Lampel, who explored a range of social issues growing out of the distress and misery of working people in the big cities. Two particular books to be remembered are: the pacifist *All Quiet on the Western Front*, published in 1928 by Erich Maria von Remarque, as an ex-soldier from the First World War; and *Berlin Alexanderplatz* written by Alfred Döblin, whose epic examined the role of a worker in Weimar society.

## Theatre

Theatre was very popular and highly regarded in Berlin and the provinces, and attracted large audiences until the depression. *Neue Sachlichkeit* developed into what was called *Zeittheater* (theatre of the time), which introduced new dramatic methods often with explicit left-wing sympathies – and was most evident in the plays of Bertolt Brecht and Erwin Piscator. They used innovative techniques such as banners, slogans, film and slides, but they also adopted controversial elements that portrayed characters' behaviour in their everyday life.

## Mass culture

The 1920s were a time of dramatic changes that saw the emergence of a modern mass culture. Germany was no exception – indeed, many of the tendencies were more exaggerated in Germany because of its particular circumstances (page 92). It saw the development of mass communication methods and international influences, especially from USA, such as jazz music and consumerism.

**Key question**
In what ways did Weimar culture reach out to ordinary people?

### Film

The German film industry was relatively insignificant until 1918, but during the 1920s it became the most advanced in Europe. Germany had more cinemas than any other European country and produced more films than all the other European countries put together. Moreover, German film-makers were generally respected for their high-quality work, though their styles varied considerably. The most famous films were:

- *Metropolis* (1926) by the film-maker Fritz Lang, was a sci-fi classic that raised frightening issues about the direction of modern industrialised society.
- *Fridericus Rex*, King Frederick the Great (1922), was a traditional, patriotic epic.
- *Blue Angel* (1930), with the young actress Marlene Dietrich, was the first big German 'talkie' that openly played on female glamour and touched on sexual issues.

However, although the German film market was very much dominated by the organisation UFA, run by Alfred Hugenberg (see page 80), from the mid-1920s American 'movies' quickly made an exceptional impact. The popular appeal of the comedy of Charlie Chaplin shows that Weimar culture was part of an international mass culture and was not exclusively German.

### Radio

Radio also emerged very rapidly as another mass medium. The German Radio Company was established in 1923 and by 1932, despite the depression, one in four Germans owned a radio.

### Cabaret

Berlin had all the traditional features of high culture but in the 1920s a vibrant nightlife also developed. Cabaret clubs opened up with a permissiveness that mocked the conventions of the old Germany: satirical comedy, jazz music, and women dancers (and even wrestlers) with varying degrees of nudity. At parties there was an interest in sexual experimentation that included transvestitism and homosexuality.

## The conflict of cultures

**Key question**
Who reacted against *Neue Sachlichkeit* and why?

It is all too easy to assume that Weimar was an exciting and vibrant era that celebrated its liberal creativity and culture. That was not the case. There were some respected conservative intellectuals, like Arthur Möller and Oswald Spengler, who condemned democratic and industrial society. Moreover many of the writers in the 1920s opposed pacifism and proudly glorified the sacrifices of the First World War.

However, in many respects the really fundamental reaction against *Neue Sachlichkeit* was not overt – it was simply responding to the doubts and tensions in Weimar society. Berlin was definitely not typical of all Germany, but it left a very powerful impression – both positive and negative. Some could enjoy and appreciate the cultural experimentation, but most Germans were horrified by what they saw as the decline in established moral and cultural standards.

One minor incident underlines how Weimar culture was seen as decadent: in the local elections of 1931 at Dessau the Nazis campaigned against financial support for the Bauhaus. Their victory resulted in the demolition of the building.

The last point also suggests that Weimar culture never established a genuinely tolerant attitude. The *avant garde* and the conservatives were clearly at odds with each other. However, more significantly, both sides took advantage of the freedoms and permissiveness of Weimar liberalism to criticise it, whilst not being genuinely tolerant or sympathetic. The Weimar Republic was therefore caught between the opposing sides of the two cultures. This conflict shows how Weimar society was becoming increasingly **polarised** before the onset of the political and economic crisis in 1929.

**Key term**

**Polarisation**
The division of society into opposite views (e.g. north and south poles).

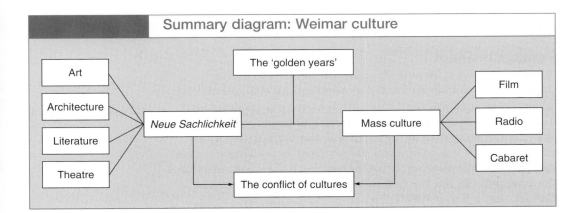

Summary diagram: Weimar culture

Art
Architecture
Literature
Theatre
→ *Neue Sachlichkeit* — The 'golden years' — Mass culture ← Film, Radio, Cabaret
The conflict of cultures

# 6 | Weimar 1924–9: An Overview

The years 1924–9 marked the high point of the Weimar Republic. By comparison with the periods before and after, these years do appear stable. The real increase in prosperity experienced by many, and the cultural vitality of the period, gave support to the view that these years were indeed the 'golden years'. However, historians have generally tended to question this stability because it was in fact limited in scope. This is the reason why the historian Peukert describes these years as a 'deceptive stability'.

**Key question**
Were the years 1924–9 deceptively stable?

## An unstable economy

Germany's economic recovery was built on unstable foundations that created a false idea of prosperity. Problems persisted in the economy and they were temporarily hidden only by an increasing reliance on credit from abroad. In this way Germany's economy became tied up with powerful external forces over which it had no control. Hindsight now allows historians to see that, in the late 1920s, any disruption to the world's trade or finance markets was bound to have a particularly damaging effect on the uncertain German economy.

## A divided society

German society was still divided by deep class differences as well as by regional and religious differences that prevented the development of national agreement and harmony. The war and the years of crisis that followed had left bitterness, fear and resentment between employers and their workers. Following the introduction of the state scheme for settling disputes in 1924, its procedure was used as a matter of course, whereas the intention had been that it would be the exception, not the rule. As a result, there was arbitration in some 76,000 industrial disputes between 1924 and 1932.

In 1928, workers were locked out from their place of work in the Ruhr ironworks when the employers refused to accept the arbitration award. It was the most serious industrial confrontation of the Weimar period. A compromise solution was achieved, but it showed the extent of the bitterness of industrial relations even before the start of the world depression.

## Political division

Tension was also evident in the political sphere where the parliamentary system had failed to build on the changes of 1918. The original ideals of the Constitution had not been developed and there was little sign that the system had produced a stable and mature system. In particular, the main democratic parties had still not recognised the necessity of working together in a spirit of compromise. It was not so much the weaknesses of the Constitution, but the failure to establish a shared political outlook that led to its instability.

## Foreign affairs

Even the successes of Stresemann in the field of foreign affairs were offset by the fact that significant numbers of his fellow countrymen rejected his policy out of hand and pressed for a more hardline approach.

In reality, the middle years of the Weimar Republic were stable only in comparison with the periods before and after. Weimar's condition suggested that the fundamental problems inherited from war and the years of crisis had not been resolved. They persisted, so that when the crisis set in during 1929–30 the Weimar Republic did not prove strong enough to withstand the storm.

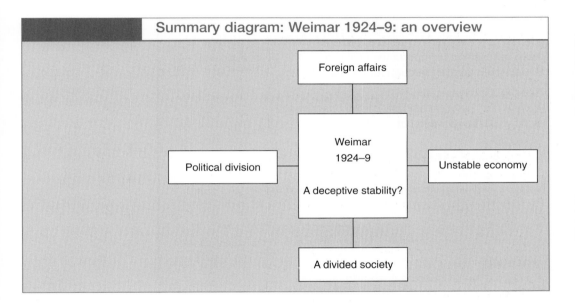

Summary diagram: Weimar 1924–9: an overview

# Study Guide: AS Questions

## In the style of AQA

How important was the part played by Gustav Stresemann in the establishment of stability within Germany between 1923 and 1929?

---

### Study tips

It is very easy to be drawn into writing a potted biography of Gustav Stresemann. Do not be tempted. You must show a good understanding of the detail of Stresemann's role, but you must also work towards making an assessment of his political influence in the broadest sense. Note carefully the years mentioned in the question; they clearly imply that the question covers Stresemann's chancellorship. One good way is to pose a series of questions about the relevant themes. In that way, you are more likely to be able to keep assessing the importance of Stresemann's political influence in establishing stability throughout the essay:

The 1923 inflation crisis
- How did he solve Germany's inflationary crisis?
- Why did his coalition not survive longer?

Extremists
- Were the extremists completely defeated? In the short term and in the long term?
- Can you distinguish between his treatment of the left and right?

Economic stability
- In what ways did he help the German economy to recover?
- Did he overcome Germany's fundamental economic weaknesses?

Leadership
- Why did he not become chancellor again?
- Did he really unite the German people?

This type of planning and thought will then provide you with a very good basis for an overall conclusion.

---

## In the style of Edexcel

(a) Describe the key features of Weimar culture.      (15 marks)
(b) Why was Weimar Germany strengthened in the years 1924–9?
(15 marks)

---

### Exam tips

*The cross-references are intended to take you straight to the material that will help you to answer the questions.*

(a) Question (a) is relatively straightforward and you should be able to earn good marks, as long as you bear in mind several points. It is vital to make reference to all the sections:
- defining *Neue Sachlichkeit* (page 93)
- art, literature, theatre, architecture (pages 93–6)
- mass culture (pages 96–7).

In a conclusion, it is worth underlining that the new culture was not universally accepted.

**(b)** In question **(b)** you must focus on the key word 'strengthened' and you should refer to it regularly in your answer. You should examine each one of these themes in turn:
- the German economy (pages 71–4)
- the political system in Weimar Germany (pages 75–82)
- Germany's position in international relations (pages 85–92).

You should also make reference to the limitations and weaknesses of Weimar Germany, 1924–9. You could refer in the conclusion to the short-term nature of its being 'strengthened'.

## In the style of OCR

'By 1929 the Weimar Republic had a good chance of survival'. How far do you agree with this judgement of the Weimar Republic?

### Exam tips

*The cross-references are intended to take you straight to the material that will help you answer the question.*

- This is a very broad question that involves all the content of Chapters 1–5, though you must refer specifically to pages 18–19, 28, 35–8, 50–2, 65–8 and 98–9.
- The question provides a specific end date with the year 1929 marking a clear turning point. Remember – a high mark depends on answering the actual question set so you should not go beyond this date in your answer.
- Either: Evaluate various arguments for the 'good chances of the survival' of the Weimar Republic and then all the ones against. But that simple structure can also lead to confusion between the different elements.

  Or: It is better to plan a structure that allows you to analyse effectively throughout by dividing the content into four themes that list the 'good chances' and 'bad chances'. This thinking and planning will also help you to use your time effectively in an exam essay. See the diagram below as an example:

| Themes | Good chances | Bad chances | Assessment of each theme |
|---|---|---|---|
| Political system | | | |
| Economy | | | |
| Foreign policy | | | |
| Culture | | | |
| Conclusion | | | |

# 6 The Early Years of the Nazis 1919–29

**POINTS TO CONSIDER**

In the 1920s Hitler and the Nazi Party enjoyed a rather chequered history and they did not made any real political impact until the onset of the Great Depression. However, Nazism did take root. The purpose of this chapter is to examine the role of the Nazis in 1920s' Germany through the following themes:

- The personal background of Adolf Hitler and the creation of the Nazi Party
- The Munich Beer Hall *putsch*
- Nazi ideas
- Mixed fortunes of Nazism in the 1920s

## Key dates

| | | |
|---|---|---|
| 1919 | | Creation of German Workers' Party (DAP) by Anton Drexler |
| 1920 | February | Party name changed to NSDAP (National Socialist German Workers' Party) |
| | | 25-points party programme drawn up by Drexler and Hitler |
| 1923 | November 8–9 | Beer Hall *putsch* in Munich |
| 1924 | | Hitler in Landsberg prison |
| | | *Mein Kampf* written |
| 1925 | February | NSDAP re-founded in Munich |
| 1926 | February | Bamberg conference: Hitler's leadership of the Party re-established |
| 1928 | May | *Reichstag* election result |
| 1929–33 | | The Great Depression |

## 1 | Adolf Hitler and the Creation of the Nazi Party

### Hitler's early years

There was little in the background of Adolf Hitler (1889–1945) to suggest that he would become a powerful political figure. Hitler was born at Braunau-am-Inn in 1889 in what was then the Austro-Hungarian Empire. He failed to impress at school, and after the death of his parents he moved to Vienna in 1907. There he

**Key question**
How did Hitler become involved in politics?

Key terms

**Anti-Semitism**
The hatred of Jews. It became the most significant part of Nazi racist thinking. For Hitler, the 'master-race' was the pure Aryan (the people of northern Europe) and the Germans represented the highest caste. The lowest race for Hitler was the Jews.

*Volk*
Often translated as 'people', although it tends to suggest a nation with the same ethnic and cultural identities and with a collective sense of belonging.

applied unsuccessfully for a place as a student at the Academy of Fine Arts. For the next six years he led an aimless and unhappy existence in the poorer districts of the city. It was not until he joined the Bavarian Regiment on the outbreak of war in 1914 that he found a real purpose in life. He served bravely throughout the war and was awarded the Iron Cross First Class.

When the war ended he was in hospital recovering from a British gas attack. By the time he had returned to Bavaria in early 1919 he had already framed in his mind the core of what was to become National Socialism:

- fervent German nationalism
- support of authoritarianism and opposition to democracy and socialism
- a racially inspired view of society which exhibited itself most obviously in a rabid **anti-Semitism** and a veneration of the German *Volk* as the master race.

Such a mixture of ideas in a man whose personal life was much of a mystery – he had no close family and few real friends – has excited some historians to resort to psychological analysis leading to extraordinary speculation. Did his anti-Semitism originate from contracting syphilis from a Jewish prostitute? Could his authoritarian attitude be explained by his upbringing at the hands of an old and repressive father? Such psychological diagnoses – and there are many – may interest the student, but the supporting evidence for such explanations is at best flimsy. As a result, the conclusions reached are highly speculative and do not really help to explain the key question of how and why Hitler became such an influential political force.

**Key question**
How significant was the NSDAP by 1922?

Key term

**Anti-capitalism**
Rejects the economic system based upon private property and profit. Early Nazi ideas laid stress upon preventing the exploitation of workers and suggesting social reforms.

## The creation and emergence of the Nazi Party

It was because of his committed right-wing attitudes that Hitler was employed in the politically charged atmosphere of 1919 as a kind of spy by the political department of the Bavarian section of the German Army. One of his investigations brought him into contact with the DAP (*Deutsche Arbeiterpartei* – German Workers' Party) which was not a movement of the revolutionary left, as Hitler had assumed on hearing its name, but one committed to nationalism, anti-Semitism and **anti-capitalism**. Hitler joined the tiny party and immediately became a member of its committee. His energy, oratory and propaganda skills soon made an impact on the small group and it was Hitler who, with the Party's founder, Anton Drexler, drew up the Party's 25-points programme in February 1920 (see Figure 6.1). At the same time, it was agreed to change the Party's name to the NSDAP, the National Socialist German Workers' Party. (For analysis of Nazi ideology, see pages 109–12.)

By mid-1921 it was clear Hitler was the driving-force behind the Party. Although he still held only the post of propaganda chief, it was his powerful speeches that had impressed local audiences and had helped increase party membership to 3300. He had encouraged the creation of the armed squads to protect

Key date

Creation of the German Workers' Party (DAP) by Anton Drexler: 1919

Name of the DAP party changed to NSDAP (National Socialist German Workers' Party): February 1920

Party's programme of 25 points drawn up by Drexler and Hitler: February 1920

Key dates

1. We demand the union of all Germans in a Greater Germany on the basis of the right of national self-determination.
2. We demand equality of rights for the German People in its dealings with other nations, and the revocation of the peace treaties of Versailles and Saint Germain.
3. We demand land and territory (colonies) to feed our people and to settle our surplus population.
4. Only members of the *Volk* (nation) may be citizens of the State. Only those of German blood, whatever their creed may be members of the nation. Accordingly no Jew may be a member of the nation.
7. We demand that the State shall make it its primary duty to provide a livelihood for its citizens. If it should prove impossible to feed the entire population, non-citizens must be deported from the Reich.
10. It must be the first duty of every citizen to perform physical or mental work. The activities of the individual must not clash with the general interest, but must proceed within the framework of the community and be for the general good.
14. We demand profit sharing in large industrial enterprises.
15. We demand the extensive development of insurance for old age.
18. We demand the ruthless prosecution of those whose activities are injurious to the common interest. Common criminals, usurers, profiteers must be punished with death, whatever their creed or race.
22. We demand the abolition of the mercenary army and the formation of a people's army.
23. We demand legal warfare on deliberate political mendacity and its dissemination in the press.
25. We demand the creation of a strong central power of the Reich.

**Figure 6.1:** Extracts from the 25 points of the programme of the German Workers' Party

Party meetings and to intimidate the opposition, especially the communists. It was his development of early propaganda techniques – the Nazi salute, the swastika, the uniform – that had done so much to give the Party a clear and easily recognisable identity.

Alarmed by Hitler's increasing domination of the Party, Drexler and some other members of the committee tried to limit his influence. However, it was here, for the first time, that Hitler showed his political ability to manoeuvre and to gamble. He was by far the most influential speaker and the Party knew it, so, shrewdly, he offered to resign. In the ensuing power struggle he was quickly able to mobilise support at two meetings in July 1921. He was invited back in glory. Embarrassed, Drexler resigned and Hitler became chairman and Führer (leader) of the Party.

Having gained supreme control over the Party in Munich, Hitler aimed to subordinate all the other right-wing groups under his Party's leadership and certainly, in the years 1921–3, the Party was strengthened by a number of significant developments:

- The armed squads were organised and set up as the **SA** in 1921 as a paramilitary unit led by Ernst Röhm. It was now used to organise planned thuggery and violence. Most notoriously, the conflict in the town of Coburg degenerated into a pitched battle between the Communists and the SA, but it showed how politically vital it was to win to control of the streets.

**SA**
*Sturm Abteilung* became known in English as the Stormtroopers. They were also referred to as the Brownshirts after the colour of the uniform. They supported the radical socialist aspects of Nazism.

Key term

- The Party established its first newspaper in 1921, the *Völkischer Beobachter* (the *People's Observer*).
- In 1922 Hitler won the backing of Julius Streicher, who previously had run a rival right-wing party in northern Bavaria. Streicher also published his own newspaper, *Der Stürmer*, which was overtly anti-Semitic with a seedy range of articles devoted to sex and violence.
- Hitler was also fortunate to win the support of the influential Hermann Göring, who joined the Party in 1922. He was born into a Bavarian landowning family, while his wife was a leading Swedish aristocratic. They made many very helpful social contacts in Munich, which gave Hitler and Nazism respectability.

## Profile: Hermann Göring 1893–1946

| | | |
|---|---|---|
| 1893 | | – Born in Bavaria, the son of the governor of German Southwest Africa |
| 1914–18 | | – Served in the First World War and became a pilot officer of the Richthofen Squadron |
| 1922 | | – Dropped out of university and joined the Party as an SA commander |
| 1923 | November | – Took part in the Munich *putsch* and was seriously injured |
| 1928 | May | – Elected to the *Reichstag* |
| 1933 | January | – Appointed to the cabinet of Hitler's government as Minister without Portfolio (a minister with no specific responsibility) |
| | February | – Exploited the *Reichstag* Fire to discredit the Communists |
| 1934 | June | – Helped to arrange the purge in the Night of Long Knives |
| 1935 | | – Commander-in-Chief of the new *Luftwaffe* (airforce) |
| 1936 | | – Economic dictator of Germany after the creation of the Four-Year Plan |
| 1939 | | – Named as Hitler's successor, although his influence declined from 1941 |
| 1946 | | – Committed suicide just after being sentenced to death at the Nuremberg trials |

Göring played a crucial role in the rise of Nazism and the consolidation of its power. He came from a well-to-do family background and with his status and the contacts provided by his aristocratic wife, he was able to present Nazism with a more respectable image in high society. At first, he was popular because of his witty and charming conversation, but he became increasingly resented for his ambition and greed. Göring's approach was uncompromising and brutal. During 1933–4 he organised the infiltration of the German police with the SA and SS – and willingly used violence and murder in the terror to secure Nazi power. He was deeply involved in the *Reichstag* Fire (see page 168–9) and the Night of the Long Knives, which purged the SA.

By 1923, the Party had a membership of about 20,000. Hitler certainly enjoyed an impressive personal reputation and, as a result, Nazism successfully established an influential role on the extreme right in Bavaria. However, despite Nazi efforts, it still proved difficult to control all the radical right-wing political groups, which remained independent organisations across Germany. The Nazi Party was still very much a fringe party, limited to the region of Bavaria.

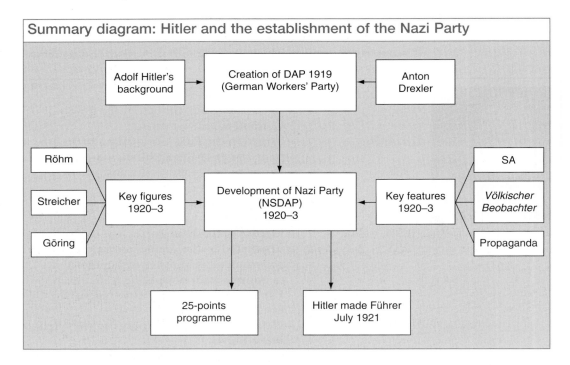

Summary diagram: Hitler and the establishment of the Nazi Party

## 2 | The Beer Hall *Putsch* 1923

The successful takeover of power by Mussolini in Italy in October 1922, combined with the developing internal crisis in Germany, convinced Hitler that the opportunity to seize power had arrived. Indeed, a leading Nazi introduced Hitler at one of his speeches in Munich by saying: 'Germany's Mussolini is called Adolf Hitler'. However, the Nazis were far too weak on their own to stage any kind of political takeover and Hitler himself was still seen merely as a 'drummer' who could stir up the masses for the national movement. It was the need for allies which led Hitler into negotiations with Kahr and the Bavarian State Government and the Bavarian section of the German army under Lossow (see pages 47–9).

It was with these two men that Hitler plotted to 'March on Berlin' (in the style of Mussolini's *coup* which, only the previous year, had become known as the 'March on Rome'). They aimed to mobilise all the military forces from Bavaria – including sections of the German army, the police, the SA and other paramilitaries –

Key question
How did Hitler manage to turn the failure of the Munich Beer Hall *putsch* to his advantage?

The Beer Hall *putsch* in Munich:
8–9 November 1923

Key date

and then, by closing in on Berlin, to seize national power. With hindsight, Hitler's plan was unrealistic and doomed because:

- he grossly over-estimated the level of public support for a *putsch* – despite the problems faced by Weimar's democratic government in 1923
- he showed a lack of real planning
- he relied too heavily on the promise of support of Ludendorff
- most significantly, at the eleventh hour, Kahr and Lossow, fearing failure, decided to hold back.

Hitler was not so cautious and preferred to press on rather than lose the opportunity. On 8 November, when Kahr was addressing a large audience in one of Munich's beer halls, Hitler and the Nazis took control of the meeting, declared a 'national revolution' and forced Kahr and Lossow to support it. The next day Hitler, Göring, Streicher, Röhm, Himmler (and Ludendorff) marched into the city of Munich with 2000 SA men, but they had no real military backing, and the attempted take-over of Munich was easily crushed by the Bavarian police. Fourteen Nazis were killed and Hitler himself was arrested on a charge of treason.

A photograph of the main leaders of the Beer Hall *putsch* posing before the trial in February 1924. Frick (A), Ludendorff (B), Hitler (C), and Röhm (D) can be identified by the letters.

## The consequences

In many respects the *putsch* was a farce. Hitler and the *putschists* were arrested and charged with treason and the NSADP itself was banned. However, Hitler gained significant political advantages from the episode:

- He turned his trial into a great propaganda success both for himself and for the Nazi cause. He played on all his rhetorical skills and evoked admiration for his patriotism. For the first time he made himself a national figure.
- He won the respect of many other right-wing nationalists for having had the courage to act.
- The leniency of his sentence – five years, the minimum stipulated by the Weimar Constitution and actually reduced to 10 months – seemed like an act of encouragement on the part of the judiciary.
- He used his months in prison to write and to reassess his political strategy (see page 113).

Hitler imprisoned in Landsberg prison: 1924

Key date

'Hitler's entry into Berlin'. A cartoon published by the *Simplicissimus* magazine in April 1924 just after Hitler's trial. It mocks Hitler's march on Berlin and shows Ebert in chains.

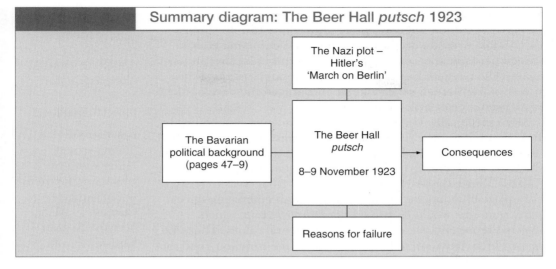

Summary diagram: The Beer Hall *putsch* 1923

The Bavarian political background (pages 47–9)

## 3 | Nazi Ideas

**Key question**
What were the main elements of Nazi thinking?

Nazism always emphasised the importance of action over thought. However, whilst in Landsberg prison, Hitler dictated the first part of **Mein Kampf** which, in the following years, became the bible of National Socialism. Together with the 25-points programme of 1920, it provides the basic framework of Hitler's ideology and of Nazism itself.

### Racism

Hitler's ideas were built upon his concept of race. He believed that humanity consisted of a hierarchy of races and that life was no more than 'the survival of the fittest'. He argued that **social Darwinism** necessitated a struggle between races, just as animals fought for food and territory in the wild. Furthermore, he considered it vital to maintain racial purity, so that the blood of the weak would not undermine the strong.

It was a crude philosophy, which appears even more simplistic when Hitler's analysis of the races is considered. The *Herrenvolk* (master-race) was the **Aryan** race and was exemplified by the Germans. It was the task of the Aryan to remain pure and to dominate the inferior races. In the following extract from *Mein Kampf* Hitler writes:

> The adulteration of the blood and racial deterioration conditioned thereby are the only causes that account for the decline of ancient civilisations; for it is never by war that nations are ruined, but by the loss of their powers of resistance, which are exclusively a characteristic of pure racial blood. In this world everything that is not of sound stock is like chaff. Every historical event in the world is nothing more nor less than a manifestation of the instinct of racial self-preservation, whether for weal or woe [for better or for worse].

(See also the 25-points programme, page 104: points 4 and 7.)

**Key terms**

**Mein Kampf**
'My struggle'. The book written by Hitler in 1924, which expresses his political ideas.

**Social Darwinism**
A philosophy that portrayed the world as a 'struggle' between people, races and nations. Hitler viewed war as the highest form of 'struggle' and was deeply influenced by the theory of evolution based upon natural selection.

**Aryan**
Broadly refers to all the peoples of the Indo-European family. However, the term was more specifically defined by the Nazis as the non-Jewish people of northern Europe.

## Anti-democracy

In Hitler's opinion there was no realistic alternative to strong dictatorial government. Ever since his years in Vienna he had viewed parliamentary democracy as weak and ineffective. It went against the German historical traditions of militarism and the power of the State. Furthermore, it encouraged the development of an even greater evil, communism.

More specifically, Hitler saw Weimar democracy as a betrayal. In his eyes, it was the democratic and socialist politicians of 1918, 'the November criminals', who had stabbed the German army in the back, by accepting the armistice and establishing the Republic (page 7). Since then Germany had lurched from crisis to crisis.

In place of democracy Hitler wanted an all-embracing one-party state that would be run on the *Führerprinzip*, which rejected representative government and liberal values. Thus, the masses in society were to be controlled for the common good, but an individual leader was to be chosen in order to rouse the nation into action, and to take the necessary decisions. (See also the 25-points programme, page 104: points 18 and 25.)

## Nationalism

A crucial element in Nazi thinking was an aggressive nationalism, which developed out of the particular circumstances of Germany's recent history. The armistice of 1918 and the subsequent Treaty of Versailles had to be overturned, and the lost territories had to be restored to Germany (see pages 30–2). But Hitler's nationalism called for more than a mere restoration of the 1914 frontiers. It meant the creation of an empire (*Reich*) to include all those members of the German *Volk* who lived beyond the frontiers of the Kaiser's Germany: the Austrian Germans; the Germans in the Sudetenland; the German communities along the Baltic coast; all were to be included within the borderlands of Germany.

Yet, Hitler's nationalist aims did not end there. He dreamed of a Greater Germany, a superpower, capable of competing with the British Empire and the United States. Such an objective could be achieved only by territorial expansion on a grand scale. This was the basis of Hitler's demand for *Lebensraum* for Germany. Only by the conquest of Poland, the Ukraine and Russia could Germany obtain the raw materials, cheap labour and food supplies so necessary for continental supremacy. The creation of his 'New Order' in eastern Europe also held one other great attraction: namely, the destruction of the USSR, the centre of world communism.

In *Mein Kampf* Hitler wrote:

> The German people must be assured the territorial area which is necessary for it to exist on earth ... People of the same blood should be in the same Reich. The German people will have no right to engage in a colonial policy until they shall have brought all their children together in one state. When the territory of the Reich embraces all the Germans and finds itself unable to assure them a livelihood, only then can the moral right arise, from the need of the

*Führerprinzip*
'The leadership principle'. Hitler upheld the idea of a one-party state, built on an all-powerful leader.

*Lebensraum*
'Living space'. Hitler's aim to create an empire by establishing German supremacy over the eastern lands in Europe.

people, to acquire foreign territory ... Germany will either become a World Power or will not continue to exist at all. ... The future goal of our foreign policy ought to be an Eastern policy, which will have in view the acquisition of such territory as is necessary for our German people.

(See also the 25-points programme, page 104: points 1, 2 and 3.)

### The socialist aspect of Nazism

A number of points in the 1920 programme demanded socialist reforms and, for a long time, there existed a faction within the Party that emphasised the anti-capitalist aspect of Nazism, for example:

- profit-sharing in large industrial enterprises
- the extensive development of insurance for old age
- the nationalisation of all businesses.

Hitler accepted these points in the early years because he recognised their popular appeal but he himself never showed any real commitment to such ideas. As a result they were the cause of important differences within the Party and were not really dropped until Hitler had fully established his dominant position by 1934. (See also the 25-points programme, page 104, points 7, 10, 14 and 25.)

What Hitler did promote was the concept of the *Volksgemeinschaft* (people's community). This remained the vaguest element of the Nazi ideology, and is therefore difficult to define precisely. Firstly, it was intended to overcome the old differences of class, religion and politics. But secondly, it aimed to bring about a new collective national identity by encouraging people to work together for the benefit of the nation and by promoting 'German values'. Such a system could of course only benefit those who racially belonged to the German *Volk* and who willingly accepted the loss of individual freedoms in an authoritarian system.

### The ideology of National Socialism

Early historians and biographers of Hitler simply saw him as a cynical opportunist motivated by the pursuit of power. Others have now generally come to view him as a committed political leader influenced by certain key ideas that he used to lay the basis of a consistent Nazi programme.

However, to describe Hitler's thinking, or Nazism, as an ideology is really to flatter it. An 'ideology' suggests a coherent thought-through system or theory of ideas, as found, for example, in Marxism. Nazism lacked coherence and was intellectually superficial and simplistic. It was not genuinely a rational system of thought. It was merely a collection of ideas not very cleverly pieced together. It was not in any positive sense original – every aspect of Hitler's thinking was to be found in the nationalist and racist writings of the nineteenth century:

- His nationalism was an outgrowth of the fervour generated in the years leading up to Germany's unification of 1871.
- His idea of an all-German *Reich* was a simple repetition of the demands for the 'Greater Germany' made by those German nationalists who criticised the limits of the 1871 unification.
- Even the imperialism of *Lebensraum* had already found expression in the programme of 'Germanisation' supported by those writers who saw the German race as somehow superior.
- The growing veneration for the *Volk* had gone hand-in-hand with the development of racist ideas, and in particular of anti-Semitism.

Thus, even before Hitler and other leading Nazis were born, the core of what would become Nazism was already current in political circles. It was to be found in the cheap and vulgar pamphlets sold to the masses in the large cities; in the political programme of respectable pressure groups, such as the Pan-German League; within the corridors of Germany's great universities; and in the creative works of certain cultural figures, such as the composer Richard Wagner.

However, despite these links, one must avoid labelling Nazi ideology as the logical result of German intellectual thinking. It is all too easy to emphasise those elements that prove the linkage theory, whilst ignoring the host of other evidence that points to entirely different views, e.g. the strong socialist tradition in Germany. Moreover, it is well to remember that a number of countries, but especially Britain and France, also witnessed the propagation of very similar ideas at this time. In that sense nationalism and racism were an outgrowth of nineteenth-century European history. Nazi ideology may not have been original, but it should not therefore be assumed that it was an inevitable result of Germany's past.

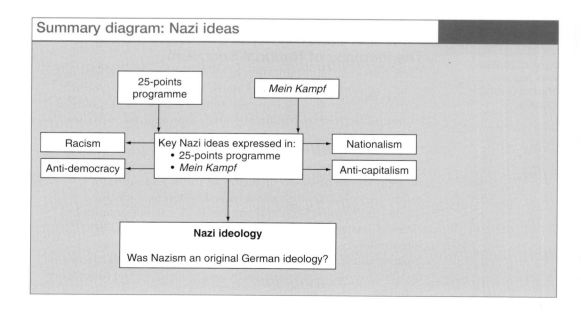

**Summary diagram: Nazi ideas**

**Key question**
In what ways was the Nazi Party revitalised?

**Key dates**

NSDAP re-founded in Munich: 27 February 1925

Bamberg conference: Hitler established his leadership of the Party: 14 February 1926

# 4 | Nazi Fortunes in the 1920s

When Hitler left prison in December 1924 the future for Nazism looked bleak. The Party was in disarray; its leading members were split into factions and the membership was in decline. More significantly, the atmosphere of crisis that had prevailed in the early years of the Republic had given way to a period of political and economic calm (see pages 71–5). Nevertheless, the Party was officially re-founded on 27 February 1925 and at the same time Hitler wrote a lengthy editorial for the *Völkischer Beobachter* with the heading 'A new beginning'.

## Strategy and leadership

In Landsberg prison Hitler, reflecting on the failure of the 1923 *putsch*, became convinced of two vital points:

- He must establish his own absolute control over the Party.
- An armed *coup* was no longer an appropriate tactic and the only sure way to succeed was to work within the Weimar Constitution and to gain power by legal means. Such a policy of legality would necessitate the creation of a party structure geared to gaining success in the elections. As Hitler himself said in prison in 1924:

> … we shall have to hold our noses and enter the *Reichstag* against the Catholic and Marxist deputies. If out-voting them takes longer than our shooting them, at least the result will be guaranteed by their own Constitution. Any lawful process is slow.

However, the Party remained deeply divided in a number of ways:

- Not everyone agreed with the new policy of legality.
- Traditional regional hostilities continued to exist, particularly between the Party's power base in Bavaria and the branches in northern Germany.
- Most importantly, policy differences had got worse between the nationalist and anti-capitalist wings of the Party (see page 111).

For over a year Hitler struggled with this internal friction. The problem was highlighted by the power and influence of Gregor Strasser and also his brother Otto. Gregor Strasser joined the NSDAP in 1920 and stood loyally next to Hitler in the Munich *putsch*, but he epitomised the opposing standpoint within the Party. He favoured the more socialist anti-capitalist policies for the workers and he was in effect the leader of the movement in northern Germany.

Eventually, in February 1926, the differences within the Party came to head at a special party conference in Bamberg. On the one hand it was a significant victory for Hitler, as he mobilised sufficient support to re-establish his supremacy. The Nazi Party was to be run according to the *Führerprinzip* and there was to be no place for disagreements. On the other hand, the Party declared that the original 25 points of the programme with its socialist elements remained unchangeable. So, although Hitler had cleverly outmanoeuvred his greatest threat and he had re-established a degree of unity within the Party, there were still significant rivalries and differences.

---

### Profile: Gregor Strasser 1892–1934

| | | |
|---|---|---|
| 1920 | | – Joined the NASDP. Supported the anti-capitalist 'left-wing' socialist faction and interestingly argued against anti-Semitism |
| 1923 | November | – Took part in the Munich *putsch* |
| 1926 | February | – Defeated by Hitler over the issue of the Party's leadership at the Bamberg Conference, but he continued to criticise Hitler's policies. Given responsibility for Party propaganda |
| 1926–32 | | – An excellent administrator, he was responsible for building up the mass movement of the Party in 1920s. Led the NSDAP in northern Germany. |
| 1932 | December | – Offered the post of vice-chancellor by Schleicher (see page 164). Differences with Hitler came to a head in a major row and he was expelled from the Party |
| 1934 | June | – Murdered in the Night of the Long Knives |

Because Gregor Strasser was murdered in 1934 and because he played no role in the government of the Third Reich, it is easy to ignore his significance in the rise of Nazism. Yet, until the day he resigned from the Party, Strasser was, in effect, second to Hitler. He was always a supporter of the anti-capitalist 'left-wing' socialist faction, which became increasingly disillusioned when Hitler courted big business. Like Hitler, an inspiring political speaker, he also showed the administrative skills to develop a mass movement for the Party. (He also worked closely with his brother until Otto left the Party in 1930.)

---

## The creation of the Party structure

The most significant development in the years before the Great Depression lay in the reorganisation of the Party structure. The whole of Germany was divided into regions (*Gaue*), which reflected the electoral geography of Weimar's system of proportional representation. The control of each region was placed in the hands of a **Gauleiter**, who then had the responsibility of creating district (*Kreis*) and branch (*Ort*) groups. In this way a vertical Party structure was created throughout

*Gauleiter*
Means 'leader of a regional area'. The Nazi Party was organised into 35 regions from 1926.

Key term

Germany, which did not detract from Hitler's own position of authority as leader.

Perhaps, the most renowned of the *Gauleiters* was the holder of the Berlin post, Joseph Goebbels. Goebbels had originally been a sympathiser of Gregor Strasser's socialist ideas, but from 1926 he gave his support to Hitler. He was then rewarded by being given the responsibility for winning over the capital – a traditionally left-wing stronghold of the SPD. He showed a real interest in propaganda and created the newspaper, *Der Angriff* (*The Attack*) – but was not appointed chief of party propaganda until 1930 (see page 156).

The Nazis also founded a number of new associated Nazi organisations that were geared to appeal to the specific interests of particular groups of Germans. Among these were:

- The Hitler Youth
- The Nazi Teachers' Association
- Union of Nazi Lawyers
- The Order of German Women.

Gregor Strasser was mainly responsible for building up an efficient Party structure and this was reflected in its increasing membership during these years (see Table 6.1).

**Table 6.1:** NSDAP membership

| Year | Membership numbers |
|------|--------------------|
| 1925 | 27,000 |
| 1926 | 49,000 |
| 1927 | 72,000 |
| 1928 | 108,000 |

**Key term**

**SS**
*Schutz Staffel* (protection squad); became known as the Blackshirts, named after the uniform.

One other significant initiative in these years was the creation of the **SS**. It was set up in 1925 as an élite body of black-shirted guards, sworn to absolute obedience to the Führer. In 1929 it had only 200 members. At first, it was just Hitler's personal bodyguard though, when it was placed under the control of Himmler later that year, it soon developed its own identity.

**Key question**
How strong was the Nazi Party by the end of the 1920s?

## The *Reichstag* election of May 1928

By 1928 it can be seen clearly that the Party had made progress and was really an effective political machine, most obviously because:

- the structure was effectively organised
- the membership had increased four-fold since 1925
- Hitler's leadership was authoritative and secure (despite the ongoing challenge from the Strasser faction).

As a result, the Nazi Party had also successfully taken over many of the other right-wing racist groups in Germany.

Such advances, however, could not compensate for Nazi disappointment after the *Reichstag* election in May 1928. When the votes were counted, the Party had won only 2.6 per cent of the vote and a mere 12 seats (see page 76). It seemed as if

**Key date**

*Reichstag* election result, very disappointing Nazi performance: May 1928

Hitler's policy of legality had failed to bring political success, whereas in the favourable socio-economic circumstances Weimar democracy had managed to stabilise its political position. So, Nazism may have taken root, but there was no real sign that it could flourish in Germany.

If this evidence confirmed the belief of many that Hitler was nothing more than an eccentric without the personal leadership to establish a really broad national appeal, there was just one telling sign. In the election, the Party made significant gains in the northern part of Germany amongst the rural and middle and lower middle classes of areas such as Schleswig-Holstein.

This trend was reflected in the regional state elections of 1929, which suggested that the fall in agricultural prices was beginning to cause discontent – demonstrations and protests were giving way to bankruptcies and violence. Most significantly, in the province of Thuringia, in central Germany, the Nazi Party trebled its vote and broke the 10 per cent barrier for the first time, recording 11.3 per cent. Such figures suggested that the Nazis could exploit the increasingly difficult economic times of the Great Depression.

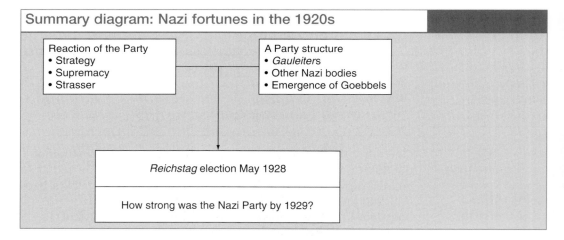

Summary diagram: Nazi fortunes in the 1920s

Reaction of the Party
• Strategy
• Supremacy
• Strasser

A Party structure
• *Gauleiters*
• Other Nazi bodies
• Emergence of Goebbels

*Reichstag* election May 1928

How strong was the Nazi Party by 1929?

# Study Guide: AS Questions

## In the style of Edexcel

Study Sources 1–5 below and answer the questions that follow.

### Source 1

*From: A. Hitler,* Mein Kampf, *describing early Nazi public meetings in 1920.*

The meetings nearly always started with the subject of War Guilt, about which nobody then bothered, and then went on to the Peace Treaties; violent methods of speech were found suitable and, indeed necessary.

In those days, if a public mass meeting, at which ordinary workers were present, dealt with the Versailles Treaty, it was taken as being an attack on the Weimar Republic. The moment Versailles was criticised, there would regularly be interruptions; 'And Brest-Litovsk?' The crowd would continue to shout until it gradually got more heated or the Speaker gave up trying to persuade them. We felt inclined to dash our heads against the wall with despair at such people! They would not understand that Versailles was a shame and a disgrace, or that a dictated peace was a frightful plundering of our nation.

### Source 2

*From: the Party Programme of the NSDAP February 1920. There were 25 points.*

The programme of the German Workers' Party is designed to be of limited duration. The leaders have no intention, once the aims announced in it have been achieved, of establishing fresh ones, merely in order to increase artificially the discontent of the masses to ensure the continued existence of the party.

1. We demand the union of all Germans in a greater Germany on the basis of the right of national self-determination.
2. We demand equality of rights for the German people in its dealings with other nations, and the revocation of the peace treaties of Versailles and St Germain.
3. We demand land and territory (colonies) to feed our people and settle our surplus population …

### Source 3

*Cartoon from a 1924 Nazi election poster: 'First Bread! Then Reparations'.*

## Source 4

*From: a speech by Nazi Reichstag deputy Wilhelm Kube to the rural population of Oldenburg in north-west Germany in 1928.*

We have recognised that the distress of agriculture is inseparably bound up with the political misery of the whole German people; the parliamentarianism which is corrupt through and through and a weak government are unable to overcome the German political and economic emergency.

Let us do away with this Marxist-capitulation extortion system that has made Germany our homeland, powerless without honour, defenceless and that has turned us free German farmers and middle class people into poor, misused slaves of the world stock exchange.

## Source 5

*From: I. Kershaw,* Hitler: Vol. 1 1889–1936.

Between the refoundation of the NSDAP in February 1925 and the beginning of the new political and economic turmoil that was to usher in the shattering of the world economic crisis, the Nazi movement was no more than a fringe irritant in German politics. Its leader, Hitler, faced with the rebuilding of his party from scratch after it had fractured into warring factions during his imprisonment in 1924, and banned from speaking in public in most of Germany until 1927. ... A confidential report by the Reich Minister of the Interior in 1927, pointing out that the NSDAP 'was not advancing', realistically describing the party as 'a numerically insignificant ... radical revolutionary splinter group'.

(a) **Study Source 1**

What does this source reveal about the difficulties the Nazis faced in 1920 when putting over their message about the Treaty of Versailles? (3 marks)

*Source: Edexcel June 2001*

(b) **Use your own knowledge**

Use your own knowledge to explain the importance, to Germany in the 1920s, of 'war guilt' and 'dictated peace' in Source 1. (5 marks)

*Source: Edexcel June 2001*

(c) **Study Sources 2 and 3**

How far does a study of Sources 2 and 3 offer support for the view that the policies of the NSDAP had changed between 1920 and 1924? (5 marks)

(d) **Study Sources 1 and 4**

How useful are these two sources to an historian studying the reason for the appeal of Nazism in the years 1920–8?

(5 marks)

(e) **Study Sources 4 and 5 and use your own knowledge**

Do you agree with the view that the Nazi Party had taken root in the 1920s? (12 marks)

Explain your answer, using these two sources and your own knowledge.

## Exam tips

*The cross-references are intended to take you straight to the material that will help you to answer the questions.*

**(a)** The answer to question **(a)** is to be found entirely within Source 1. You have to show that you generally understand the contents of the document. But you must also refer to particular points showing what the Nazis felt about Versailles and why they found it difficult to put over their message. You do not have to use your own knowledge. Keep your answer to the point.

**(b)** For question **(b)**, you must understand exactly the references to the 'war guilt' and the 'dictated peace'. Then, you have to use your own knowledge to explain the link between the references and Germany in the 1920s, for example:

- The effect of unilateral disarmament in weakening Germany's military position (pages 80–1 and 81–92).
- The effect of reparations being legally built upon Article 231 (page 59).

**(c)** In question **(c)** you must make certain you understand the meaning of the two sources and point to any similarities and differences – as many as possible. You should draw attention to elements of continuity as well as change, although the emphasis of the question is geared to fundamental change. As the question asks 'how far', it is also worth drawing attention to:

- Source 2 covers only 3 of the 25 points.
- The poster was produced in 1924, immediately in the wake of the inflationary economic crisis in 1923.

**(d)** In question **(d)** you must go beyond describing the content of the sources and you have to think about the reliability of the two sources. To do this, it is important to:

- explore the nature and origin of the sources
- explain the significance of the author and the circumstances of the writing.

In a conclusion, it is worth assessing the usefulness of the two sources from Hitler and Kube to understand the appeal of Nazism in the 1920s.

**(e)** Question **(e)** carries by far the most number of marks and you must spend nearly half the time in this exam on this question. You must use the same analytical skills as when writing an essay, so you have to:

- refer to the evidence of Sources 4 and 5. It is worth noting Kershaw's reference that '*the Nazi movement was no more than a fringe irritant in German politics*'. But show your own knowledge of the whole topic
- describe the state of the Nazi Party in the 1920s – its strengths and weaknesses.

Make an assessment as to whether the Nazi Party was strong enough to survive – though it would also be worth highlighting the *potential* power of Nazism in the different circumstances of the 1930s.

## In the style of OCR

Assess the reasons why the Nazis enjoyed only limited political success in the years 1919–29.

---

### Exam tips

*The cross-references are intended to take you straight to the material that will help you to answer the question.*

You have to adopt an analytical approach and you must be careful not to get lost in too much detail. Also, be careful not simply to describe the Nazis' progress. Identify a number of key reasons to explain why the success of Nazism was *limited*, for example:

- the limitations of the Nazi Party in its early years (pages 102–6)
- the failure of the Beer Hall *putsch* (pages 106–8)
- the problems faced by the Party when Hitler came out of gaol (pages 113–114)
- divisions in the Party (page 113–14).
- the recovery and stability in Weimar Germany, 1924–29 (pages 71–5)
- the *Reichstag* election 1928 (page 76–115).

Try to prioritise the reasons and justify your choice(s). Make an overall judgement.

# 7

# The Decline of Weimar and the Rise of Nazism 1929–32

**POINTS TO CONSIDER**

Weimar already faced pressures before 1929, but the Wall Street Crash, in the very same month as the death of Gustav Stresemann, ushered in the Great Depression that precipitated a political and economic crisis in Germany. This chapter focuses on the collapse of the Weimar Republic and the emergence of the Nazis, which, although closely linked, raises two questions. The first one is why did the Weimar Republic collapse? This is the subject of this chapter. Its main themes are:

- The effects of the world economic crisis on Germany
- The breakdown of parliamentary government
- The advent of presidential government under Brüning, 1930–2
- The appointment of Papen as chancellor
- The death of the Weimar Republic

The next and final chapter of this book will concentrate on why the Nazis became so politically popular and why Hitler was appointed chancellor in January 1933.

## Key dates

| | | |
|---|---|---|
| 1929 | October | Wall Street Crash |
| 1930 | March | Resignation of Müller's government. Brüning appointed chancellor |
| | | Young Plan approved by the *Reichstag* |
| | September | *Reichstag* election: Nazis emerged as second largest party in the *Reichstag* |
| | December | Brüning's economic measures imposed by presidential decree |
| 1931 | July | Five leading German banks failed |
| | October | Formation of Harzburg Front |
| 1932 | January | Unemployment peaked at 6.1 million |
| | April | Re-election of Hindenburg as president of Germany |
| | May | Brüning resigned |
| | | Von Papen appointed chancellor |
| | July | *Reichstag* election: Nazis emerged as largest party in the *Reichstag* |

# 1 | The Impact of the World Economic Crisis on Germany

**Key question**
Did the Wall Street Crash cause the economic crisis in Germany?

There is no dispute amongst historians that the world economic crisis, which is known as the Great Depression, was an event of major significance. Its effects were felt throughout the world – although not in the Soviet Union.

Germany undoubtedly felt it in a particularly savage way. It suffered the consequences of the Wall Street Crash – the collapse of share prices on the New York Stock Exchange in October 1929 – more than any other country. Almost immediately the American loans and investment dried up and this was quickly followed by demands for the repayment of those short-term loans. At the same time, the crisis caused a further decline in the price of food and raw materials as the industrialised nations reduced their imports. As demand for exports collapsed, so world trade slumped. In this situation, German industry could no longer pay its way. Without overseas loans and with its export trade falling, prices and wages fell and the number of bankruptcies increased.

The Wall Street Crash: October 1929

Key date

**Table 7.1:** Economic effects of the world economic crisis in Germany

| Economic effects | Key features |
|---|---|
| **Trade**<br>Slump in world trade. Demand for German exports fell rapidly, e.g. steel, machinery and chemicals | Exports value fell by 55 per cent<br>1929 = £630m<br>1932 = £280m |
| **Employment**<br>Workers laid off – mass unemployment | Number of registered unemployed (annual averages)<br>1929 = 1.8m<br>1932 = 5.6m |
| **Industry**<br>Industrial production declined sharply | Production: (1928 = 100)<br>1929 = 100<br>1932 = 58<br>50,000 businesses collapsed |
| **Agriculture**<br>Wages and incomes fell sharply. Many farms sold off | Agricultural prices (1913 = 100)<br>1927 = 138<br>1932 = 77 |
| **Finance**<br>Banking sector dislocated by loss of confidence | Five major banks collapsed in 1931<br>50,000 businesses bankrupted |

However, it is all too easy to put Germany's economic crisis down to the Wall Street Crash. It should be borne in mind that there were fundamental weaknesses in the German economy *before* the Wall Street Crash (see also pages 72–5):

- the balance of trade was in the red, i.e. in debt
- the number of unemployed averaged 1.9 million in 1929, even before the Wall Street Crash

- many farmers were already in debt and had been facing falling incomes since 1927
- German government finances from 1925 were continually run in deficit.

So, although the Wall Street Crash contributed to Germany's economic problems, it is *probable* that the Germany economy faced a chance of a serious depression without it. This suggests that the world economic crisis should really be seen as simply the final push that brought the Weimar economy crashing down. In that sense, it could be said that the Wall Street Crash was merely the occasion, not the cause of Germany's economic crisis.

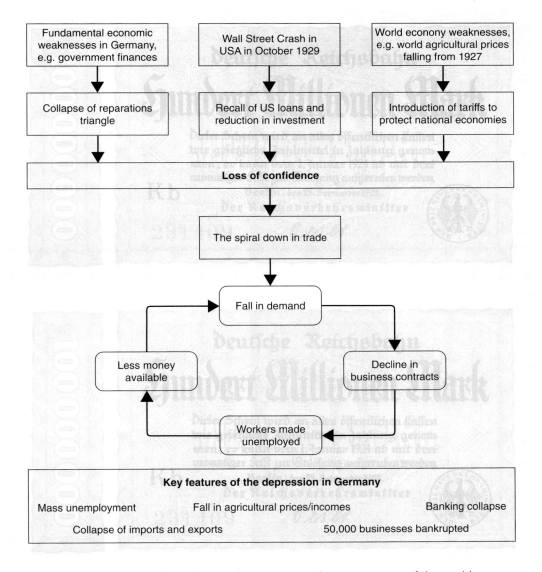

**Figure 7.1:** Germany in the Great Depression: causes and consequences of the world economic crisis

A camp for the unemployed and homeless in Berlin. Because there were so many poor people, large camps of tents were set up. These camps gave the impression of orderliness: numbered tents in neat rows with names, like streets.

## The human effects of the Great Depression

During the winter of 1929–30, unemployment rose above two million and only 12 months after the Crash, it had reached three million. By January 1932 it stood at 6.1 million, which did not substantially fall until the spring of 1933. On their own, such figures can provide only a limited understanding of the effects of the depression of this magnitude. Unemployment figures, for example, do not take into account those who did not register. Nor do they record the extent of part-time working throughout German industry.

Above all, statistics fail to convey the extent of the human suffering that was the consequence of this disaster because the depression in Germany affected virtually everyone; few families escaped its effects.

Many manual industrial workers, both skilled and unskilled, faced the prospect of long-term unemployment. For their wives, there was the impossible task of trying to feed families and keep homes warm on the money provided by limited social security benefits.

However, such problems were not to be limited to the working class. This depression dragged down the middle classes. From the small shopkeepers to the well-qualified professionals in law and medicine, people struggled to survive in a world where there was little demand for their goods and services. For such people, the decline in their economic position and the onset of poverty were made more difficult by the loss of pride and respectability.

The situation in the countryside was no better than in the towns. As world demand fell further, the agricultural depression deepened, leading to widespread rural poverty. For some tenant farmers there was even the ultimate humiliation of being evicted

**Key question**
How did the economic crisis affect the German people's lives?

Unemployment peaked at 6.1 million: January 1932

*Key date*

from their homes, which had often been in their families for generations.

In the more prosperous times we live in today, it is difficult to appreciate the scale of the suffering that struck German people in the early 1930s. The city of Cologne could not pay the interest on its debts, banks closed their doors and, in Berlin, large crowds of unemployed youngsters were kept occupied with open-air games of chess and cards. To many ordinary respectable Germans it seemed as if society itself was breaking down uncontrollably. It is not surprising that many people lost faith in the Weimar Republic, which seemed to offer no end to the misery, and began to see salvation in the solutions offered by political extremists. This was why the economic crisis in Germany quickly degenerated into a more obvious political crisis.

## The political implications

**Key question**
Why did the economic crisis turn into a political one?

The impact of the depression in Germany was certainly more severe than in either Britain or France, but it was on a par with the American experience. In Germany, one in three workers was unemployed in 1933 and by 1932 industrial production had fallen by 42 per cent of its 1929 level. In the USA, the comparable figures were one in four and 46 per cent.

However, in Germany the economic crisis quickly became a political crisis, simply because there was a lack of confidence that weakened the Republic's position in its hour of need. Britain, France and the USA were all well-established democracies and did not face the possibility of a wholesale collapse of their political systems.

Taken together these two points suggest that the Great Depression hastened the end of the Weimar Republic, but only because its economy was already in serious trouble, and the democratic basis of its government was not sufficiently well established.

Summary diagram: The impact of the world economic crisis on Germany

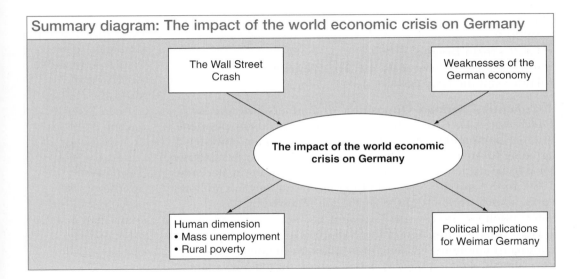

# 2 | Parliamentary Government's Breakdown

In 1929 the German government was in the hands of Hermann Müller's Grand Coalition, which had been formed after the general election of May 1928 (see page 76). Yet, at the very time when unity and firm government were required to tackle the economic crisis, the Weimar Republic was being torn apart by the re-emergence of the emotive issue of reparations.

The Dawes Plan (1924) successfully overcame the reparations crisis of the early 1920s by rescheduling payments based on Germany's capacity to pay but, from the outset, it was seen as a temporary measure until Germany regained its economic strength (see page 67). In early 1929 the IARC (Inter-Allied Reparations Commission) formed a committee of international financiers under the chairmanship of the American banker Owen Young. Its report in June 1929 suggested a new scheme of payments. Germany was to continue paying reparations until 1988 but the final sum was reduced to £1850 million (only one-quarter of the figure demanded in 1921). So, after some negotiation by Stresemann with the Allies, the German government accepted the Young Plan shortly before Stresemann's death.

However, in right-wing circles in Germany, Stresemann's diplomatic achievement was seen as yet another betrayal of national interests to the Allies. In the view of the right wing, any payment of reparations was based upon the 'lie' of Germany's war guilt (Article 231 of the Treaty of Versailles) and the new scheme had, therefore, to be opposed. A national committee, led by the new leader of the Nationalists, Alfred Hugenberg, was formed to fight the Young Plan (see page 89). Hugenberg was also Germany's greatest media tycoon. He owned 150 newspapers and a publishing house, as well as UFA, a world-famous film organisation. He now used all his resources to promote his message. Moreover, he generated support from a wide variety of right-wing nationalist factions:

- DNVP
- *Stahlhelm* (the largest ex-servicemen's organisation) led by Franz Seldte
- **Pan-German League**
- some leading industrialists, e.g. Fritz Thyssen
- Hitler and the Nazi Party.

Together this '**National Opposition**' drafted a *Law against the Enslavement of the German People*, which denounced any payment of reparations and demanded the punishment of any minister agreeing to such a treaty. The proposal gained enough signatures for it to be made the issue of a national referendum in December 1929. In the end the National Opposition won only 5.8 million votes, a long way short of the 21 million required by the constitution for success.

However, the campaign of the National Opposition had stirred nationalist emotions, focusing opposition on the democratic government at a vital time. It had also brought together many

**Key question**
How and why did the Young Plan increase political exposure for the Nazis?

**Key date**

Young Plan approved by *Reichstag*: March 1930

**Key terms**

**Pan-German League**
A movement founded at the end of the nineteenth century campaigning for the uniting of all Germans into one country.

**National Opposition**
A title given to various political forces that united to campaign against Weimar. It included the DNVP, the Nazis, the Pan-German League and the Stahlhelm – an organisation of ex-soldiers. The 'National Opposition' was forged out of the Young Plan in 1929 to oppose all reparations payments.

right-wing opponents of the Republic. For Hitler, the campaign showed clear-cut benefits:

- The Party membership grew to 130,000 by end of 1929.
- Nazism really gained a national standing for the first time.
- The main Party rally at Nuremberg had been a great propaganda success on a much more grandiose scale than any before.
- Hitler made influential political contacts on the extreme right wing.
- The opportunity of having access to Hugenberg's media empire.

## The collapse of Müller's Grand Coalition

Müller's coalition government successfully withstood the attack from the 'National Opposition'. However, it was not so successful in dealing with its own internal divisions. Müller, a Social Democrat, struggled to hold the coalition together but, not surprisingly, it was an issue of finance which finally brought down the government in March 1930.

The sharp increase in unemployment had created a large deficit in the new national insurance scheme, and the four major parties in the coalition could not agree on how to tackle it. The SPD, as the political supporters of the trade unions, wanted to increase the contributions and to maintain the levels of welfare payments. The DVP, on the other hand, had strong ties with big business and insisted on reducing benefits. Müller could no longer maintain a majority and he had no option but to tender the resignation of his government.

## The appointment of Heinrich Brüning

President Hindenburg granted the post of chancellor to Heinrich Brüning. At first sight, this appeared an obvious choice, since he was the parliamentary leader of the ZP, the second largest party in the *Reichstag*. However, with hindsight, it seems that Brüning's appointment marked a crucial step towards the end of true parliamentary government. This was for two reasons.

First, because he was manoeuvred into office by a select circle of political intriguers, who surrounded the ageing President Hindenburg:

- Otto Meissner, the president's State Secretary
- Oskar von Hindenburg, the president's son
- Major General Kurt von Schleicher, a leading general who had held a series of government and military posts.

All three were conservative-nationalists and had no real faith in the democratic process. Instead, they looked to the president and the emergency powers of Article 48 of the constitution (see pages 24 and 27) as a means of creating a more authoritarian government. In Brüning, they saw a respectable, conservative figure, who could offer firm leadership.

Second, Brüning's response to the growing economic crisis led to a political constitutional crisis. His economic policy was to propose cuts in government expenditure, so as to achieve a balanced budget and prevent the risk of reviving inflation. However, the budget was rejected in the *Reichstag* by 256 votes to 193 in July

**Key question**
Why could the Grand Coalition not agree?

**Key dates**

Resignation of Müller's government: March 1930

Brüning appointed chancellor: March 1930

**Key question**
How was parliamentary government weakened by the leadership of Heinrich Brüning?

1930. When, despite this, Brüning put the proposals into effect by means of an emergency decree, signed by the president according to Article 48, the *Reichstag* challenged the decree's legality and voted for its withdrawal. Deadlock had been reached. Brüning, therefore, asked Hindenburg to dissolve the *Reichstag* and to call an election for September 1930.

## Nazi breakthrough

Brüning had hoped that in the developing crisis the people would be encouraged to support the parties of the centre-right from which a coalition could be formed. However, the election results proved him wrong and the real beneficiary was the Nazi Party, which increased its vote from 810,000 to a staggering 6,409,600 (see Figure 7.2).

**Key question**
Why was the 1930 *Reichstag* election so significant?

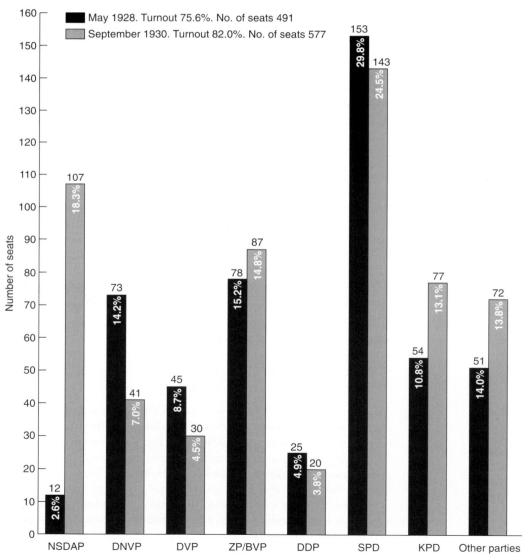

**Figure 7.2:** *Reichstag* election results for 1928 and 1930

**Key date**

Reichstag election –
Nazis emerged as
second largest party
in Reichstag:
September 1930

The key features about the performance of the political parties
are as follows:

- Nazis: With 107 seats and 18.3 per cent, the NSDAP became
  the second largest political party in Germany.
- Nationalists: The vote of the DNVP was halved from 14.2 per
  cent to 7 per cent, largely benefiting the Nazis.
- Middle-class democratic parties: The DDP and the DVP lost 20
  seats between them.
- Left-wing parties: The vote of the SPD declined from 29.8 per
  cent to 24.5 per cent, though in contrast the vote of the KPD
  increased from 10.8 per cent to 13.1 per cent.

Because the result of the 1928 *Reichstag* election had been so
disappointing, not even Hitler could have expected the dramatic
gains of 1930. Nevertheless, there are several key factors to
explain the Nazi breakthrough:

- Since 1928 the Nazi leaders had deliberately directed their
  propaganda at rural and middle-class/lower middle-class
  audiences. Nazi gains were at the expense of the DNVP, DVP
  and DDP.
- Nazi success cannot just be explained by these 'protest votes'.
  Nearly half of the Nazi seats were won by the Party's attracting
  'new' voters:
  – The electorate had grown by 1.8 million since the previous
    election because a new generation of voters had been added
    to the roll.
  – The turn-out had increased from 75.6 per cent to 82 per cent.

It would seem that the Nazis had not only picked up a fair
proportion of these young first-time voters, but a also persuaded
many people who had not previously participated in elections to
support their cause.

The implications of the 1930 *Reichstag* election were profound. It
meant that the left and right extremes had made extensive gains
against the pro-democratic parties. This now made it very difficult
for proper democratic parliamentary government to function.

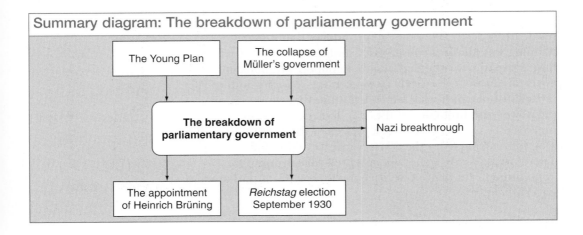

**Summary diagram: The breakdown of parliamentary government**

The Young Plan

The collapse of
Müller's government

**The breakdown of
parliamentary government**

Nazi breakthrough

The appointment
of Heinrich Brüning

Reichstag election
September 1930

# 3 | Brüning: Presidential Government

**Key question**
Was Brüning simply a victim of the circumstances?

Brüning's political position after the election was undoubtedly very difficult. His plan of reinforcing his parliamentary support from the centre–right had not succeeded. Instead, he faced the committed opposition of the more powerful extremes of left and right. However, he was not dismissed as chancellor. Brüning still enjoyed the support of Hindenburg and the SPD decided to 'tolerate' his cabinet. So, although the SPD did not join the government, given the threat now facing the Republic from the extremists it was not prepared to defeat the emergency decrees by the use of Article 48.

In this way, true parliamentary democracy gave way to 'presidential government' with some backing from the *Reichstag*. From 1930–2 Brüning remained as chancellor and he governed Germany by the use of Article 48 through President Hindenburg. He was almost a semi-dictator, as can be seen from his growing use of presidential decrees (see Table 7.2).

**Table 7.2:** Presidential government, 1930–2

|  | 1930 | 1931 | 1932 |
|---|---|---|---|
| Presidential decree laws (Article 48) | 5 | 44 | 66 |
| *Reichstag* laws | 98 | 34 | 5 |
| Sitting days of the *Reichstag* | 94 | 42 | 13 |

Initially, many historians were sympathetic to Brüning and saw him as a sincere statesman struggling in the face of enormous difficulties to save democracy. They believed that his decision to use Article 48 was an understandable reaction to the failure of party government in the crisis. Others, however, saw him as a reactionary, opposed to democracy, who used his position to introduce emergency powers that paved the way to destroying the Republic and to building the road towards Hitler's dictatorship.

Surprisingly, original defenders of Brüning were forced to give way after the publication of his *Memoirs, 1918–34* following his death in 1970. This shows beyond any doubt that Brüning was an ultra-conservative and monarchist, who had little sympathy for the democratic Republic. His aims in government were decisively to weaken the *Reichstag* and to re-establish an authoritarian constitution that would ignore the power and influence of the left. To these ends, he was prepared to use the emergency powers of the presidency and to look for backing from the conservative vested interests. Therefore, it is now generally accepted that Brüning's appointment did mark a decisive move away from parliamentary government.

## Das tote Parlament

The Dead Parliament. A cartoon/photomontage published by the German communist John Heartfield in October 1930. It shows an empty *Reichstag* with the number 48 superimposed on it, reflecting Brüning's use of the emergency decrees. The caption below the picture reads: 'The dead parliament. It's what's left from 1848! That's what the parliament looks like which is going to open on 13 October'.

**DAS BLIEB VOM JAHRE 1848 ÜBRIG!**
So sieht der Reichstag aus, der am 13. Oktober eröffnet wird.

**Key question**
What were the aims and effects of Brüning's economic policy?

## Economic policy

Brüning's economic policy was at least consistent. Throughout his two years in office his major aims were imposed by presidential decree:

- to balance the budget
- to prevent the chance of restarting inflation
- to get rid of the burden of German reparations.

And so, his policy's main measures were:

- to cut spending drastically
- to raise taxes.

This clearly lowered demand and it led to a worsening of the slump. Most obviously, there was a large increase in the number of unemployed and a serious decline in the welfare state provision. Soon he was mocked with the title 'the Hunger Chancellor'.

Brüning's economic measures imposed by presidential decree: December 1930

Key date

## Key debate

Bearing in mind the widespread effects of the Great Depression in Germany, Brüning's economic decisions have become the focus of considerable attention. It really raises the question:

### Was Brüning economically incompetent?

After 1945, historians generally condemned Brüning's economic policy. It was believed that governments should have followed policies that would have expanded the economy and so have reduced the harmful effects of depression. It was generally believed that by sticking to a policy of reducing expenditure Brüning had seriously worsened the situation and made possible the rise of the Nazis.

The historian Borchardt's work has already been mentioned in the discussion on Weimar's economy (see pages 73–4). He considered Brüning's reputation more sympathetically. He viewed Weimar by the late 1920s as having been 'abnormal' and 'incurably sick' and this formed an important part of his assessment of Brüning. In simple terms, Borchardt claimed that Brüning had no real choice in his economic policy and that he had no feasible alternative to his measures. This was because the German economy entered the depression with severe weaknesses:

- excessively high wage levels
- an already large government deficit
- low investment dependent on credit from abroad.

Therefore, he believed that any German government was not in a position to expand the economy. Finally, Borchardt argues that even if the money had been available, the severity of the depression was not really recognised until the summer of 1931. By that time it was already too late to introduce measures to prevent unemployment rising above six million. In this context, Borchardt sees Brüning as a relatively innocent pawn, at the mercy of economic forces.

Borchardt's defence of Brüning has been disputed because it challenged long-established views. Leading the opposition has been Holtfrerich in the 1980s, who claims that Brüning could have implemented other policies, which would have improved the situation. Holtfrerich makes three main claims:

- That there were weaknesses in Weimar's economy, but the economy was not doomed to collapse on the eve of the depression.
- That Brüning had remained committed to his economic policy because his real aim was to exacerbate the depression in order to prove to the Allies that the payment of reparations was no longer realistic. It was not so much that circumstances

prevented Brüning from facing the problems of the depression; it was simply that he had another priority.
- That Brüning did have alternative options. Economic measures in the summer of 1931, such as work creation schemes in the construction industry and the reduction of agricultural subsidies to make spending possible elsewhere, might just have been enough to lessen the worst effects of the depression during 1932.

The conflict between Borchardt and Holtfrerich has been fierce. It is now generally accepted that Brüning was motivated on political grounds to show that Germany could not afford to pay reparations, but there is no real agreement between the historians on the main issue of Brüning's responsibility. In his analysis Holtfrerich has continued to highlight the severity of the depression and the failure of Brüning to rescue the situation over the two years. By contrast, Borchardt has pointed out that there were no easy solutions to the crisis. Any alternative approach would have had serious consequences, especially at a time when Germany would have been acting differently from the rest of the world. Instead, he has successfully broadened the discussion beyond the narrow limits of 1929–32 and has shown the serious nature of the Weimar Republic's economic condition before the onset of the world depression. Borchardt's interpretation is an attractive one and his defence of Brüning's economic policy has proved to be very influential, although it is not yet universally accepted in all its details.

## Foreign policy

**Key question**
What were the main features of the foreign policy of Brüning's government?

Clearly Brüning's approach was not so conciliatory compared to the Stresemann years and the results were mixed:

- In 1930 he was able to bask in the glory of the evacuation of the last Allied troops from the Rhineland, but this had really been agreed in the previous year because of Stresemann's negotiations for the Young Plan.
- After long discussions he pushed for the reparations to be ended. In July 1931 the Hoover Moratorium temporarily suspended debts and reparations and eventually they were all abolished by the Lausanne Conference of June 1932 – ironically a few days after Brüning's resignation.
- Similarly, he decided to pursue the idea of a **customs union** between Austria and Germany. He hoped to encourage a revival in trade, but also to satisfy nationalist desires for the *Anschluss* (the union of Germany and Austria). However, the announcement of such a scheme in March 1931 backfired badly when it was rejected by the League of Nations because it was contrary to the Treaty of Versailles. This was a major blow for Brüning and his Foreign Minister, Curtius, felt compelled to resign.

**Key term**

**Customs union**
An agreement between two or more countries to abolish customs and tariffs. It aims to create free trade within the area and to encourage business.

## Brüning's fall from power

**Key question**
Why did Hindenburg force Brüning to resign?

In the spring of 1932, Hindenburg's first seven-year term of office as president came to an end. Brüning committed himself to securing the old man's re-election and after frenetic campaigning

Hindenburg was re-elected on the second ballot. He gained 19.3 million votes (53 per cent) compared with Hitler's 13.4 million (36.8 per cent). However, it was a negative victory. Hindenburg had been chosen because he was the only alternative to Hitler and the KPD candidate, Ernst Thälmann. Also, Hitler had doubled the Nazi vote, despite losing, and had projected an even more powerful personal image. Moreover, Hindenburg showed no real gratitude to Brüning and, at the end of May 1932, the president forced his chancellor to resign by refusing to sign any more emergency decrees. Why was this?

Brüning did not resign until May 1932, but by the end of 1931 confidence in him had begun to wane as the effects of the depression began to take their toll. In June 1931, even one of Germany's major banks, the Danat, closed its doors to customers, and several others soon followed suit. This meant that all those who had their savings there were unable to gain access to them – and it revived the fears of financial crisis. By the end of the year unemployment was approaching five million and, not surprisingly, there were demonstrations in the streets. Moreover, in October 1931 the 'National Opposition' (see page 126) was reborn as the Harzburg Front. It brought together again a range of right-wing political, military and economic forces who demanded the resignation of Brüning and a new *Reichstag* election. The Front arranged a massive rally to denounce Brüning, but in the winter of 1931–2 the chancellor still enjoyed the support of Hindenburg.

The immediate cause of Brüning's fall from grace was the president's displeasure at his aim to issue an emergency decree to turn some *Junker* estates in East Prussia into 600,000 allotments for unemployed workers. Landowners regarded the plan as a threat to their property interests, which they dubbed as 'agrarian bolshevism'. It resulted in Germany's landed classes pressurising Hindenburg into dropping the unpopular chancellor.

Brüning's unpopularity spurred the group of intriguers that surrounded the old president to exert political changes. It was the scheming and ambitious Kurt von Schleicher who was convinced that the Nazis could no longer be ignored. He wanted them to be included in a right-wing government and it was he who persuaded Hindenburg to force the chancellor's resignation at the end of May 1932 by refusing to sign any more emergency decrees.

One might be tempted to view Brüning as an innocent sacrifice, who was removed by Hindenburg without consultation with the *Reichstag*. However, it should also be borne in mind that he had only survived as chancellor because he enjoyed the personal backing of the president. Brüning had agreed with the creation of presidential government based on the powers granted by Article 48 of the constitution, but he was not astute enough to recognise the precarious nature of his own position. He depended solely on retaining the confidence of the president. This makes it harder to sympathise with him, when he became the victim of the intrigue of the presidential court.

**Key dates**

Re-election of Hindenburg as president of Germany: April 1932

Five leading German banks failed: July 1931

Formation of Harzburg Front: October 1931

Brüning resigned. Von Papen appointed chancellor: May 1932

## Profile: Heinrich Brüning 1885–1970

| | | |
|---|---|---|
| 1885 | | – Born into a Catholic trading family |
| 1904–11 | | – Attended the universities of Munich and Strasbourg and awarded a doctorate in economics |
| 1915–18 | | – Volunteered to fight in the First World War and gained a commission in the Machine Gun Corps |
| 1918 | | – Won the Iron Cross First Class |
| 1920 | | – Entered politics after the war and joined the ZP |
| 1924–33 | | – Elected to the *Reichstag* and rapidly rose up the ranks of the ZP |
| 1929 | | – Chosen as leader of the ZP |
| 1930 | March | – Appointed chancellor by Hindenburg |
| | July | – Tried to pass the budget with a presidential decree, but rejected by *Reichstag*. This resulted in the *Reichstag* election of September 1930 |
| 1931 | July | – Hoover Moratorium on reparations |
| 1932 | April | – Proposed the land reform of the Prussian estates |
| | May | – Dismissed by Hindenburg |
| 1934 | | – Fled to Holland and then emigrated to America. Lectured at Harvard University |
| 1947 | | – Returned to Germany and lectured at Cologne University |
| 1970 | | – Died |

The significance of Brüning's career is almost completely concentrated into the two years of his chancellorship, 1930–2. He was very much on the right wing of the ZP so, when he became the leader of the Party, his anti-socialism made it impossible for him to work with the left-wing parties. In his heart, he remained a monarchist and he hoped to amend the Weimar Constitution to make it a more authoritarian system. However, he was opposed to the Nazis – his real mistake was that he underestimated the extent of their threat.

His policies and decisions have been heavily criticised on various fronts:

• He called for the *Reichstag* election in September 1930 and misread the political consequences.
• He remained committed to the economic programme of balancing the budget, which resulted in enormous economic and political pressures.
• He relied on Hindenburg for the use of emergency decrees – and he failed to recognise his over-dependence on the president.

In his defence, it may be claimed that he was a man of integrity and a victim of exceptional circumstances. His historic reputation is perhaps overshadowed by the later development of the Nazi dictatorship.

## Assessment of Brüning

Brüning was an honest, hard-working and honourable man who failed. He was not really a committed democrat, but neither was he sympathetic to Nazism, and it is very important to remember that last point. In many respects, Brüning was making good progress towards his aims, when he was dismissed:

Key question
Was Brüning a failure?

- He succeeded in ending the payment of reparations.
- He sympathised with the reduction of the democratic powers of the *Reichstag*.

However:

- He was not clever enough to appreciate how dangerous and unstable the economic crisis had become in Germany by 1932.
- Neither did he realise how insecure was his own position. For as long as Brüning retained the confidence of Hindenburg, presidential government protected his position.

With no real hope of improvement in the economic crisis, it is not surprising that large sections of the population looked to the Nazis to save the situation. Brüning would have nothing to do with Hitler and the Nazis and he continued to uphold the **rule of law**. Sadly, presidential rule had accustomed Germany again to rule by decree. In this way democracy was undermined and the way was cleared for more extreme political parties to assume power. In the end, it is hard to escape the conclusion that Brüning's chancellorship was a dismal failure, and, in view of the Nazi tyranny that was soon to come, a tragic one.

Key term

**Rule of law**
Governing a country according to its laws.

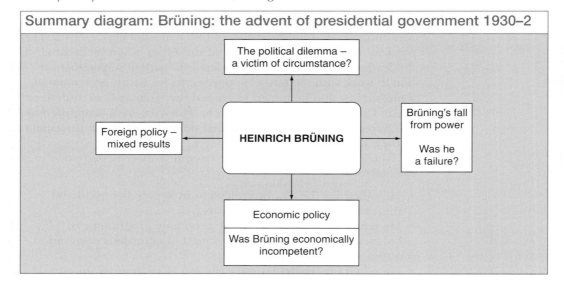

Summary diagram: Brüning: the advent of presidential government 1930–2

The political dilemma – a victim of circumstance?

Foreign policy – mixed results

**HEINRICH BRÜNING**

Brüning's fall from power

Was he a failure?

Economic policy

Was Brüning economically incompetent?

## 4 | From Brüning to Papen

Key question
What was Papen's political aim?

Schleicher had recommended the new chancellor, Franz von Papen, to Hindenburg. As an aristocrat, Papen had good connections with high society; as a Catholic he was a member of the Centre Party, although his political views mirrored those of

## Profile: Franz von Papen 1879–1969

| | | |
|---|---|---|
| 1879 | | – Born into a Catholic aristocratic family |
| 1913–18 | | – Having been trained as a cavalry officer, he embarked on his diplomatic career and served in the USA, Mexico and Turkey |
| 1921 | | – Elected to the Prussian regional state as a member of ZP |
| 1932 | May | – Appointed as chancellor by Hindenburg to head the so-called 'Cabinet of Barons', which did not include any member of the *Reichstag* |
| | | – Decided to call for the *Reichstag* election of July 1932, with serious consequences |
| | July | – Removed the state regional government of Prussia and appointed himself as Reich Commissioner of Prussia |
| | September | – Personally defeated by a massive vote of 'no confidence' in the *Reichstag* (512 votes to 42) |
| | November | – Dismissed by Hindenburg but schemed to replace Schleicher and to recover his power |
| 1933 | January | – Appointed as vice-chancellor in Hitler's Nazi–Nationalist coalition |
| 1934 | July | – Resigned after the Night of Long Knives |
| 1934–44 | | – Ambassador for Germany in Austria and then Turkey |
| 1946 | | – Charged with war crimes in the Nuremberg trials, but found not guilty |
| 1947 | | – Sentenced by a German de-nazification court to eight years in a labour camp (released after two years) |
| 1969 | | – Lived privately until his death |

There have been few political careers that were so short and so disastrous as that of Franz von Papen. He had limited political experience and was out of his depth. His advance was mainly due to his connections with the aristocracy, the Catholic Church and big business (his wife was the daughter of a very rich industrialist).

He was always a monarchist and a nationalist (although he remained nominally a member of ZP). When he became chancellor, he aspired to undo the Weimar Constitution and so he was quite happy to rule by presidential decrees and to denounce the state government of Prussia. Despite his failings, he pursued his personal ambitions but was quickly outmanoeuvred by Hitler in the early months of 1933.

the Nationalists. His outlook quickly formed the basis for a close friendship with Hindenburg.

Papen was also politically ambitious, but his understanding and experience of politics was limited (he did not even hold a seat in the *Reichstag*). If many greeted the choice of Papen with disbelief, it was the man's very lack of ability which appealed to Schleicher, who saw the opportunity to influence events more directly through him.

The new cabinet was called a non-party government of 'national concentration', though it was soon nicknamed the 'Cabinet of Barons'. It was a presidential government dominated by aristocratic landowners and industrialists – and many were not even members of the *Reichstag*. In order to strengthen the government, Papen and Schleicher wanted to secure political support from the Nazis – though Hitler only agreed not to oppose the new government in return for two concessions:

- The dissolution of the *Reichstag* and the calling of fresh elections.
- The ending of a government ban on the SA and SS, which had been introduced in the wake of violence during the presidential campaign.

In this way, Papen and Schleicher hoped that this agreement with the Nazis would result in the creation of a right-wing authoritarian government with a measure of popular support in the form of the Nazis. The *Reichstag* was therefore dissolved and an election was arranged to take place on 31 July 1932.

## *Reichstag* election: July 1932

The election campaign was brutal, as street violence once again took hold in the large cities. In the month of July alone 86 people died as a result of political fights.

**Key question**
Why was the *Reichstag* election of July 1932 so politically significant?

Yet, such bloodshed provided Schleicher and Papen with the excuse to abolish the most powerful regional state government in Germany, Prussia. This government of Prussia had long been a coalition of the SPD and the ZP and had been the focus of right-wing resentment since 1919. So, on 20 July 1932, it was simply removed by Papen who declared a state of emergency and appointed himself as Reich Commissioner of Prussia. This was of immense significance:

- It was an arbitrary and unconstitutional act.
- It replaced a parliamentary system with a presidential authoritarian government.
- Democrats – especially the SPD and the trade unions – gave in without any real opposition. Their passive response shows how far the forces of democracy had lost the initiative.

Many on the right wing congratulated Papen on the Prussian *coup*. However, it did not win him any additional electoral support. When the election results came in, it was again the Nazis who had cause to celebrate. They had polled 13.7 million votes and had won 230 seats. Hitler was the leader of by far the largest party in Germany and constitutionally he had every right to form a government.

It is worth bearing in mind the following key features about the performance of the political parties:

- Nazis: With 230 seats and 37.3 per cent the NSDAP became the largest political party in Germany.
- Nationalists: The vote of the DNVP fell further to 5.9 per cent.

**Key date**
Nazis emerged as the largest party in the *Reichstag* election: July 1932

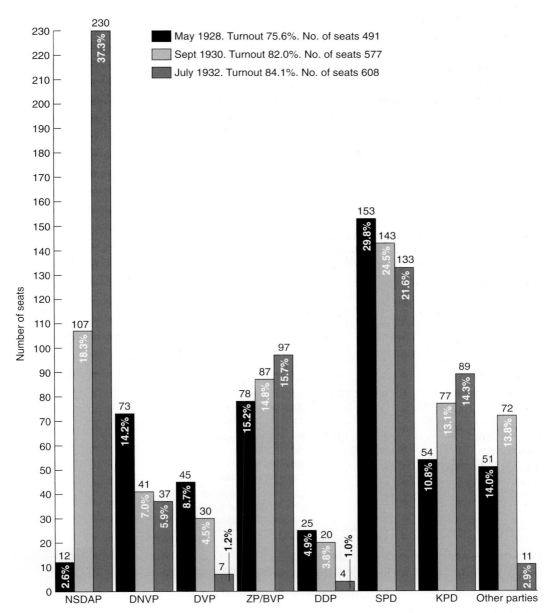

**Figure 7.3:** *Reichstag* election results 1928–32

- Middle-class democratic parties: The DDP and the DVP collapsed disastrously. They polled only 2.2 per cent of the vote and gained just 11 seats between them.
- Left-wing parties: The vote of the SPD declined further to 21.6 per cent, though in contrast the vote of the KPD increased to 14.3 per cent.

In electoral terms the gains of the Nazis could be explained by:

- the collapse of the DDP and DVP vote
- the decline of the DNVP
- a small percentage of disgruntled workers changing from SPD to NSDAP

- the support for the 'other parties' falling from 13.8 per cent to 2.9 per cent, which suggests their loyalty transferred to the Nazis
- the turnout increasing to 84 per cent which indicated the same trend as September 1930 that the Party was attracting even more 'new voters'.

Two further points worth remembering about the *Reichstag* election of July 1932 are:

- Only 39.5 per cent voted for the pro-democratic parties.
- Added together, the percentage of votes for the KPD and NSDAP combined to 51.6 per cent.

These two political facts are telling indeed. The German people had voted to reject democracy.

**Table 7.3:** Germany's governments 1928–33

| Chancellors | Dates in office | Type of government |
| --- | --- | --- |
| Hermann Müller (SPD) | May 1928– March 1930 | Parliamentary government. A coalition cabinet of SPD, ZP, DDP, DVP |
| Heinrich Brüning (ZP) | March 1930– May 1932 | Presidential government dependent on emergency decrees. A coalition cabinet from political centre and right |
| Franz von Papen (ZP, but very right wing) | May 1932– December 1932 | Presidential government dependent on emergency decrees. Many non-party cabinet members |
| General Kurt von Schleicher (Non-party) | December 1932– January 1933 | Presidential government dependent on emergency decrees. Many non-party cabinet members |
| Adolf Hitler (NSDAP) | 1933–45 | Coalition cabinet of NSDAP and DNVP but gave way to Nazi dictatorship |

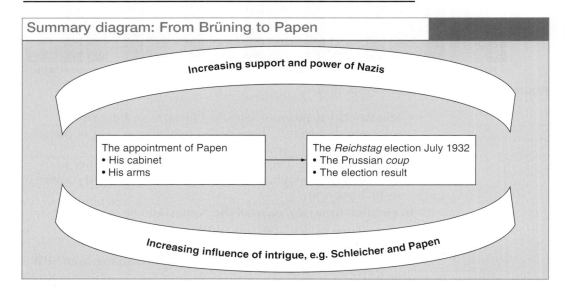

Summary diagram: From Brüning to Papen

Increasing support and power of Nazis

The appointment of Papen
- His cabinet
- His arms

The *Reichstag* election July 1932
- The Prussian *coup*
- The election result

Increasing influence of intrigue, e.g. Schleicher and Papen

Key question
Why did Weimar
democracy fail?

# 5 | The Death of the Weimar Republic

It is now clear that Weimar democracy was really dead before the establishment of the Nazi dictatorship in early 1933 (see pages 167–70). The problem for the historian is trying to determine when the Weimar Republic expired and why.

Three major themes stand out as fundamental weaknesses of the Weimar Republic.

## (i) The hostility of Germany's vested interests

From the very start, the Weimar Republic faced the hostility of Germany's established élites. Following military defeat and the threat of revolution, this opposition was at first limited. However, the fact that so many key figures in German society and business rejected the idea of a democratic republic was a major problem for Weimar. They worked against the interests of Weimar and hoped for a return to the pre-war situation. This was a powerful handicap to the successful development of the Republic in the 1920s and, in the 1930s, it was to become a decisive factor in its final collapse.

## (ii) Ongoing economic problems

The Republic was also troubled by an almost continuous economic crisis that affected all levels of society. It inherited the enormous costs of the First World War followed by the burden of post-war reconstruction, Allied reparations and the heavy expense of the new welfare benefits. So, even though the inflation crisis of 1923 was overcome, problems in the economy were disguised and remained unresolved. These were to have dramatic consequences with the onset of the world economic crisis in 1929.

## (iii) Limited base of popular support

Weimar democracy never enjoyed widespread political support. There was never total acceptance of, and confidence in, its system and its values. From the Republic's birth its narrow base of popular support was caught between the extremes of left and right. But, as time went by, Weimar's claims to be the legitimate government became increasingly open to question. Sadly, Weimar democracy was associated with defeat and the humiliation of the Treaty of Versailles and reparations. Its reputation was further damaged by the crisis of 1922–3. Significantly, even the mainstays of the Weimar Republic had weaknesses:

- The main parties of German liberalism, DDP and DVP, were losing support from 1924.
- The ZP and DNVP were both moving to the political right.
- Even the loyalty and the commitment of the SPD to democracy has to be balanced against its failure to join the coalitions in the mid-1920s and its conflict with its left-wing partner, the KPD.

In short, a sizeable proportion of the German population never had faith in the existing constitutional arrangements and, as the years passed, more were looking for change.

These unrelenting pressures meant that Weimar democracy went through a number of phases:

- The difficult circumstances of its birth in 1918–19 left it handicapped. It was in many respects, therefore, a major achievement that it survived the problems of the period 1919–23.
- The years of relative stability from 1924 to 1929, however, amounted to only a short breathing space and did not result in any strengthening of the Weimar system. On the eve of the world economic crisis it seemed that Weimar's long-term chances of survival were already far from good.
- In the end, the impact of the world depression, 1929–33, intensified the pressures that brought about Weimar's final crisis.

In the view of some historians, Weimar had been a gamble with no chance of success. For others, the Republic continued to offer the hope of democratic survival right until mid-1932, when the Nazis became the largest party in the July *Reichstag* election. However, the manner of Brüning's appointment and his decision to rule by emergency decree created a particular system of presidential government. This fundamentally undermined the Weimar system and was soon followed by the electoral breakthrough of the Nazis. From this time, democracy's chance of surviving was very slim indeed. Democracy lived on with ever increasing weakness before it reached to its demise in July 1932. However, in truth, democratic rule in Germany was terminal from the summer of 1930.

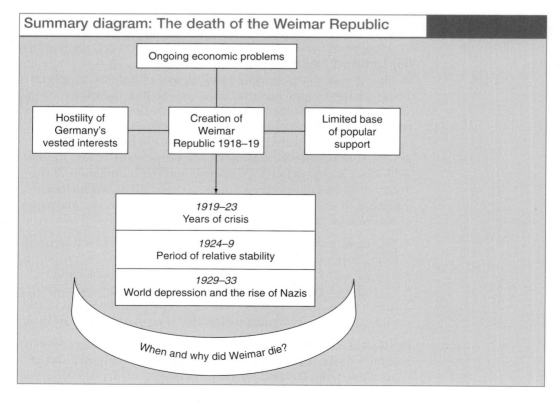

Summary diagram: The death of the Weimar Republic

Ongoing economic problems

Hostility of Germany's vested interests — Creation of Weimar Republic 1918–19 — Limited base of popular support

1919–23
Years of crisis

1924–9
Period of relative stability

1929–33
World depression and the rise of Nazis

When and why did Weimar die?

## Study Guide: AS Questions

### In the style of AQA

Explain the main reasons why the Weimar Republic was unable to resist the pressures of non-democratic forces in the period 1930–2.

*Source: AQA, June 2001*

---

*Study tips*

You will not be short of material in this question. The real problems in writing this answer are making certain to:

- Select the most relevant content within your word allocation, usually 1000–1500.
- Stick to the analytical point effectively and avoiding drifting on to description.

So you must use the preparation time very well. It should also be noted from the wording in the question that:

- The 'non-democratic forces' will require reference to the Nazis, but also the communists and the nationalist/conservatives of the extreme right.
- The dates 1930–2 provide a focus, so there is no need to include Hitler's appointment in January 1933, but at the same time you will have to refer to the broader background of Weimar before 1930.

Some of the key factors to refer to are:

- The weaknesses of the Weimar Republic before 1930.
- The crucial significance of the economic crisis.
- Brüning's decision to use presidential government from 1930.
- The personalities and intrigue of Hindenburg, Papen and Schleicher (and the influence of conservative/nationalist forces, e.g. the army).
- The rise of the Nazis and the Communists and how they destabilised Weimar.

It is important to maintain an analytical approach throughout the essay and you will effectively work towards a strong conclusion with a reasoned judgment. Then, you are more likely to earn higher marks.

---

### In the style of Edexcel

Study Sources 1–5 below and answer the questions that follow.

#### Source 1

*From: the memo by Dr Kulz, the Minister of the Interior.*

Looked at politically, objectively, the result of the election [Summer 1932] is so fearful because it seems clear that the present election will be the last normal *Reichstag* election for a long time to come. The so-called race of thinkers and poets is hurrying with flags flying towards dictatorship …

… the situation is such that more than half the German people have declared themselves against the present state, but have not said what sort of state they would accept …. As the lesser of many evils to be feared, I think, would be the open assumption of dictatorship by the present government.

## Source 2

*From: the recollections of a middle-aged civil servant who joined the NSDAP in 1930.*

One day early in 1927, I bought a copy of a weekly magazine called *Der Angriff* (*The Attack*). The name of the magazine attracted me. After a study of the first copy, I could not wait to see the next, and I eagerly read its attacks on the Republican regime. From then on, I became a regular reader of *Der Angriff*, which brought me in close contact with the party fighting for a new Germany.

## Source 3

*A cartoon by Paul Weber, published in Germany in 1932 and called* The Fate, *showing the German people tumbling into a coffin.*

## Source 4

*From: the recollections of a young middle-class professional man who joined the NSDAP in 1929.*

In 1927, I obtained a copy of *Der Angriff*. Its language was harsh and crude, yet there was something about the contents which attracted me. This opinion was outweighed by my low opinion of National Socialists, often described in other magazines and newspapers as a murderous plague.

Following this, in 1928 I became acquainted with a colleague of my own age, with whom I had frequent conversations. He was a calm, quiet person and I thought very highly of him. When I found that he was one of the local leaders of the National Socialist party, my opinion of it as a group of criminals changed completely. My friend asked me to attend a meeting and after this my new attitude was confirmed through my contacts with other National Socialists. I came to value many of them as good comrades and honest, sincere fellows.

Source 5

*From: Martin Collier and Philip Pedley,* Germany 1919–45, *2000.*

By the early 1930s, the Nazis were the only party that could present itself as a national one that could cut across class and interest lines. This was due to the attractions of the Nazis as a party of protest and lofty but ill-defined ideals such as Volksgemeinschaft. Nazi policy was vague but deliberately so, style being more important than substance. It was this that made the Nazis successful electorally.

A crucial factor in the rise to power of the Nazis was the ability of the party to expand and provide a political home for the discontented, particularly after the Crash of 1929. The use of rallies, speeches, lectures and 'aeroplane campaigns' in certain areas were effective in raising the profile of the party and increasing the vole at elections.

(a) **Study Source 1**
    What can you learn from Source 1 about Dr Kulz's attitude to the voters in the electorate? (3 marks)
(b) **Use your own knowledge**
    Use your own knowledge to explain the importance of Article 48 in contributing to the decline of the Weimar Republic.
    (5 marks)
(c) **Study Sources 2 and 4**
    How far do the two sources agree on the impact and importance of the magazine *Der Angriff*? (5 marks)

*Source: Edexcel, June 2003*

(d) **Study Sources 1 and 3**
    How useful are these two sources to an historian studying the political condition of the Weimar Republic in 1932? (5 marks)
(e) **Study Sources 1 and 5 and use your own knowledge**
    Do you agree with the view that Weimar collapsed in the years 1929–32 mainly because of the Wall Street Crash? (12 marks)

Exam tips to these questions are on page 146.

*Exam tips*

*The cross-references are intended to take you straight to the material that will help you to answer the questions.*

**(a)** The answer to question **(a)** is to be found entirely within Source 1. You have to show that you generally understand the contents of the document. But you must also refer to particular points showing why Dr Kulz thought the election was so significant. You do not have to use your own knowledge. Keep your answer to the point.

**(b)** Firstly, you must understand exactly the reference to 'Article 48'. Then, you have to use your own knowledge to explain how 'Article 48' links with the collapse of Weimar Germany. For example:
- Brüning's use of emergency decrees to put into effect the economic policy (page 130)
- the weakness of the *Reichstag* (pages 127–30)
- the dependence on Hindenburg's authority (page 130).

**(c)** You must make certain you understand the meaning of the two sources and point to any similarities and differences. Focus on the use of the words 'impact' and 'importance' of the magazine. You should be able to distinguish elements between the two sources and assess who made the greater impact. As the question asks 'how far', you should make some conclusion.

**(d)** You must go beyond describing the content of the sources and you have to think about the reliability of the two sources. To do this, it is important to:
- explore the nature and origin of the sources
- explain the significance of the author and the circumstances of the writing.

In a conclusion, it is worth assessing the usefulness of the two sources of the memo and the cartoon to understand the political condition of Germany in 1932.

**(e)** This question carries by far the most number of marks and you must spend nearly half the time in the exam on this question. You must use the same analytical skills of an essay and show your own knowledge of the whole topic, as well as your understanding of Sources 1 and 5.

You have to:
- describe the effects and consequences of the Great Depression (pages 121–5)
- draw attention to other weaknesses of the Weimar Republic (pages 141–2)
- show how the rise of Nazism reflected and exacerbated the decline of Weimar (pages 128–9 and 138–40).

Make an assessment as to whether the Wall Street Crash was the 'main' reason for the decline of Weimar (see pages 122–3).

## In the style of OCR

'The Weimar Republic was weak from the start; its collapse was always likely'. How far do you agree with this judgement on the period 1919–33?

*Source: OCR, June 2003*

---

*Exam tips*

*The cross-references are intended to take you straight to the material that will help you to answer the question.*

This is a very broad question, which covers elements of all chapters in the book. You must choose the relevant material carefully and not get lost in too much detail. So you must not drift into just telling the story, but instead, aim to analyse the strengths and weaknesses of Weimar at each stage. Remember the 'condition' of Weimar Germany was not static – it changed over time.

- The weaknesses (and strengths) of the Weimar Republic in its early years, 1918–24 (pages 18–19, 28, 35–6, 50–2 and 65–8).
- The problems (and strengths), which developed over the main period, 1924–9 (pages 98–9).
- The fundamental problems (and any strengths), which overtook Weimar in 1929–33 (pages 141–2).

In your conclusion, you have to focus on Weimar's weaknesses to explain when and why exactly it collapsed. It would also be helpful to bear in mind that Weimar's collapse was not inevitable and various alternative scenarios were possible.

# 8 The Nazi Road to Dictatorship 1932–3

## POINTS TO CONSIDER

Although Weimar democracy was, in effect, dead by the summer of 1932, it should not be assumed that Hitler's appointment was inevitable. The purpose of this chapter is to consider two questions that are inextricably linked: 'Why did Hitler and the Nazis become so politically popular?' and 'Why was Hitler appointed chancellor in January 1933?'

The main themes are:

- The creation of a Nazi mass movement: who voted for the Nazis and why?
- Nazi political methods: propaganda and violence
- Political intrigue: the appointment of Hitler as chancellor
- The establishment of the Nazi dictatorship, January–March 1933
- Why the Nazis replaced the Weimar Republic

## Key dates

| | | |
|---|---|---|
| 1932 | May | Brüning dismissed as chancellor and replaced by von Papen |
| | July | *Reichstag* election: Nazis won 230 seats (37.3 per cent) |
| | September | *Reichstag* passed a massive vote of 'no confidence' in Papen's government (512 to 42) |
| | November | *Reichstag* election: Nazis' vote dropped to 33.1 per cent, winning 196 seats |
| | December | Papen dismissed as chancellor and replaced by Schleicher |
| 1933 | January 30 | Schleicher dismissed and Hitler appointed as chancellor |
| | February 27 | *Reichstag* fire: Communists blamed |
| | March 5 | Last *Reichstag* elections according to Weimar Constitution |
| | March 21 | The 'Day of Potsdam' |
| | March 23 | Enabling Act passed |

Key question
Who voted for the
Nazis?

# 1 | The Creation of a Nazi Mass Movement

The point is often made that Hitler and the Nazis never gained an overall majority in *Reichstag* elections. However, such an occurrence was unlikely because of the number of political parties in Weimar Germany and the operation of the proportional representation system. Considering this, Nazi electoral achievements by July 1932 were very impressive. The 13,745,000 voters who had supported them represented 37.3 per cent of the electorate, thus making Hitler's party the largest in the *Reichstag*. Only one other party on one other occasion had polled more – the SPD in the revolutionary atmosphere of January 1919. Nazism had become a mass movement with which millions identified and, as such, it laid the foundations for Hitler's coming to power in January 1933. Who were these Nazi voters and why were they attracted to the Nazi cause?

The results of the elections 1928–32 show the changing balance of the political parties (see pages 128 and 129), although really these figures on their own are limited in what they show us about the nature of Nazi support. However, the graph and table in Figure 8.1 reveal a number of significant points about the kind of people who actually voted for the Nazis.

Key date

Nazis won 230 seats out of 608 (37.3 per cent) in *Reichstag* election: July 1932

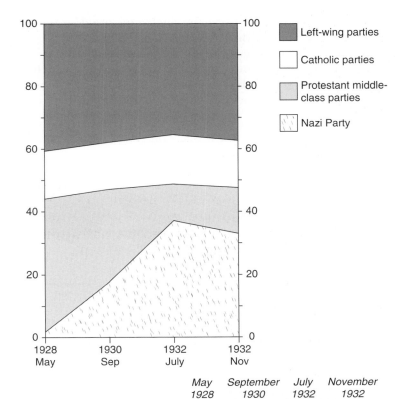

**Figure 8.1:**
Percentage of vote gained by each major political grouping in the four *Reichstag* elections 1928–32

| | May 1928 | September 1930 | July 1932 | November 1932 |
|---|---|---|---|---|
| Nazi Party | 2.6 | 18.3 | 37.3 | 33.1 |
| Protestant middle-class parties (DNVP, DDP, DVP and others) | 41.8 | 29.3 | 11.1 | 14.6 |
| Catholic parties (ZP and BVP) | 15.2 | 14.8 | 15.7 | 15.0 |
| Left-wing parties (SPD and KPD) | 40.4 | 37.6 | 35.9 | 37.3 |

From this it seems fairly clear that the Nazis made extensive gains from those parties with a middle-class and/or a Protestant identity. However, it is also apparent that the Catholic parties, the Communist Party and, to a large extent, the Social Democrats were able to withstand the Nazi advances.

## Geography and denomination

These political trends are reflected in the geographical base of Nazi support, which was generally higher in the north and east of the country and lower in the south and west. Right across the North German Plain, from East Prussia to Schleswig-Holstein, the Nazis gained their best results. This seems to reflect the significance of two important factors – religion and the degree of urbanisation.

In those areas where Catholicism predominated, the Nazi breakthrough was less marked, whereas the more Protestant regions were more likely to vote Nazi. Likewise, the Nazis fared less well in the large industrial cities, but gained greater support in the more rural communities and in residential suburbs.

The Nazi vote was at its lowest in the Catholic cities of the west, such as Cologne and Düsseldorf. It was at its highest in the Protestant countryside of the north and north-east, such as Schleswig-Holstein and Pomerania. Ironically, therefore, Bavaria, a strongly Catholic region and the birthplace of Nazism, had one of the lowest Nazi votes in Germany. Such a picture does not of course take into account the exceptions created by local circumstances. For instance, parts of the province of Silesia, though mainly Catholic and urbanised, still recorded a very high Nazi vote. This was probably the result of nationalist passions generated in a border province, which had lost half its land to Poland.

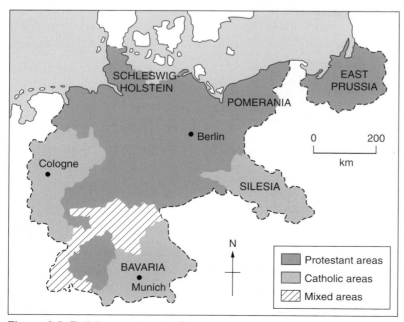

**Figure 8.2** Religious regions in Germany

## Class

Nazi voters also reflected the rural/urban division in terms of their social groupings. It seems that the Nazis tended to win a higher proportion of support from:

- the peasants and farmers
- the '*Mittelstand*' (the lower middle classes, e.g. artisans, craftsmen and shopkeepers)
- the established middle classes, e.g. teachers, **white-collar workers**, public employees.

This tendency is shown in the figures of the Nazi Party's membership lists, which can be seen in Figure 8.3 and Table 8.1.

A significantly higher proportion of the middle-class subsections, i.e. government officials/employees, self-employed, white-collar workers, tended to join the Nazi Party than the other classes. However, it is worth bearing in mind two other points.

**Key term**

**White-collar workers**
Workers not involved in manual labour.

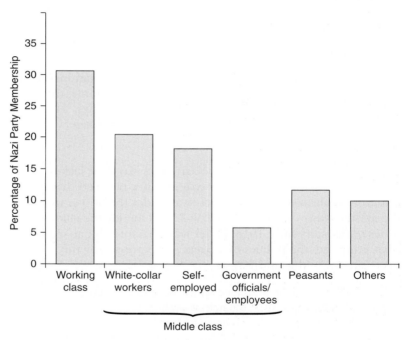

**Figure 8.3:** Nazi Party members in 1932

**Table 8.1:** German society as a whole in 1933 (%)

| Working class | Middle class | | | Peasants | Others |
| --- | --- | --- | --- | --- | --- |
| | White-collar workers | Self-employed | Government officials/ employees | | |
| 46.3 | 12.4 | 9.6 | 4.8 | 20.7 | 6.2 |

First, although the working class did join the Nazi party in smaller proportions, it was still the largest section in the NSDAP. Second, although the peasants tended to vote for the Nazis, the figures show they did not join the NSDAP in the same proportion.

## The appeal of Nazism

It is clear that more of the Protestants and the middle classes voted for Nazism in proportion to their percentage in German society. The real question is why were those with a loyalty to Catholicism or socialism not so readily drawn in to voting for the Nazis?

**Key question**
Why were the Protestants, the middle classes and the young more attracted to Nazism?

- First, both of them represented well-established ideologies in their own right and both opposed Nazism on an intellectual level.
- Second, the organisational strength of each movement provided an effective counter to Nazi propaganda. For socialism, there was the trade union structure. For Catholicism, there was the Church hierarchy, extending right down to the local parish priest.
- Third, both movements had suffered under the Imperial German regime. As so often happens, persecution strengthened commitment. It was, therefore, much harder for the Nazis to break down the established loyalties of working-class and Catholic communities and their traditional '**associationism**', or identity, remained strong. In contrast, the Protestants, the farmers and the middle classes had no such loyalties. They were therefore more likely to accept the Nazi message.

**Associationism**
Having a strong identity or affiliation with a particular group.

Key term

### The 'politics of anxiety'

What was common among many Nazi voters was their lack of faith in, and identity with, the Weimar system. They believed that their traditional role and status in society was under threat. For many of the middle classes the crisis of 1929–33 was merely the climax of a series of disasters since 1918. Hitler was therefore able to exploit what is termed 'the politics of anxiety', as expressed by the historian T. Childers in his book *The Nazi Voter*:

> [By 1930] the NSDAP had become a unique phenomenon in German electoral politics, a catch-all party of protest, whose constituents, while drawn primarily from the middle class electorate were united above all by a profound contempt for the existing political and economic system.

In this way Hitler seemed able to offer to many Germans an escape from overwhelming crisis and a return to former days.

### The young

Another clearly identifiable group of Nazi supporters was the youth of Germany. The Depression hit at the moment when youngsters from the pre-war baby-boom came of age and, however good their qualifications were, many had little chance of finding work. In a study of Nazi Party membership 41.3 per cent of those who joined before 1933 had been born between 1904 and 1913, despite this age group representing only 25.3 per cent of the total population. Equally strikingly, of the youngsters aged 18–30 who became members of political parties, 61 per cent joined the Nazis. Thus, it was the young who filled the ranks of the SA – often unemployed, disillusioned with traditional politics and without hope for the future. They saw Nazism as a movement for change, not a search for respectability. Equally, the SA activities gave them something to do. All ages were prepared to vote for the Nazis, but the younger members of society were actually more likely to become involved by joining the Party.

**Key question**
Why has Nazism been described as a 'people's party'?

## Nazism: the people's party

However, the previous analysis should not obscure the fact that the Nazis still boasted a broader cross-section of supporters than any other political party. Unlike most of the other parties, the Nazis were not limited by regional, religious or class ties. So, by 1932 it is fair to say that the NSDAP had become Germany's first genuine *Volkspartei* or broad-based people's party. This point was made in a recent study of voting habits that suggests the Nazis became a mass party only by making inroads into the working-class vote. Hitler therefore succeeded in appealing to *all* sections of German society – it is simply that those from Protestant, rural and middle-class backgrounds supported in much greater numbers.

## Profile: Adolf Hitler 1889–1945

| 1889 | April | – Born at Braunau-am-Inn |
|---|---|---|
| 1905 | | – Left school with no real qualifications |
| 1907–13 | | – After the death of his mother, moved to Vienna where he lived as a dropout in the poorest slum areas |
| | | – Applied twice for a place at the Academy of Fine Arts, but was rejected |
| 1913 | | – Moved to Munich to avoid conscription from the Austro-Hungarian empire |
| 1914 | | – At the outbreak of the First World War, volunteered and joined the Bavarian Infantry Regiment of the German army. |
| 1916 | | – Wounded by shrapnel |
| 1918 | August | – Awarded the Iron Cross, First Class, but only promoted to corporal |
| | October | – Gassed and stayed in hospital at the time of Germany's surrender |
| 1919 | | – Worked as an education officer for the political department of the German army in Bavaria |
| | September | – Joined the DAP |
| 1920 | February | – Drew up the Party's 25-points programme with the party's leader, Drexler. The Party was renamed the NSDAP |
| 1921 | July | – Appointed leader of the Party |

| 1923 | November 8–9 | – Led the unsuccessful Beer Hall *putsch* at Munich |
|---|---|---|
| 1924 | | – Found guilty of treason and sentenced to five years, reduced to nine months. Imprisoned in Landsberg. Wrote *Mein Kampf* |
| 1925 | February 27 | – NSDAP re-founded at Munich |
| 1925–33 | | – Committed the Party to a legality policy |
| | | – Re-structured the Party |
| 1926 | February 14 | – Leadership of the Party re-established at the Bamberg conference |
| 1929 | | – Nationalist reputation enhanced by his opposition to the Young Plan |
| 1930 | September | – *Reichstag* election |
| | | – Nazi breakthrough |
| 1932 | July | – *Reichstag* election |
| | | – Nazis became the largest party |
| | August | – Requested the post of chancellor, but rejected by Hindenburg |
| 1933 | January 30 | – Appointed chancellor of coalition government by Hindenburg |
| | March 23 | – Given dictatorial powers by the Enabling Act |
| 1933–45 | | – Dictator of Germany |
| 1934 | June 30 | – Ordered the purge of the SA, known as the Night of the Long Knives |
| | August 2 | – Combined the posts of chancellor and president on the death of Hindenburg. Thereafter, referred to as *Der Führer* |
| 1945 | April 30 | – Committed suicide in the ruins of Berlin |

## Background

Hitler rose from a very humble background in Austria to become one of the most notorious dictators in history. Yet, although he is universally recognised as evil, his character, ideas and actions have still remained the subject of immense discussion.

His upbringing has provoked much psychological analysis and the character that has emerged has been seen as repressed, lonely and moody. It also seems that much of his outlook on life was shaped by his unhappy years in Vienna, 1907–13, when he failed to become an art student. It was here too that the real core of his political ideas was firmly established – anti-Semitism, German nationalism, anti-democracy and anti-Marxism.

## The war experience

It was only in the First World War that Hitler found a real purpose. His belief in the cause of German nationalism and the camaraderie of the soldiers in the trenches combined to give him direction. However, the shock of hearing of Germany's surrender in November 1918 confirmed all his prejudices. He had fought bravely in the war and he had seen many German comrades die – so, not surprisingly, he was convinced by the view that Germany had been 'stabbed in the back' by forces such as the Jews, the democrats and the Communists.

### The early years of the Nazi party

Hitler in 1919 was drawn to the DAP which was just one of many ultra-right-wing racist parties in post-war Germany. His dynamic speeches and his commitment quickly resulted in him becoming the NSDAP's leader by 1921 and it was he who prompted many of the Party's early features that gave it such a dynamic identity. Nevertheless, despite all the noise and trouble he caused, Hitler was still only the leader of a fringe political party in Bavaria. So when Germany hit the problems of 1923, Hitler grossly over-estimated the potential of the *putsch* in November 1923 and it ended in disaster and his own arrest.

### Rebuilding of the Party 1924–9

Hitler used the next few months to good effect. He exploited his trial by turning himself into a hero of the right-wing nationalists and in prison he wrote *Mein Kampf*. He also re-assessed his long-term strategy to one based on legality.

The following years were relatively stable and economically prosperous years for Weimar and the election results for Hitler and the Nazi Party in 1928 were very disappointing. Nevertheless, he managed to restore his leadership and restructure the Party and its organisation.

### The road to power 1929–33

There is no doubt that the onset of the Great Depression created the environment in which Hitler could exploit his political skills. His charisma, his speeches and his advanced use of propaganda, directed by his disciple Goebbels, were the key features of his political success. Nevertheless, although he emerged by 1932 as the leader of the largest party and the most serious opponent to Weimar democracy, he was only invited to be chancellor in January 1933 when he joined a coalition with other nationalists and conservatives.

### Dictator 1933–45

Hitler established his dictatorship with immense speed and authority. He was given unlimited powers by the Enabling Act, which provided the legal basis for the suppression of political opposition. After the death of Hindenburg, he styled himself *Führer* of Germany and took full direction of the nation's fate for the duration of the Third Reich. It was only when the Russian Red Army closed in on the ruins of Berlin that the spell of the *Führer's* power was finally broken – by his own suicide in the bunker on 30 April 1945.

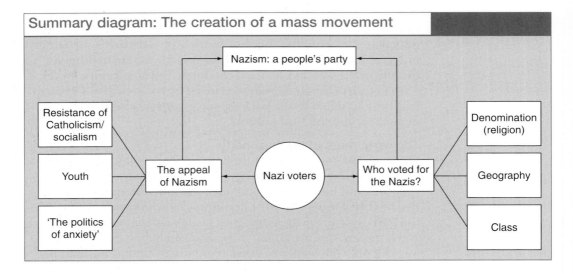

Summary diagram: The creation of a mass movement

## 2 | Nazi Political Methods

It would be wrong to assume that voters for the Nazi Party were simply won over by the appeal of a radical political ideology at a time of economic crisis. There were still various fringe parties on the extreme right, which publicised similar messages. What made the Nazis stand out for the voters was their revolutionary political style. Or, to use present-day jargon, it was the presentation and packaging of the Party and its programme.

### Propaganda

From his earliest days in politics Hitler had shown an uncanny but cynical awareness of the power of propaganda. In 1924 in *Mein Kampf* he had written:

> The receptive powers of the masses are very restricted, and their understanding is feeble. On the other hand, they quickly forget. Such being the case, all effective propaganda must be confined to a few bare essentials and those must be expressed as far as possible in stereotyped formulas. These slogans should be persistently repeated until the very last individual has come to grasp the idea that has been put forward.

Such thinking was to remain the basis of Nazi propaganda, and there can be little doubt that its implementation in the years 1929–33 played a vital part in Nazi success.

The whole process of Nazi propaganda was highly organised. From April 1930 Joseph Goebbels was promoted and put in complete charge of the Party's propaganda machine, which reached right down to branch level. In this way, information and instructions could be sent out from Party headquarters and adapted to local circumstances. It also allowed the Party to target its money and efforts in the key electoral districts. Finally, it encouraged feedback from the grass roots, so that particularly effective ideas could be put into practice elsewhere.

**Key question**
What were the main aims of Nazi propaganda?

'Our Last Hope'. Nazi poster of the 1932 presidential election. Note the image of despair portrayed and the range of Germans – class, age and sex.

## Canvassing

Posters and leaflets had always played an important role in Nazi electioneering, but Goebbels was able to initiate a new approach. He practised mass politics on a grand scale. The electorate was deluged with material with a range of propaganda techniques and an increasingly sophisticated application. He showed a subtlety and an understanding of psychology, which we now associate with advertising agencies.

Yet, Goebbels also correctly recognised the need to direct propaganda according to people's social and economic interests.

## Profile: Josef Goebbels 1897–1945

| | | |
|---|---|---|
| 1897 | | – Born in the Rhineland. Disabled by a clubbed foot which affected his walking |
| 1914–18 | | – Was excused military service on the grounds of his disability |
| 1917–21 | | – Attended the University of Heidelberg and graduated with a Doctor of Philosophy |
| 1924 | August | – Joined the Nazi Party. Originally a supporter of the radical Gregor Strasser |
| 1926 | February | – Broke with Strasser after the Bamberg conference (see pages 113–14) and sided with Hitler |
| | October | – Hitler appointed him as *Gauleiter* of Berlin |
| 1927 | | – Created the Nazi newspaper *Der Angriff* |
| 1928 | May | – Appointed member of the *Reichstag* – a post he technically held until 1945 |
| 1930 | | – Put in charge of Party propaganda |
| 1933 | March | – Joined the cabinet and appointed Minister of Public Enlightenment and Propaganda, which he held until 1945 |
| 1933–45 | | – A key figure throughout the history of the Nazi regime |
| 1945 | April | – Committed suicide after poisoning his children and shooting his wife |

Goebbels was one of the few intellectuals in the Nazi leadership, but he suffered from a strong inferiority complex over his physical limitations and he became embittered and an anti-Semite. Although, originally, he supported the radical socialist wing of the Strassers, from 1926 he became a long-term loyal supporter of Hitler. As propaganda chief of the party from 1930, he played a crucial role in exploiting every possible method to sell the Nazi image and to promote the cult of Hitler in the series of elections, 1930–3. He was a highly skilled orator, although unscrupulous and amoral in his methods. Once he became Minster of Propaganda, he developed the whole range of the regime's propaganda techniques that were frighteningly ahead of their time. He remained a central figure until the collapse of the regime, although many other leading Nazis, such as Göring, distrusted him.

Specific leaflets were produced for different social groups, and Nazi speakers paid particular attention to the worries and concerns of the individual clubs and societies they addressed. In this way, the Nazi propaganda message was tailored to fit a whole range of people. For example:

- To appeal to farmers and peasants by offering special benefits to offset the collapse of agricultural prices.

- To appeal to the unemployed and the industrial workers by aiming to overcome the depression and offering 'Bread' and 'Work'.
- To appeal to the *Mittelstand*, for example, by limiting the control of large department stores.
- To appease the industrialists by playing down the fear of nationalisation and the state control of the economy.

## Technology

Modern technology was also exploited. Loudspeakers, radio, film and records were all used. Expensive cars and aeroplanes were hired, not only for the practical purpose of transporting Hitler quickly to as many places as possible, but also to project a statesman-like image. In 1932, three major speaking programmes were organised for Hitler called 'Flight over Germany'. At a local level the political message was projected by the Party arranging social events and entertainments – sports, concerts and fairs.

## Mass suggestion

However, it was in the organisation of the mass rallies that the Nazis showed their mastery of propaganda. The intention was to create an atmosphere so emotional that all members of the crowd would succumb to the collective will. This is the idea of '**mass suggestion**' and every kind of device was used to heighten the effect: uniforms, torches, music, salutes, flags, songs and anthems, and speeches from leading personalities. Many people have since described how they were converted as a result of such meetings.

## Scapegoats and unifying themes

In order to project itself as a mass people's party, Nazism tried to embrace and bring together many of the disparate elements in Germany. This was partly achieved by Goebbels who showed an astute ability to play on social and psychological factors in Nazi propaganda. Three key unifying themes dominated Nazi propaganda:

- The Führer cult. Hitler was portrayed as a messiah-type figure, who could offer strong authoritarian leadership and a vision for Nazi Germany's future.
- The *Volksgemeinschaft* (national community). To appeal to the people for the development of a unifying idea, regardless of class.
- German nationalism. To play on German nationalism and to exploit the discontent since the First World War. To make Germany great again.

Through these themes Nazi propaganda successfully portrayed itself as both revolutionary and reactionary. The Party aimed to destroy the Republic, while at the same time promising a return to a glorious bygone age.

> **Key term**
>
> **Mass suggestion**
> A psychological term suggesting that large groups of people can be unified simply by the atmosphere of the occasion. Hitler and Goebbels used their speeches and large rallies to particularly good effect.

In addition, Nazism cynically played on the idea of 'scapegoats'. It focused on several identifiable groups, which were denounced and blamed for Germany's suffering:

- The 'November criminals'. The politicians responsible for the Armistice and the creation of the Republic became representative of all aspects associated with Weimar democracy.
- Communists. By playing on the fears of communism – the KPD was a sizeable party of 13–17 per cent in 1930–2 – and the increasing threat of Communist USSR.
- Jews. It was easy to exploit the long established history of anti-Semitism in Europe as a whole and in Germany in particular.

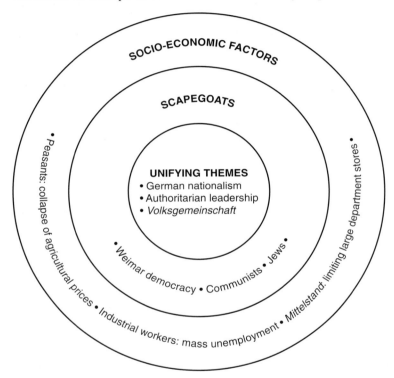

**Figure 8.4:** Nazi propaganda

## Violence

There was one other strand to the political style of this Nazi revolution: the systematic encouragement and use of violence. Weimar politics had been a bloody affair from the start but the growth of the SA and SS unleashed an unprecedented wave of violence, persecution and intimidation.

The growth of unemployment resulted in a phenomenal expansion of the SA, led by Röhm, 1921–3 and 1930–4. Understandably, many joined as members of the SA out of desperation, for food and accommodation, though much of it was just thuggery. The SA was mainly responsible for the violence against the opposition, especially the Communists. All this helped to destabilise the already difficult situation in Germany and, in the wake of the presidential election (see pages 133–4), the SA

Key question
Did SA violence advance the rise of Nazism?

was actually banned for three months. However, it was restored by the new chancellor, Papen, in June 1932. So, during the campaign of July 1932, there were 461 political riots in Prussia alone: battles between Communists and Nazis on 10 July left 10 dead; a week later, 19 died after the Nazis marched through a working-class suburb of Hamburg.

Such violent activities were encouraged by the Nazi leadership, as control of the streets was seen as vital to the expansion of Nazi power. The ballot box of democracy remained merely a means to an end, and, therefore, other non-democratic tactics were considered legitimate in the quest for power. The Nazis poured scorn on rational discussion and fair play. For them the end did justify the means. For their democratic opponents, there was the dilemma of how to resist those who exploited the freedoms of a democratic society merely to undermine it.

---

## Profile: Ernst Röhm 1887–1934

| 1887 | | – Born in Munich |
| 1914–18 | | – Served in the First World War and reached the level of captain |
| 1919 | | – Joined the *Freikorps* |
| | | – Met Hitler and joined the DAP (see page 104) |
| 1921 | | – Helped to form the SA and became its leader in the years 1921–3 |
| 1923 | November | – Participated in the Munich Beer Hall *putsch* |
| 1924 | | – Initially jailed, but soon released on probation |
| 1925–30 | | – Left for Bolivia in South America |
| 1930 | | – Returned to Germany at Hitler's request and re-appointed as SA leader, 1930–4 |
| 1933 | December | – Invited to join the cabinet |
| 1934 | June | – Arrested and then murdered in the 'Night of the Long Knives' |

Röhm was always a controversial character. He was a blatant homosexual, a heavy drinker and enjoyed the blood and violence of war and political street battles. Yet, he was one of Hitler's closest friends in the years 1919–34, which partially explains why Hitler found it so hard to destroy the SA and its leader.

He played a key role in the earliest years, when he introduced Hitler to the DAP in 1919 and he formed the SA. Most significantly, in the years 1930–3 Röhm was given the responsibility by Hitler to reorganise the SA and to restore its discipline. By intimidation and street violence Röhm's SA turned itself into a potent powerful force by 1931 – though conflict between the Party leadership and the SA grew increasingly serious, which culminated in the 'Night of the Long Knives' and his own death.

## The Stennes' revolt

Despite the Nazi violence, Hitler became increasingly keen to maintain the policy of legality. He felt it was vital to keep discipline, so he could maintain the image of a party, which could offer firm and ordered government. The SA had generally supported the radical socialist aspects of Nazism and yet Hitler was increasingly concerned with appealing to the middle-class conservative Nazi voters. The most serious disagreement between the SA and the Party leadership has become known as the Stennes' revolt in February 1931.

Walther Stennes, the leader of the Berlin SA, rebelled against the orders of Hitler and Goebbels to act legally and to limit the violence. Hitler defeated the revolt with a small purge, but it underlined the fact that the relationship between the Party leadership and the SA was at times very difficult. These differences were not really resolved until the infamous **Night of the Long Knives** in 1934.

**Key term**

**Night of the Long Knives**
A crucial turning point when Hitler arranged for the SS to purge the SA leadership and murder about 200 victims, including Ernst Röhm, Gregor Strasser and Kurt von Schleicher on 30 June 1934.

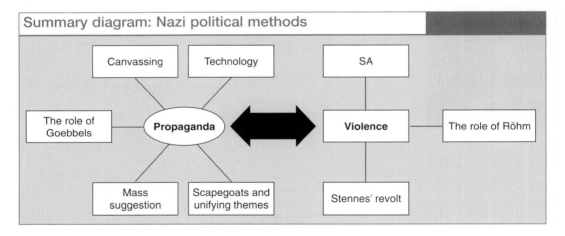

Summary diagram: Nazi political methods

# 3 | Political Intrigue, July 1932–January 1933

The political strength of the Nazi Party following the July 1932 *Reichstag* election was beyond doubt (see page 138–40). However, there still remained the problem for Hitler of how to translate this popular following into real power. He was determined to take nothing less than the post of chancellor for himself. This was unacceptable to both Schleicher and Papen, who were keen to have Nazis in the cabinet, but only in positions of limited power. Therefore, the meeting between Hitler, Papen and Hindenburg on 13 August ended in deadlock.

## Papen's failure

As long as Papen retained the sympathy of Hindenburg, Hitler's ambitions would remain frustrated. Indeed, a leading modern historian, Noakes, describes the period from August to December 1932 as 'the months of crisis' for the Nazis, since 'it appeared the policy of legality had led to a cul-de-sac'. Party morale declined and some of the wilder SA members again became increasingly restless.

**Key question**
Why did Papen fail to prevent Hitler's coming to power?

On the other hand, Papen was humiliated when on 12 September the *Reichstag* passed a massive vote of 'no confidence' in Papen's government (512 votes to 42). Consequently, he dissolved the new *Reichstag* and called for another election. In some respects Papen's reading of the situation was sound. The Nazis were short of money, their morale was low and the electorate was growing tired of repeated elections. These factors undoubtedly contributed to the fall in the Nazi vote on 6 November to 11.7 million (33.1 per cent), which gave them 196 seats. However, Papen's tactics had not achieved their desired end, since the fundamental problem of overcoming the lack of majority *Reichstag* support for his cabinet remained. Hitler stood firm – he would not join the government except as chancellor.

**Key dates**

*Reichstag* passed a massive vote of 'no confidence' in Papen's government (512 votes to 42): September 1932

Nazi votes dropped to 33.1 per cent and won 196 seats in the *Reichstag* election: November 1932

'A Breakdown: A Pleasing Phenomenon!' Cartoon by Oskar Garvens mocking the German people in 1932 for showing no interest in the competing political parties.

In his frustration, Papen began to consider a drastic alternative; the dissolution of the *Reichstag*, the declaration of martial law and the establishment of a presidential dictatorship. However, such a plan was completely opposed by Schleicher, who saw Papen's growing political desperation and his friendship with President Hindenburg as additional causes for concern. Schleicher still believed that the popular support for the Nazis could not be ignored, and that Papen's plan would give rise to civil commotion and perhaps civil war. When he informed Hindenburg of the army's lack of confidence in Papen, the president was forced, unwillingly, to demand the resignation of his friendly chancellor.

**Key date**
Papen dismissed as chancellor and replaced by Schleicher: December 1932

## Schleicher's failure

Schleicher at last came out into the open. Over the previous two years he had been happy to play his role behind the scenes, but he now decided to become the dominant player, when he gained the favour of Hindenburg and was appointed chancellor on 2 December. Schleicher's aims, rather ambitiously, were to achieve political stability and restore national confidence by creating a more broadly based government. He had a two-pronged strategy:

**Key question**
Why did Schleicher fail to prevent Hitler's coming to power?

- First, to gain some support from elements of the political left, especially the trade unions, by suggesting a programme of public works to create jobs.
- Second, to split the Nazis and attract the more socialist wing of the Nazi Party, under Gregor Strasser, by offering him the position of vice-chancellor.

With these objectives Schleicher, therefore, intended to project himself as the chancellor of national reconciliation. However, his political manoeuvres came to nothing.

First, the trade unions remained deeply suspicious of his motives and, encouraged by their political masters from the SPD, they broke off negotiations. Moreover, the idea of public works alienated some of the landowners and businessmen.

Second, although Schleicher's strategy to offer Strasser the post of vice-chancellor was a very clever one, in the end it did not work. Strasser himself responded positively to Schleicher's overtures and he was keen to accept the post but the fundamental differences between Hitler and Strasser led to a massive row. Hitler retained the loyalty of the Party's leadership and Strasser was left isolated and promptly forced to resign from the Party. Nevertheless, the incident had been a major blow to Party morale and tensions remained high in the last few weeks of 1932, as the prospect of achieving power seemed to drift away.

## Hitler's success

Hitler's fortunes did not begin to take a more favourable turn until the first week of 1933. Papen had never forgiven Schleicher for dropping him. Papen was determined to regain political office and he recognised he could only achieve this by convincing Hindenburg that he could muster majority support in the *Reichstag*. Consequently, secret contacts were made with Nazi

**Key question**
Why did President Hindenburg eventually appoint Hitler as chancellor?

## Profile: Kurt von Schleicher 1882–1934

| | | |
|---|---|---|
| 1882 | | – Born at Brandenburg in Prussia |
| 1900–18 | | – Professional soldier and became an officer in Hindenburg's regiment |
| 1919–32 | | – Worked in the German civil service in the Defence Ministry |
| 1932 | June | – Appointed defence minister in Papen's presidential government |
| | December | – Chancellor of Germany, until his forced resignation on 28 January 1933 |
| 1933 | January | – Dismissed by Hindenburg |
| 1934 | June | – Murdered in the 'Night of the Long Knives' |

Schleicher was a shadowy figure and yet he still had an important influence in the years 1930–3. He really preferred to exert political power behind the scenes and he did not take any high-ranking post until he became defence minister in June 1932. Nevertheless, he was undoubtedly the 'fixer', who set up the appointments of Brüning and Papen before, he finally contrived his own chancellorship through Hindenburg. As a general, his primary aim was to preserve the interests and values of the German army, but in the end he was unable to control the intrigue – and a year later he lost his own life.

leaders, which culminated in a meeting on 4 January 1933 between Papen and Hitler. Here it was agreed in essence that Hitler should head a Nazi–Nationalist coalition government with Papen as vice-chancellor.

Back-stage intrigue to unseat Schleicher now took over. Papen looked for support for his plan from major landowners, leaders of industry and the Army. It was only now that the conservative establishment thought that they had identified an escape from the threat of communism and the dangerous intrigues of Schleicher. But, above all, Papen had to convince the president himself. Hindenburg, undoubtedly encouraged by his son, Oskar, and his state secretary, Meissner, eventually gave in. Schleicher had failed in his attempt to bring stability. In fact, he had only succeeded in frightening the powerful vested interests with his ambitious plans. Hindenburg, therefore, heeded the advice of Papen to make Hitler chancellor of a coalition government, secure in the knowledge that those traditional conservatives and Nationalists would control the Nazis. On 28 January 1933, Hindenburg withdrew his support for Schleicher as chancellor.

It was only in this situation that Hindenburg finally agreed, on the suggestion of Papen, to appoint Hitler as chancellor in the mistaken belief Hitler could be controlled and used in the interests of the conservative establishment. Papen believed that Hitler would be a chancellor in chains.

Two days later on 30 January Hindenburg appointed Hitler to head a coalition government of 'national concentration' (a government that aims to bring together a range of interested groups).

**Key date**

Schleicher dismissed and Hitler appointed as chancellor: 30 January 1933

Nazi parade celebrating Hitler's appointment as chancellor near the Brandenburg Gate during the evening of 30 January 1933.

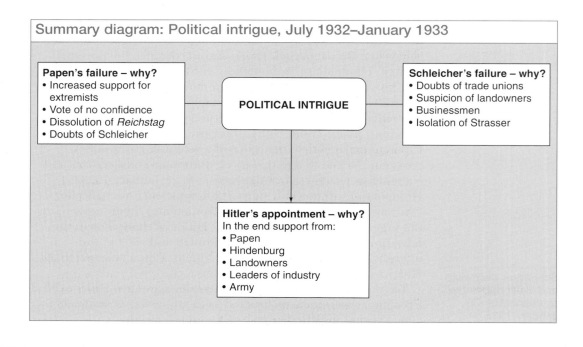

Summary diagram: Political intrigue, July 1932–January 1933

**Papen's failure – why?**
• Increased support for extremists
• Vote of no confidence
• Dissolution of *Reichstag*
• Doubts of Schleicher

**POLITICAL INTRIGUE**

**Schleicher's failure – why?**
• Doubts of trade unions
• Suspicion of landowners
• Businessmen
• Isolation of Strasser

**Hitler's appointment – why?**
In the end support from:
• Papen
• Hindenburg
• Landowners
• Leaders of industry
• Army

## 4 | The Establishment of the Nazi Dictatorship, January–March 1933

**Key question**
What were the political constraints on Hitler?

Although Hitler had been appointed chancellor, his power was by no means absolute. Hindenburg had not been prepared to support Hitler's appointment until he had been satisfied that the chancellor's power would remain limited. Such was Papen's confidence about Hitler's restricted room for manoeuvre that he boasted to a friend, 'In two months we'll have pushed Hitler into a corner so hard that he'll be squeaking'.

At first sight the confidence of the conservatives seemed to be justified, since Hitler's position was weak in purely constitutional terms:

- There were only two other Nazis in the cabinet of 12 – Wilhelm Frick as Minister of the Interior, and Hermann Göring as a Minister without Portfolio. There were, therefore, nine other non-Nazi members of the cabinet, all from conservative-nationalist backgrounds, such as the army, industry and landowners.
- Hitler's coalition government did not have a majority in the *Reichstag* which suggested it would be difficult for the Nazis to introduce any dramatic legislation.
- The chancellor's post, as the previous 12 months had clearly shown, was dependent on the whim of President Hindenburg, and he openly resented Hitler. Hindenburg had made Hitler chancellor but he could as easily sack him.

Hitler was very much aware of the potential power of the army and the trade unions. He could not alienate these forces, which could break his government. The army could arrange a military *coup*; whereas the trade unions could organise a general strike, as they did against the Kapp *putsch* (see pages 45–7).

### Hitler's strengths

**Key question**
What were Hitler's main political strengths?

Yet, within two months, these were shown not to be real limitations when Hitler became a dictator. Moreover, this was to be achieved by a continuation of the policy of legality, which the Party had pursued since 1925. Hitler already possessed several key strengths when he became chancellor:

- He was the leader of the largest political party in Germany, which was why the policy of ignoring him had not worked. During 1932 it had only led to the ineffectual governments of Papen and Schleicher. Therefore, political realism forced the conservatives to work with him. They probably needed him more than he needed them. The alternative to Hitler was civil war or a Communist *coup* – or so it seemed to many people at the time.
- More importantly, the Nazi Party had now gained access to the resources of the State. For example, Göring not only had a place in the cabinet but also was Minister of the Interior in Prussia, with responsibility for the police. It was a responsibility that he used blatantly to harass opponents, while ignoring Nazi

crimes. Goebbels, likewise, exploited the propaganda opportunities on behalf of the Nazis. 'The struggle is a light one now,' he confided in his diary, 'since we are able to employ all the means of the State. Radio and Press are at our disposal.'

- Above all, however, Hitler was a masterly political tactician. He was determined to achieve absolute power for himself whereas Papen was really politically naïve. It soon became clear that Papen's political puppet was too clever to be strung along by a motley collection of ageing conservatives.

## The *Reichstag* election of 5 March 1933

Hitler lost no time in removing his strings. Within 24 hours of his appointment as chancellor, new *Reichstag* elections had been called. Anyway, he felt new elections would not only increase the Nazi vote, but also enhance his own status.

**Key question**
How did Hitler create the dictatorship in two months?

The campaign for the last *Reichstag* elections held according to the Weimar Constitution had few of the characteristics expected of liberal democracy: violence and terror dominated; and meetings of the Socialists and Communists were regularly broken up by the Nazis. In Prussia, Göring used his authority to enrol an extra 50,000 into the police – nearly all were members of the SA and SS. Altogether 69 people died during the five-week campaign.

However, the atmosphere of hate and fear generated by the Nazis was also used to great effect in their election propaganda. Hitler set the tone in his 'Appeal to the German People' of 31 January 1933. He blamed the prevailing conditions on democratic government and the terrorist activities of the Communists. He cultivated the idea of the government as a 'National Uprising' determined to restore Germany's pride and unity. In this way he played on the deepest desires of many Germans, but never committed himself to the details of a political and economic programme.

Another key difference in this election campaign was the improved Nazi financial situation. At a meeting on 20 February with 20 leading industrialists, Hitler was promised three million *Reichsmarks*. With such financial backing and Goebbels' exploitation of the media, the Nazis were confident of securing a parliamentary majority.

## The *Reichstag* fire

As the campaign moved towards its climax, one further bizarre episode strengthened the Nazi hand. On 27 February the *Reichstag* building was set on fire, and a young Dutch Communist, van der Lubbe, was arrested in incriminating circumstances. At the time, it was believed by many that the incident was a Nazi plot to support the claims of a Communist *coup*, and thereby to justify Nazi repression. However, to this day the episode has defied satisfactory explanation. A major investigation in 1962 concluded that van der Lubbe had acted alone; a further 18 years later the West Berlin authorities posthumously acquitted him;

**Key date**
The *Reichstag* fire – Communists blamed by the Nazis: 27 February 1933

whereas the recent biography of Hitler by Ian Kershaw remains convinced that van der Lubbe acted on his own in a series of three attempted arsons within a few weeks. So, it is probable that the true explanation will never be known. The real significance of the *Reichstag* fire is the cynical way it was used by the Nazis to exploit the incident to their advantage.

On the next day, 28 February, Frick drew up and Hindenburg signed the 'Decree for the Protection of People and State'. In a few short clauses most civil and political liberties were suspended and the power of central government was strengthened. The justification for the Decree was the threat posed by the Communists. Following this, in the last week of the election campaign, hundreds of Nazi political opponents were arrested, and the violence reached new heights.

### Election result

In this atmosphere of fear Germany went to the polls on 5 March. The election had a very high turnout of 88 per cent – a reflection of intimidation by the SA, corruption by officials and an increased government control of the radio.

Somewhat surprisingly, the Nazis increased their vote from 33.1 per cent to only 43.9 per cent, thereby securing 288 seats. Hitler could claim a majority in the new *Reichstag* only with the help of the 52 seats won by the DNVP. It was not only disappointing; it was also a political blow, since any change in the existing Weimar Constitution required a two-thirds majority in the *Reichstag*.

## The Enabling Act, March 1933

Despite this constitutional hurdle, Hitler decided to propose to the new *Reichstag* an Enabling Bill that would effectively do away with parliamentary procedure and legislation and that would instead transfer full powers to the chancellor and his government for four years. In this way the dictatorship would be grounded in legality. However, the successful passage of the Enabling Bill depended on gaining the support of, or abstention from, some of the other major political parties in order to get a two-thirds majority.

A further problem was created by the fact that the momentum built up within the lower ranks of the Party was proving increasingly difficult for Hitler to contain in the regional areas. They were impatient and taking the law into their own hands and this gave the impression of a '**revolution from below**'. It threatened to destroy Hitler's image of legality, and antagonise the conservative vested interests and his DNVP coalition partners. Such was his concern that a grandiose act of reassurance was arranged. On 21 March, at Potsdam Garrison Church, Goebbels orchestrated the ceremony to celebrate the opening of the *Reichstag*. In the presence of Hindenburg, the Crown Prince (the son of Kaiser Wilhelm II), and many of the Army's leading generals, Hitler symbolically aligned National Socialism with the forces of the old Germany.

---

**Key dates**

Last elections according to the Weimar Constitution: 5 March 1933

Day of Potsdam ceremony: 21 March 1933

Enabling Act passed: 23 March 1933

---

**Key term**

'**Revolution from below**'
The radical elements in the Party, e.g. the SA, that wanted to direct the Nazi revolution from a more local level rather than from the leadership in Berlin.

Two days later the new *Reichstag* met in the Kroll Opera House to consider the Enabling Bill, and on this occasion the Nazis revealed a very different image. The Communists (those not already in prison) were refused admittance, whilst the deputies in attendance faced a barrage of intimidation from the ranks of the SA who surrounded the building.

However, the Nazis still required a two-thirds majority to pass the bill and, on the assumption that the Social Democrats would vote against, they needed the backing of the ZP. Hitler thus promised in his speech of 23 March to respect the rights of the Catholic Church and to uphold religious and moral values. These were false promises, which the ZP deputies deceived themselves into believing. In the end only the Social Democrats voted against, and the Enabling Bill was passed by 444 to 94 votes.

Germany had succumbed to what Karl Bracher, a leading German scholar, has called 'legal revolution'. Within the space of a few weeks Hitler had legally dismantled the Weimar Constitution. The way was now open for him to create a one-party totalitarian dictatorship.

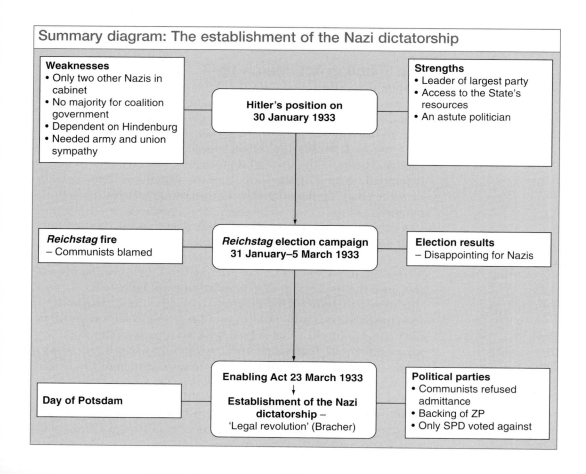

**Summary diagram: The establishment of the Nazi dictatorship**

**Weaknesses**
- Only two other Nazis in cabinet
- No majority for coalition government
- Dependent on Hindenburg
- Needed army and union sympathy

**Hitler's position on 30 January 1933**

**Strengths**
- Leader of largest party
- Access to the State's resources
- An astute politician

*Reichstag* fire
– Communists blamed

*Reichstag* election campaign 31 January–5 March 1933

**Election results**
– Disappointing for Nazis

**Day of Potsdam**

Enabling Act 23 March 1933

Establishment of the Nazi dictatorship –
'Legal revolution' (Bracher)

**Political parties**
- Communists refused admittance
- Backing of ZP
- Only SPD voted against

Key question
Why did the Nazis, and not any of the other parties, replace Weimar?

# 5 | Conclusion

In 1932 only 43 per cent of the electorate voted in the July *Reichstag* elections for pro-republican parties. The majority of the German people had voted in a free (and reasonably fair) election to reject democracy, despite the fact that there was no clear alternative. By this time Weimar's problems had accumulated to serious proportions:

- its birth in military defeat
- its association with the Treaty of Versailles
- the compromise constitution
- its chronic economic problems
- the political uncertainties created by short-lived coalition governments.

However, its problems did not have to end in a Nazi dictatorship, so why was it that Hitler assumed the mantle of power just six months later?

The Great Depression transformed the Nazis into a mass movement. Admittedly, 63 per cent of Germans never voted for them, but 37 per cent of the electorate did, so that the Nazis became by far the strongest party in a multi-party democracy. The Depression had led to such profound social and economic hardship that it created an environment of discontent, which was easily exploited by the Nazis' style of political activity. Indeed, it must be questionable whether Hitler would have become a national political figure without the severity of that economic downturn. However, his mixture of racist, nationalist and anti-democratic ideas was readily received by a broad spectrum of German people, and especially by the disgruntled middle classes.

Yet, other extreme right-wing groups with similar ideas and conditions did not enjoy similar success. This is partially explained by the impressive manner in which the Nazi message was communicated: the use of modern propaganda techniques, the violent exploitation of scapegoats – especially the Jews and Communists – and the well-organised structure of the Party apparatus. All these factors undoubtedly helped but, in terms of electoral appeal, it is impossible to ignore the powerful impact of Hitler himself as a **charismatic** leader with a cult following. Furthermore, he exhibited a quite extraordinary political acumen and ruthlessness when he was involved in the detail of political in-fighting.

Nevertheless, the huge popular following of the Nazis, which helped to undermine the continued operation of democracy, was insufficient on its own to give Hitler power. In the final analysis, it was the mutual recognition by Hitler and the representatives of the traditional leaders of the army, the landowners and heavy industry that they needed each other, which led to Hitler's appointment as chancellor of a coalition government on 30 January 1933. Ever since September 1930 every government had been forced to resort almost continuously to the use of presidential emergency decrees because they lacked a popular mandate.

**Key term**

**Charismatic**
Suggests a personality that has the ability to influence and to inspire people.

In the chaos of 1932 the only other realistic alternative to including the Nazis in the government was some kind of military regime – a presidential dictatorship backed by the army, perhaps. However, that, too, would have faced similar difficulties. Indeed, by failing to satisfy the extreme left and the extreme right there would have been a very real possibility of civil war. A coalition with Hitler's Nazis, therefore, provided the conservative élites with both mass support and some alluring promises: a vigorous attack on Germany's political left wing; and rearmament as a precursor to economic and political expansion abroad. For Hitler, the inclusion of Papen and Hugenberg gave his cabinet an air of conservative respectability.

In the end, Hitler became chancellor because the political forces of the left and centre were too divided and too weak, and because the conservative right wing was prepared to accept him as a partner in government in the mistaken belief that he could be tamed. With hindsight, it can be seen that 30 January 1933 was decisive. The dictatorship did not start technically until the completion of the 'legal revolution' in February–March 1933, but Hitler was already entrenched in power and, as one historian has claimed, now he 'could only be removed by an earthquake'.

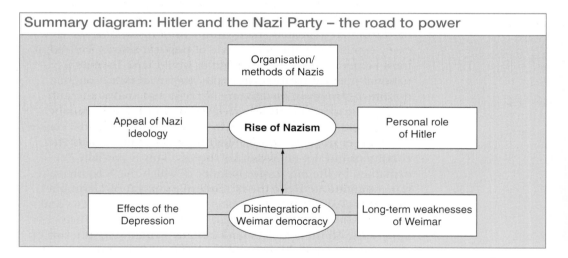

Summary diagram: Hitler and the Nazi Party – the road to power

## 6 | The Key Debate

The rise of Hitler and the Nazis stands as one of the most controversial and intriguing historical debates. One key question continues to dominate the discussion:

> Why did the Weimar Republic collapse and why did it give way to Hitler and Nazism?

Historians have various different interpretations:

### Left-wing Marxists: Nazism, the result of crisis capitalism

In the 1930s many left-wing analysts sought to explain the unexpected rise of Nazism (and the rise of fascism in Italy). They

**Left-wing Marxists**
A school of historians who believe that history has been deeply influenced by economic circumstances. They sympathise with the ideology of Karl Marx.

Key term

came to believe that there was a close connection between the rise of Nazism and the crisis of capitalism faced by Germany in 1929–33. Consequently, big business lost faith in the Weimar Republic and supported the Nazis who were seen as mere 'agents' for the controlling capitalists who sought to satisfy their desire for profits.

### Anti-German determinists: Hitler, the inevitable result of German history

However, left-wing arguments were matched by some equally unquestioning views outside Germany. Clearly, anti-German feelings can be put down to the requirements of wartime propaganda in Britain. Nevertheless, some academic historians after the war portrayed Nazism as the natural product of German history. The renowned English historian A.J.P. Taylor wrote in *The Course of German History* in 1945:

> It was no more a mistake for the German people to end up with Hitler than it is an accident when a river flows into the sea.

**Key terms**

**Anti-German determinists**
Believed that the collapse of Weimar democracy and the rise of Nazi dictatorship were bound to happen because of Germany's long-term history and the national character of its people.

The culmination of this kind of **anti-German determinist** view was probably reached with the publication in 1959 of William Shirer's *Rise and Fall of the Third Reich*. This monumental work, written by an American journalist who had worked as a correspondent in Germany between 1926 and 1941, had a profound impact on the general public. In it he explained how Nazism was 'but a logical continuation of German history'. He argued that Germany's political evolution, its cultural and intellectual heritage and the people's national character all contributed to the inevitable success of Hitler.

### Gerhard Ritter: Nazism, the result in Germany of a 'moral crisis' in Europe

Not surprisingly, the implicit anti-German sentiments were not kindly received in Germany, especially amongst those intellectuals who had opposed Hitler. As a consequence, there emerged in the post-war decade in West Germany a school of thought that emphasised the 'moral crisis of European society'. It was epitomised above all by the writings of Gerhard Ritter, who focused on the European circumstances in which Nazism had emerged. In his view, it was hard to believe that Germany's great traditions, such as the power of the Prussian state, or its rich cultural history could have contributed to the emergence of Hitler. Instead, Ritter emphasised the events and developments since 1914 in Europe as a whole. It was the shock given to the traditional European order by the First World War that created the appropriate environment for the emergence of Nazism. The decline in religion and standards of morality, a tendency towards corruption and materialism and the emergence of mass democracy were all exploited by Hitler to satisfy his desire for power.

## Structuralists: Nazism, a response to Germany's social and economic 'structures'

The 1960s witnessed the beginning of a phenomenal growth in research on the Third Reich – partly due to the practical reason that the German archives in the hands of the Western Allies had been made available. By the late 1960s and early 1970s, historians, such as Martin Broszat and Hans Mommsen, had started to exert a major influence on our understanding of the rise of Hitler and the Third Reich and their approach has been dubbed '**structuralist**'.

In essence, the structuralist interpretation emphasises Germany's continuities from the 1850s to 1945. It argues that Germany had remained dominated by authoritarian forces in Germany's society and economy, such as the armed services and the bureaucracy, and had not really developed democratic institutions. As a result, the power and influence of such conservative vested interests continued to dominate Germany – even after the creation of the Weimar Republic – and therefore, these conservatives sympathised with the Nazi movement, which provided the means to uphold a right-wing authoritarian regime.

## Intentionalists: Nazism, a result of Hitler's ideology and his evil genius

However, some historians have continued to argue that there is no escape from the central importance of Hitler the individual in the Nazi seizure of power. Indeed, '**intentionalists**', like Klaus Hildebrand and Eberhard Jäckel, believe that the personality and ideology of Hitler remain so essential that Nazism can really be directly equated with the term Hitlerism. This is because although the intentionalists accept the special circumstances created by Germany's history, they emphasise the indispensable role of the individual, Hitler.

## Kershaw: Hitler's coming to power – the result of miscalculation

This latest interpretation has arisen as a result of the recently published biography by Ian Kershaw, arguably the leading British historian of Nazi Germany. However, he is keen to stress that his book goes well beyond the framework of mere biography and tries to balance the role of structuralist and intentionalist interpretations. Most significantly, he emphasises that the appointment of Hitler was not inevitable until the very last moment – 11 o'clock on 30 January 1933. Hitler's appointment as chancellor was the result of a series of miscalculations and if Brüning, Papen, Schleicher or Hindenburg had made just one different crucial decision in 1930–3, history would have been very different. In that way Kershaw shows that Hitler's 'path ought to have been blocked long before the final drama'.

**Key terms**

**Structuralists**
Interpret history by analysing the role of social and economic forces and structures. They therefore tend to place less emphasis on the role of the individual.

**Intentionalists**
Interpret history by emphasising the role (intentions) of people who shape history.

## Summary diagram: The key debate

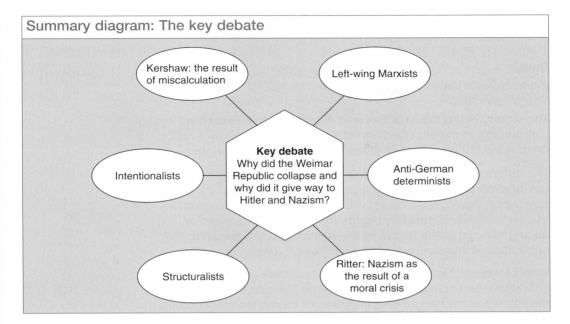

## Study Guide: AS Questions

### In the style of AQA
Examine the extent to which Nazism had become a mass movement by 1932.

> *Study tips*
> *This question is quite a significant one and you must focus your answer specifically. It should be noted from the wording in the question that:*
>
> - a 'mass movement' asks you to explain how and why the Nazis achieved 'electoral breakthrough'
> - the date 'by 1932' suggests you should concentrate on the years 1930–2, but there is a good case to refer also to the first signs of increased support from 1928 because of the agricultural depression.
>
> The main themes to bear in mind are:
>
> - which political parties declined and from which ones did the Nazis gain, e.g. DNVP
> - which types of people voted for the Nazis
> - why certain people tended to vote for the Nazis.
>
> However, the question not only asks you to 'examine', but also to measure 'the extent' of Nazism's popular influence. Therefore, it is vital for the top marks to make a judgment. It would be helpful to refer to some things such as:
>
> - the idea of Nazism as a *Volkspartei*
> - the figures of 37 per cent who voted for Nazism in July 1932 – compared to other parties in the history of Weimar.

## In the style of Edexcel

Study Sources 1–5 below and answer the questions that follow.

### Source 1

*Extracts from: the election manifesto of the NSDAP, published September 1930.*

The victory of the National Socialist Movement will mean the overcoming of the old class and status spirit. It will allow a nation once more to rise up out of status mania and class madness.

The other parties may have come to terms with the thievery of the inflation of 1923 and may recognise the fraudulent Revolution. National socialism will bring the thieves and traitors to justice. National socialism fights for the German worker by getting him out of the hands of the swindlers and destroying the protectors of international bank and Stock Exchange capital.

With its victory, the National Socialist Movement will also seek to guarantee the economic protection of the German people. As long as stock exchanges and department stores are inadequately taxed, any further tax increases on the little man are a crime.

### Source 2

*Cartoon in* Vorwarts, *the SPD newspaper in 1932, claiming that the NSDAP was backed by money from big business. The words on the placard say 'The National Socialist Workers' Party fights against capitalism'.*

## Source 3

*Order given on 17 February 1933 by Göring, to the police throughout the state of Prussia.*

The police must in all circumstances avoid giving the appearance of a hostile attitude, still less the impression of persecuting the Nazi Storm Detachments. I expect all police authorities to maintain the best relations with patriotic associations like the Nazi Storm Detachments. Patriotic activities and propaganda are to be supported by every means.

The activities of subversive organisations are to be combated with the most drastic methods. Communist terrorist acts and attacks are to be proceeded against with all severity. Weapons must be used ruthlessly when necessary. Police officers, who in the execution of this duty use their firearms, will be supported by me without regard to the effect of their shots. On the other hand, officers who fail through a false sense of consideration may expect disciplinary measures.

## Source 4

*From: a letter written by Grzesinski, a prominent member of the SPD, to the SPD secretaries in various German towns and cities, on 24 February 1933.*

Dear Comrade
The incidents of the past days at meetings of prominent speakers have prompted the Party meetings to consider withdrawing these speakers, of whom I am one. Several of my meetings have been disrupted and a considerable section of the audience taken away badly injured. In agreement with the Party committee, I therefore request the cancellation of meetings with me as speaker. As things are, there is obviously no longer any police protection sufficient to check the aggressive actions of the Nazi storm detachments.

## Source 5

*From: S.J. Lee,* Hitler and Nazi Germany, *1998.*

Within days of his appointment as chancellor, on the 30th January 1933, Hitler requested a dissolution of the *Reichstag* so that he could increase the number of seats of the NSDAP. During the election campaign he made use of emergency decrees, issued under article 48 of the constitution, to hamstring the other parties, especially the SPD and KPD; the reason given for this way the *Reichstag* fire which have blamed on the Communists. Although the NSDAP did not achieve an overall majority in the election, they did succeed in increasing the number of their seats from 196 to 288.

(a) **Study Source 1**

In what ways does Source 1 suggest that the Nazi party was a 'National Socialist' party? (3 marks)

(b) **Use your own knowledge**

Use your own knowledge to explain the importance of 'the inflation' referred to in Source 1 line 4. (5 marks)

(c) **Study Sources 3 and 4**

In what ways do the instructions shown in Source 3 explain the feelings shown in Source 4? (5 marks)

(d) **Study Sources 1 and 2**

How useful are these two sources to an historian studying the importance of the NSDAP's relationship with big business in the 1920s and early 1930s? (5 marks)

(e) **Study Sources 3 and 5 and use your own knowledge**

Do you agree with the view that the Nazis were able to consolidate their hold on power so easily in the period January to March 1933 simply because of the use of terror and intimidation?

Explain you answer, using these two sources and your own knowledge. (12 marks)

*Source: Edexcel, May 2002*

---

*Exam tips*

*The cross-references are intended to take you straight to the material that will help you to answer the questions.*

(a) The answer to question **(a)** is to be found entirely within Source 1. You have to show that you generally understand the contents of the document. But you must also refer to particular points that suggest that the Nazi Party was a 'nationalist and/or socialist' party. You do not have to use your own knowledge. Keep your answer to the point.

(b) Firstly, you must understand exactly the reference to 'the inflation' (page 60). Then, you have to use your own knowledge to explain the importance of money being lost in the inflation by the German people. For example:
  • savings were eroded (page 61)
  • fixed incomes declined (pages 62–3)
  • recipients of welfare declined (page 62).

(c) You must make certain you understand the meaning of the two sources and focus on the key words 'instructions' and 'feelings'. Point out and explain any similarities and differences between the two sources.

(d) You must go beyond describing the content of the sources and you have to think about the reliability of the two sources. To do this, it is important to:
  • explore the nature and origin of the sources
  • explain the significance of the author and the circumstances of the writing.

  In a conclusion, it is worth assessing the usefulness of the two sources of the election manifesto and the cartoon to understand the relationship between the NSDAP and big business.

**(e)** This carries by far the most number of marks and you must spend nearly half the time in this exam on this question. It is worth noting that the question suggests that the Nazi consolidation of power was 'simply because of the use of terror and intimidation'. So do refer to the evidence of Sources 3 and 5 and show your own knowledge of the whole topic, in order to examine the evidence for and against. You must use analytical skills and show your own knowledge of the months January–March 1933.

You have to:
- Describe the ways the Nazis used terror, e.g. intimidation, arrest of Communists (page 168–70)
- show the other factors employed by Nazism to consolidate its power, e.g. deception (propaganda) (page 156–60), legality (Enabling Act) (page 169–70)
- make an assessment as to whether terror was the 'main' reason for Nazi success in the months January–March 1933.

## In the style of OCR

To what extent did Hitler become the most powerful opponent of the Weimar Republic?'

*Exam tips*
*The cross-references are intended to take you straight to the material that will help you to answer the question.*

This is a very broad question, which covers many elements of Chapters 6–8. You must choose the relevant material carefully but you need not take a chronological approach. Your main aim is to assess the reason why Hitler became 'the most powerful opponent of the Weimar Republic'. Focus on such factors as:

- the effects of the depression and the general situation in Germany (pages 122–6)
- the Party's organisation/structure (pages 114–15)
- Nazi methods – propaganda and violence (pages 156–61)
- Hitler's personal charisma and political skills (pages 101–107, 109–12, 113–14, 116, 152–155, 156–61, 171).

In your conclusion, you have to prioritise the factors and, if possible, choose the most significant combination of factors.

# Glossary

**Alliance**   An agreement where members promise to support the other(s), if one or more of them is attacked.

**Annexation**   Seizing the territory of another country against international law. Taking over of another country against its will.

**Anschluss**   Usually translated as 'union'. In the years 1919–38, it referred to the paragraph in the Treaty of Versailles that outlawed any political union between Germany and Austria, although the population was wholly German.

**Anti-capitalism**   Rejects the economic system based upon private property and profit. Early Nazi ideas laid stress upon preventing the exploitation of workers and suggesting social reforms.

**Anti-German determinists**   Believed that the collapse of Weimar democracy and the rise of Nazi dictatorship were bound to happen because of Germany's long-term history and the national character of its people.

**Anti-Marxism**   Opposition to the ideology of Karl Marx.

**Anti-Semitism**   The hatred of Jews. It became the most significant part of Nazi racist thinking. For Hitler, the 'master-race' was the pure Aryan (the people of northern Europe) and the Germans represented the highest caste. The lowest race for Hitler was the Jews.

**Arbitration treaty**   An agreement to accept the decision by a third party to settle a conflict.

**Article 48**   Gave the Weimar president the power in an emergency to rule by decree and to override the constitutional rights of the people.

**Aryan**   Refers to all the peoples of the Indo-European family. However, the term was more specifically defined by the Nazis as the non-Jewish people of northern Europe.

**Associationism**   Having a strong identity or affiliation with a particular group.

**Authoritarianism**   A broad term meaning government by strong non-democratic leadership.

**Autocracy**   A system where one person (usually a hereditary sovereign) has absolute rule.

**Avant garde**   A general term suggesting new ideas and styles in art.

**Balanced budget**   A financial programme in which a government does not spend more than it raises in revenue.

**Bolsheviks**   Followers of Bolshevism – Russian communism.

**Buffer state**   The general idea of separating two rival countries by leaving a space between them. Clemenceau believed that the long-established Franco-German military aggression could be brought to an end by establishing an independent Rhineland state (though this was not implemented because Wilson saw it as against the principle of self-determination).

**Cartel**   An arrangement between businesses to control the market by exercising a joint monopoly.

**Charismatic**   Suggests a personality that has the ability to influence and to inspire people.

**Coalition government**   Usually formed when a party does not have an overall majority in parliament; it then combines with more parties and shares government positions.

**Constitution**   The principles and rules that govern a state. The Weimar

Constitution is a good example. (Britain is often described as having an unwritten constitution. It is not drawn up in one document, but built on statutes, conventions and case law.)

**Constitutional monarchy**  Where the monarch has limited power within the lines of a constitution.

**Customs union**  An agreement between two or more countries to abolish customs and tariffs. It aims to create free trade within the area and to encourage business.

**Demilitarisation**  The removal of military personnel, weaponry or forts. The Rhineland demilitarised zone was outlined by the Treaty of Versailles.

*Diktat*  A dictated peace. The Germans felt that the Treaty of Versailles was imposed without negotiation.

*Ersatzkaiser*  Means 'substitute emperor'. After Marshal Hindenburg was elected president, he provided the ersatzkaiser figure required by the respectable right wing – he was a conservative, a nationalist and a military hero.

**Exports**  Goods sold to foreign countries.

**Expressionism**  An art form that suggests that the artist transforms reality to express a personal outlook.

**Federal structure**  Where power and responsibilities are shared between central and regional governments.

**First past the post**  An electoral system that simply requires the winner to gain one vote more than the second placed candidate. It is also referred to as the plurality system and does not require 50 per cent plus one votes. In a national election it tends to give the most successful party disproportionately more seats than its total vote merits.

*Freikorps*  Means 'free corps' who acted as paramilitaries. They were right-wing, nationalist soldiers who were only too willing to use force to suppress communist activity.

**Fulfilment**  The policy of conforming to the terms of a treaty, like Versailles.

*Führerprinzip*  'The leadership principle'. Hitler upheld the idea of a one-party state, built on an all-powerful leader.

*Gauleiter*  Means 'leader of a regional area'. The Nazi party was organised into 35 regions from 1926.

**GNP**  Gross national product is the total value of all goods and services in a nation's economy (including income derived from assets abroad).

**Great Depression**  The severe economic crisis of 1929–33 that was marked by mass unemployment, falling prices and a lack of spending.

**Hard currency**  A currency that the market considers to be strong because its value does not depreciate. In the 1920s the hardest currency was the US dollar.

**Hyper-inflation**  Hyper-inflation is unusual. In Germany, in 1923, it meant that prices spiralled out of control because the government increased the amount of money being printed. As a result, it displaced the whole economy.

**Imperial Germany**  The title given to Germany from its unification in 1871 until 1918. Also referred to as the Second Reich (Empire).

**Imports**  Goods purchased from foreign countries.

**Intentionalists**  Interpret history by emphasising the role (intentions) of people who shape history.

**Kaiser**  Emperor. The last Kaiser of Germany was Wilhelm II, 1888–1918.

**Labour market**  Comprises the supply of labour (those looking for work) and the demand for labour from employers. These two forces within the labour market determine wage rates.

**League of Nations** The international body initiated by President Wilson to encourage disarmament and to prevent war.

*Lebensraum* 'Living space'. Hitler's aim to create an empire by establishing German supremacy over the eastern lands in Europe.

**Left-wing Marxists** A school of historians who believe that history has been deeply influenced by economic circumstances. They sympathise with the ideology of Karl Marx.

**Mandates** The name given by the Allies to the system created in the Peace Settlement for the supervision of all the colonies of Germany (and Turkey) by the League of Nations.

**Marxism** The political ideology of Karl Marx. His two major books, *Communist Manifesto* and *Capital*, outline his beliefs that the working classes will overthrow the industrial classes by revolution and create a classless society.

**Mass suggestion** A psychological term suggesting that large groups of people can be unified simply by the atmosphere of the occasion. Hitler and Goebbels used their speeches and large rallies to particularly good effect.

*Mein Kampf* 'My struggle'. The book written by Hitler in 1924, which expresses his political ideas.

*Mittelstand* Can be translated as 'the middle class', but in German society it tends to represent the lower middle classes, e.g. shopkeepers, craft workers and clerks. Traditionally independent and self-reliant but increasingly felt squeezed out between the power and influence of big business and industrial labour.

**Mutual guarantee agreement** An agreement between states on a particular issue, but not an alliance.

**National Opposition** A title given to various political forces that united to campaign against Weimar. It included the DNVP, the Nazis, the Pan-German League and the Stahlhelm – an organisation of ex-soldiers. The 'National Opposition' was forged out of the Young Plan in 1929.

**Nationalism** Grew from the national spirit to unify Germany in the nineteenth century. Supported a strong policy to embrace all German-speakers in eastern Europe.

**New functionalism** A form of art that developed in post-war Germany, it tried to express reality with a more objective view of the world.

**Night of the Long Knives** A crucial turning point when Hitler arranged for the SS to purge the SA leadership and murder about 200 victims, including Ernst Röhm, Gregor Strasser and Kurt von Schleicher on 30 June 1934.

**'November criminals'** Those who signed the November Armistice and a term of abuse to vilify all those who supported the democratic republic.

**Pan-German League** A movement founded at the end of the nineteenth century campaigning for the uniting of all Germans into one country.

**Paramilitary units** Informal non-legal military squads.

**'Passive resistance'** Refusal to work with occupying forces.

**Plebiscite** A vote by the people on one specific issue – like a referendum.

**Polarisation** The division of society into opposite views (e.g. north and south poles).

**Proletariat** The industrial working class who, in Marxist theory, would ultimately take power in the state.

**Proportional representation** An electoral system that allocates parliament seats in proportion to the total number of votes.

*Putsch* The German word for an uprising (though often the French phrase, *coup d'état*, is used). Normally, a *putsch* means the attempt by a small group to overthrow the government, which usually fails.

**Reactionary**   Those opposing change and supporting a return to traditional ways.

**Recession**   Period of economic slowdown, usually accompanied by rising unemployment.

**'Red Threat'**   A 'Red' was a loose term used to describe anyone sympathetic to the left and it originated from the Bolshevik use of the red flag in Russia.

*Reichstag*   The German parliament. Although created in 1871, it had very limited powers. Real power lay with the Emperor.

**Revisionism**   In general terms, the aim to modify or change an agreement. In the context of Germany in the 1920s it refers specifically to the policy of changing the terms of the Treaty of Versailles.

**'Revolution from below'**   The radical elements in the Party, e.g. the SA, that wanted to direct the Nazi revolution from a more local level rather than from the leadership in Berlin.

**Rule of law**   Governing a country according to its laws.

**SA**   *Sturm Abteilung* became known in English as the Stormtroopers. They were also referred to as the Brownshirts after the colour of the uniform. They supported the radical socialist aspects of Nazism.

**Schlieffen plan**   Its purpose was to avoid a two-front war by winning victory on the Western Front before dealing with the threat from Russia. It aimed to defeat France within six weeks by a massive German offensive in northern France and Belgium.

**Self-determination**   The right of people of the same nation to decide their own form of government. In effect, it is the principle of each nation ruling itself. Wilson believed that the application of self-determination was integral to the

Peace Settlement and it would lead to long-term peace.

*Siegfriede*   'A peace through victory' – referring to Germany fighting the First World War to victory and making major land gains.

**Social Darwinism**   A philosophy that portrayed the world as a 'struggle' between people, races and nations. Hitler viewed war as the highest form of 'struggle' and was deeply influenced by the theory of evolution based upon natural selection.

**Socialist republic**   A system of government without a monarchy that aims to introduce social changes for collective benefit.

**Soviet**   A Russian word meaning an elected council. Soviets developed during the Russian Revolution in 1917. In Germany many councils were set up in 1918, which had the support of the more radical and revolutionary left-wing working class.

**Soviet republic**   A system of government without a monarchy that aims to introduce a communist state organised by the workers' councils and opposed to private ownership.

**SS**   *Schutz Staffel* (protection squad); became known as the Blackshirts, named after the uniform.

**'Stab in the back' myth**   The distorted *view* that the army had not really lost the First World War and that unpatriotic groups, such as socialists and Jews, had undermined it. The myth severely weakened the Weimar democracy from the start.

**'State within a state'**   Where the authority and government of the state are threatened by a rival power base.

**Structuralists**   Interpret history by analysing the role of social and economic forces and structures. They therefore tend to place less emphasis on the role of the individual.

**Tariffs**   Taxes levied by an importing nation on foreign goods coming in, and paid by the importers.

**Toleration**   To accept alternative political, religious and cultural views.

**Total war**   Involves the whole population in war – economically and militarily.

**Unilateral disarmament**   The disarmament of one party. Wilson pushed for general (universal) disarmament after the war, but France and Britain were more suspicious. As a result only Germany had to disarm.

**'Unrestricted submarine warfare'** Germany's policy of attacking all military and civilian shipping in order to sink supplies going to Britain.

*Vernunftrepublikaner*   'A rational republican'. Used in the 1920s to define those people who really wanted Germany to have a constitutional monarchy but who, out of necessity, came to support the democratic Weimar Republic.

*Volk*   Often translated as 'people', although it tends to suggest a nation with the same ethnic and cultural identities and with a collective sense of belonging.

*Volksgemeinschaft*   'A people's community'. Nazism stressed the development of a harmonious, socially unified and racially pure community.

**War bonds**   In order to raise more money to pay for the war Imperial Germany encouraged people to invest into government funds in the belief they were helping to finance the war and their savings would be secure.

**Weimar Republic**   Took its name from the first meeting of the National Constituent Assembly in Weimar. The Assembly had moved there because there were still many disturbances in Berlin. Weimar was chosen because it was a town and with a great historical and cultural tradition.

*Weltpolitik*   'World policy', the imperial policy of Kaiser Wilhem II to make Germany a great power by overseas expansion.

**White-collar workers**   Workers not involved in manual labour.

**'White Terror'**   The 'Whites' were seen as the opponents (in contrast to the Reds). The 'White Terror' refers to the soviet republic in Bavaria.

# Index